Ultras

Manchester University Press

Ultras

The passion and performance of
contemporary football fandom

**Mark Doidge, Radosław Kossakowski
and Svenja Mintert**

Manchester University Press

The rights of Mark Doidge, Radosław Kossakowski and Svenja Mintert to be identified as the authors of this work have been asserted by them in accordance with the Copyright, Designs and Patents Act 1988.

Published by Manchester University Press
Oxford Road, Manchester M13 9PL

www.manchesteruniversitypress.co.uk

British Library Cataloguing-in-Publication Data
A catalogue record for this book is available from the British Library

ISBN 978 1 5261 2762 4 hardback
ISBN 978 1 5261 6371 4 paperback

First published 2020
Paperback published 2022

The publisher has no responsibility for the persistence or accuracy of URLs for any external or third-party internet websites referred to in this book, and does not guarantee that any content on such websites is, or will remain, accurate or appropriate.

Typeset in Sabon and Gill Sans by
Servis Filmsetting Ltd, Stockport, Cheshire

Contents

Acknowledgements

Writing a book is not just a collaboration between the authors, but a whole network of people. The authors would like to thank Tom Dark at Manchester University Press for his patience (and we hope it was worth the wait).

A book about ultras would not be possible without the ingenuity, passion and creativity of football fans across the globe. The dedication, desire and commitment of so many fan groups provide such a rich seam of activities which a book like this can only touch upon.

Mark would like to thank his partner, Momtaz, for her support throughout the process and the emotional labour of encouragement and reassurance. He would also like to reiterate his support and thanks to Football Supporters Europe (FSE) – and Endi and Ronan in particular – who perform such an important role in European football fandom. Their annual networking meetings and congresses bring together so many active fans to discuss the real issues affecting football supporters. Just being linked to FSE provides so many insights into what is happening across European fan cultures. Finally, he would also like to thank his colleagues in the Sport and Leisure Cultures research cluster at the University of Brighton. Discussions here, and with Tom Carter in particular, provide so much intellectual nourishment to explore ideas and analyses that hopefully find expression in these pages.

Radosław would like to thank his family for their permanent support. He appreciates also the intellectual and research journeys with many colleagues engaged in football studies and the sociology of sport.

Svenja would like to thank all the talented young researchers who were involved in realising the findings in this book. Their significant inspiration, critical thoughts and valuable insights provided constant support and were at all times highly appreciated.

We would also like to acknowledge the generosity of funders in enabling aspects of this book to come together. Consequently, some data used and analysed in this book have been collected thanks to a research grant funded by Polish National Centre of Science (no. 2013/09/D/HS/6/00238; principal investigator – Radosław Kossakowski) and within in the framework of Football Research in an Enlarged Europe (FREE), which received funding from the European Union's Seventh Framework Programme for research, technological development and demonstration under grant agreement no. 290805.

Introduction

All the hot, sweaty bodies collapsed domino-like onto the searing heat of the concrete stand. The home team, Livorno, had just scored against Pisa, their hated local rivals. The joy sparked a euphoric reaction with thousands of fans jumping, hugging and cheering. In the maelstrom of relief, ecstasy and *Schadenfreude* that the goal elicited, bodies became unstable and crumpled onto the seats of the stadium. They became one mass of flesh, clothing and flags. On the pitch, the players were running to the fans, embracing each other and raising their fists to the air in exaltation. Through their displays of emotion, they acknowledged the importance of the goal to the fans of Livorno, and by extension the city's inhabitants who have a longstanding rivalry with Pisa that pre-dates the codification of football in the nineteenth century. As play restarted, the fans were back on their feet, all the flags were waved wildly and the volume of the songs lauding the city of Livorno were significantly amplified. The intensity of the chants increased as more fans joined in, while the capos at the front exaggerated their direction of the *curva* to bring more fans into the performance. The collective outpouring of emotion was incongruous, as the goal seemed to come from nowhere; there had been no sustained passage of play that suggested a goal might be scored. Pisa had dominated possession for a few minutes, yet Livorno broke away to land the classic sucker punch and produce delirium among their fans. Only moments before that delirium there was a collective intake of breath as the home player sprinted towards goal; the Livornese had a very different set of emotions. But in the seconds after the ball hit the net there were two clear groups: Livornese and Pisans; and they were clearly divided by the emotions they felt.

The joyous, chaotic mass of bodies signifies the importance of emotions in creating the social collective. Although Livorno's defeat of Pisa was an emotional moment in the history of Livornese football, it was not unique in the football world. The atmosphere in a football stadium is a ritual that is actively performed by the fans. The ecstasy of Tottenham fans celebrating Lucas Moura's ninety-fifth-minute winner in their 2019 Champions League semi-final contrasts sharply with the deflation experienced by the fans of Ajax in the rest of the stadium. The bitterness Fiorentina fans hold towards Juventus endures decades after the Turin side snatched the 1982 Serie A title on the last day of the season. Across the globe, one particular group has taken a leading role in creating these highly passionate atmospheres: the ultras. They produce choreographies (also known as 'tifos' or 'choreos') that regularly involve collective chanting, flags, banners, clothing and pyrotechnics. For bigger matches, such as local derbies, spectacular choreographies will be displayed that can cover the whole terrace (or *curva*) and can take many weeks to fund, design, paint and prepare. These can include paintings on gargantuan sheets of fabric or designs that require a variety of coloured cards. Ultras are obsessed about the collective performance, unity and harmonisation, and this is not only what distinguishes them from other football fans but also from many other forms of collective behaviour. Ultras are one of the only groups displaying collective behaviour that pride themselves on having a shared, coherent sense of identity based on an act of consumption: that of football.

This book marks half a century of the ultras phenomenon. Although passionate fans have been following football since the beginning, and certain elements of the ultras style existed elsewhere (notably with the *Torcida* group in Split, Croatia), the ultras can date their formation back to AC Milan's *Fossa dei Leoni* in 1968. Few cultural activities engage as many people as football, and within football fandom, the ultras are overwhelmingly the most widespread and powerful group of fans in the world. It is for this reason that they represent an important group for social analysis. There are few social groups in the world that have the global reach, visibility and regular mobilisations of the ultras. Even though these groups are only loosely affiliated – some will work together, others will not – there is a coherent identification with the ultras way of life. It is for this reason that they represent an important case study in contemporary consumer culture.

To be an ultra is to subsume your individual identity into a wider collective. A piece of graffiti painted by ultras of Wydad Casablanca sums this up perfectly when they portrayed a hooded ultra with their face obscured alongside the slogan 'No Face. No Name. Just Passion.' When certain social commentators (Giddens, 1990; 1991; 1992; Beck, 1992; Putnam *et al.*, 1993; Putnam, 2000) suggest that social life is becoming more individualistic, the ultras clearly demonstrate collective action on a weekly basis. They are willing to embody the collective by removing traces of their individuality, as the individual and group become one organic body. They represent an important analysis of how groups identify, mobilise and sustain their activities over time. The regularity of the football season and the growth of social media technology ensures that these groups remain in constant contact both temporally and geographically. And most importantly, they represent an important space for the formation of social relationships and belonging.

For the uninitiated, ultras are an organised style of fandom, typically associated with football, but also supporting other sports including basketball, volleyball, ice hockey and handball. Ultras are highly organised, often with a coordinating committee headed by a capo (head) who leads the strategy of the group and, more importantly for matchdays, conducts the choreographies and chants in the *curva*. The term derives from the *ultrá-royaliste* loyal supporters of the monarchy in the French Restoration (Testa, 2009). Both 'ultrà' and 'ultras' have been adopted as terms for these hardcore fans (Cere, 2002). Early taxonomies of football fans suggest that there are spectrums or distinct styles of support (Giulianotti, 2002; Crawford, 2004). These tend to privilege a type of masculine, passionate support. In the case of the ultras, they may sit at the passionate end of the spectrum, but this should not privilege their activities. It is true that they add colour and spectacle to the stadium, so much so that clubs often use the image of the ultras to sell their brand while at the same time continuing to curb some of the activities of the ultras (Nuhrat, 2018a). These activities can include the use of pyrotechnics, abusive chants and banners, and violence. The use of violence has led to the ultras becoming a media folk devil in many countries (Cere, 2002; Marchi, 2005; Doidge, 2015a). Although most groups do not engage in this behaviour, attention has also focused on instances of racism and far-right politics (Testa and Armstrong, 2010; Doidge, 2015a; 2015b). Attempts to regulate these practices have led to a feeling of persecution that manifests itself in 'ACAB syndrome' against the police and authorities (Stefanini, 2009; Doidge, 2015a). ACAB is an acronym of the slogan 'All Cops Are Bastards' and the ultras can be characterised by a rebellious social movement who not only fight for their rights but also resist various forms of authority and regulation. This can be illustrated by Eintracht Frankfurt ultras stealing a German police banner in March 2019 and displaying it upside down, indicative of the tradition of showing symbolic victory over rivals.

The core ultras mentality is an unwavering support for their football team. 'The Ultras fans formed their identity in relation to their soccer clubs. Therefore, the soccer club became the focal point of their belief system, the entity to be valued beyond all else, to believe in, to defend and to die for if necessary' (El-Zatmah, 2012: 805). Consequently, the club provides the ritual focus of the ultras who structure their activities around the football season and its regular matches. At these matches ultras engage in a ritualistic performance which produces the spectacles and also reaffirms their belonging to a wider collective. These collectives are linked to the wider geographical area the club represents. Most teams are named after their city or region and this can lead to clubs becoming 'small mother countries', as Podaliri and Balestri (1998: 95) argue. Although this can link to racist and xenophobic behaviours, this does not automatically translate as typical for all ultras groups. Indeed, some are explicitly anti-racist or anti-fascist, while many would claim to be apolitical.

Ultras have become the most dominant form of fandom in world football. From the movement's origins in Italy in the late 1960s, it spread across southern Europe and into other parts of the continent. It is now the most dominant form of fandom in Germany, Poland, Greece, Southern France and the Balkans, as well as Indonesia and North Africa. Elements of the ultras style have been adopted in Eastern and Central Europe, Spain, Turkey, Australia, the US, Japan, Scotland and Scandinavia. It is even starting to take root in England, where the 1970s saw the development of hooliganism, a very different approach to the ultras style that was developing in Italy. As a diverse and dynamic culture, theorising the ultras becomes problematic. While it is true that there are certain similar features, there are many internal contradictions, paradoxes and local features that differentiate ultras across the world. More importantly, these contradictions can occur among groups within the same *curva*, terrace or stadium.

Football today is the largest participant and spectator sport in the world. More people across the globe engage in football-related activity than any other social pursuit. In this way, it represents the 'deep play' of wider society described by Geertz (1972) and, like Geertz's analysis, is overwhelmingly focused on masculine groups. As the ultras constitute the largest organised fandom in the most popular sport in the world, they represent a pertinent object of study. There are few social activities that operate across the globe, in virtually every community. Football is one of them. Studying football fandom gives a rare opportunity to study similar practices across local and national boundaries. As a style that has taken hold in many diverse countries, it gives us an opportunity to build forms of fandom up from the local and observe some common factors. As will be outlined in the following section, many authors have suggested that the use of certain displays and politics is what marks out the ultras as different. While these are common features, not all ultras supporting a team will share the same politics. Likewise, some ultras within a group focus on large visual displays using banners, pyrotechnics, drums, chants and flags. Others may concentrate on politics, while another group focuses on violence. Rather than focus on the local, politics or violence, this book draws a common thread through the performances enacted by the ultras and the emotional responses that exist through these regular acts. By drawing on the shared performances and emotions of the participants, we hope to show that collective mobilisation, belonging and identity are regularly and repetitively enacted. Football provides the ritual focus for these repetitive acts to be performed, as well as the space where comparisons can be made globally. It is for this reason that football represents one of the most important sites of study in contemporary society.

Ultras in scholarship

Football fans are inherently heterogeneous. The problem from an academic perspective is overgeneralisation. Ultras are often simply equated with hooliganism, the form of fandom and violence that originated in England. This is far too reductive, as Podaliri and Balestri (1998) argue. Ultras incorporate a wide range of techniques and paraphernalia into their fandom. As the example at the opening of this introduction highlighted, clothing, pyrotechnics, chanting, clapping and choreographies that utilise flags, images and banners are all part of the ultras style. While it is true that violence is also part of this culture, it is not the only aspect; and not every ultras group engages in violence. What unifies ultras is an extreme sense of loyalty and camaraderie with their fellow supporters, and they perform this with an unwavering loyalty and support for their team.

What is clear is that ultras see themselves as intimately linked to their club, which becomes an extension of their locality (Podaliri and Balestri, 1998; Doidge, 2015a). Historically, ultras emerged from the politically turbulent environment of 1970s Italy and were aligned to both left- and right-wing ideology. While Kassimeris (2011) correctly highlights the political aspect of football in Italy, he also succumbs to generalisations about ultras. He argues that 'in defence of the *curva*, the ultras will not hesitate to employ nationalistic and xenophobic rhetoric' (Kassimeris, 2011: 679). This implies that all ultras are nationalistic, racist, right-wing or ideologically driven. While it is true that *some* ultras engage in this type of abuse, it is not correct to say that *all* ultras do, or that all those who engage in this abuse are ultras. Fans of Hamburg club St Pauli, for instance, show that ultras can be involved in anti-discrimination activities and campaigns, and promote a motto '*gegen Deutschland*' ('against Germany'); another example is Ajax Amsterdam fans participating in a demonstration in support of immigrants. Many more are overly focused on local identity and this structures countless interactions (Kossakowski, 2013; Doidge, 2015a). The heterogeneity of ultras is reinforced by the fact that groups with rival political outlooks can exist side by side in support of the same club, as evidenced by the existence of groups of left-wing (*Avispero*) and right-wing (*Ligallo Fondo Norte*) ultras at Real Zaragoza. As academics, we have to be careful about generalising about *all* ultras groups, and specify that it is *certain* ultras groups.

This political generalisation becomes more problematic when assessed across the continents. Merkel (2012) succumbs to the same political essentialism in relation to German ultras. 'In sharp contrast with their Italian counterparts', Merkel (2012: 368) argues, 'German Ultras take a left-wing stance that tries to preserve an old-fashioned, romantic and idealised version of football. A huge banner that became part of the inventory of the Allianz Arena in Munich in 2008 sums up their main cause: *Gegen den modernen Fussball* (Against Modern Football).' It is not possible to say that all Italian ultras are right-wing; clubs like Livorno and Ternana have staunchly left-wing groups (Doidge, 2013). By the same extension, one cannot say that all German ultras are left-wing. Some groups of ultras who follow clubs like Dynamo Dresden have developed a reputation for nationalistic sentiments (Ziesche, 2018). Another example would be the Balkans where football fandom is often approached as being highly nationalistic and increasingly violent (Nielsen, 2010; 2013). While there is a significant level of both violence and xenophobia (see Brentin, 2016), a closer look at the intricate particularities conveys a much more complex and blurry image of ultras in South-eastern Europe (Brentin and Hodges, 2018). In Poland, considering that forty-five years of communism in the country had fostered aversion to leftist ideology, the ultras groups contesting the system can only rely on a set of conservative-patriotic-religious symbols as a means of expressing collective experience and social discontent. In most cases, however, it does not lead to nationalist excesses (Kossakowski *et al.*, 2018). Similarly, it is not correct to equate racism and xenophobia with far-right extremism. Back *et al.* (2001) highlighted that racism could be 'instrumental' and used for political purposes, or 'organic' and related to events on the pitch. While some groups do engage in these types of instrumental practices, this is not true of all ultras.

The use of politics in the stadium does not automatically translate as a clear expression of ideology. As Doidge (2013) argues, the symbols of Che Guevara and communism have become entwined as symbols of Livorno. Fans of the Tuscan team prominently display these in order to reinforce their identity as a 'left-wing club'. With their origins in a unique city that was the birthplace of the Italian Communist Party, Livorno fans emphasise their history with these symbols. Likewise, Spaaij and Viñas (2013: 185) argue:

> It should be noted that although left-wing fan groups draw on 'thick' ideologies to articulate their beliefs and legitimize their actions, we must bear in mind their often shallow ideologization, which in many cases goes no deeper than the display of symbols and paraphernalia. In that regard, it is arguably more pertinent to speak of a 'pseudo-ideology' built on image alone, lacking any coherence or depth of thought.

The use of symbols and political terminology can help reinforce a sense of collective identity without necessarily constituting instrumental political action. A useful example would be some of forms of protest action by football fans in Croatia. In order to send the governing bodies of Croatian football a clear message, and even more importantly to try and create international awareness of the problems that have taken over Croatian football, ultras have not shied away from the open evocation of fascist symbols (Holiga, 2014). Hodges and Stubbs (2016) describe this repertoire of actions as one of the 'paradoxes of politicisation' of Croatian football fans, who combine right-wing and neo-Nazi ideology with popular distrust of new elites and opposition to crony capitalism in football. Despite this, some fans do engage in political action (Testa and Armstrong, 2010; Doidge, 2013; 2015a; Totten, 2014; Guțu, 2017).

When discussing politics in the stadium, we have to be clear that this is ideological politics. Many ultras groups explicitly state that politics have no place in the stadium (Doidge, 2015a; Guțu, 2017). Yet when they state this, they are distancing themselves from the politics of left and right. As Guțu (2017: 3) argues in relation to Romanian ultras,

> Although between 2000 and 2008 ultras factions which shared right-wing or nationalist values were quite popular (Dinamo, Honor et Patria – Romanian National Team, Peluza Sud Steaua etc.), the same members participated actively in the protests against austerity measures from January 2012, against the right-wing government. Today, we notice the ultras becoming ideologically moderate, some of them getting involved in democratic causes of the civil society.

This does not mean that ultras are not political in the broadest definition of the term, nor does it mean they are not racist or xenophobic. Ultras in Poland have engaged in political events like the Independence March where the most influential ultras groups participate, marching shoulder to shoulder with no mutual hostility. Another example of political activism by ultras is the banners and protests that are frequently held to challenge the increased commercialism and regulation of the ultras style of fandom. This has become linked under the umbrella term 'Against Modern Football'. It is through this generic slogan that a broader 'ultras mentality' has developed across Europe (Doidge, 2017). In some cases, the attitude of Against Modern Football serves for groups' reflexivity (Numerato, 2015).

The cross-cultural and global style of the ultras also means that cultural and geographical aspects cannot be generalised. Pilz and Wölki-Schumacher (2010: 22) essentialise certain aspects when they state that

> The 'South European style' refers to the use of pyrotechnics, the 'East European style' more to the stealing of banners and scarves and the 'German style' perhaps more to the organisation and operation of fan policy.

As the Southern Europe geographical area is quite broad, covering Italy, Southern France, Greece and the Balkans, it is naive to suggest that all ultras in the disparate cities and nations of the region prefer to use pyrotechnics. This style is also popular in Denmark, Sweden, Poland, Austria and Turkey, for example. More importantly, while some pyrotechnics have been used in Italy, the location where the ultras phenomenon started, it is not the dominant form. As Spaaij and Viñas (2013) observe, the ultras movement is a complex web of localised activities that adapts to various local, national and transnational influences.

Other cultural aspects are also generalised. While there are many websites that seek to sell clothing for ultras, this does not translate as a uniform worn across Europe. As Kennedy (2013: 132) suggests: 'Ultras identify themselves with a certain kind of clothes and attitude and, crucially, by a specific area of their club's stadium which is considered "off-limits" for non-ultra fellow supporters.' This is not always the case. As Guțu (2017: 7) witnesses, 'in the ultras culture, apart from the group hoodie or jacket, there are no dress code rules'. This is in sharp contrast to the 'casuals' style associated with hooliganism in Britain. Casuals wear a variety of leisurewear influenced by travels to Europe, or as in Indonesia through learning about European casuals through social media and the Internet. At the same time, this style is devoid of club colours, enabling the casuals to evade police detection. Ultras, in contrast, are about public visibility.

Similarly, the territoriality of ultras varies by club. It is true that some ultras groups are very protective of 'their' space; ultras groups occupy different areas of the *curva*, terrace or stadium. In Nice the

Brigate Sud are named after the South Stand where they congregate, while the *Armada Rupetata* are in the North Stand. It is fair to say that State authorities, and those perceived to be in authority, are not welcome in the *curva* (Gabler, 2010; Doidge, 2015a). In relation to the dynamics between supporters, some groups like Lazio's *Irriducibili* have used violence against those not joining in with their chants. This does not automatically imply that all ultras are this protective or that non-ultras cannot enter the stands where the ultras congregate. The style of fandom is characterised by those who are passionately performing the rituals of the group. As the supporters ripple out from the core they engage in the chants and choreographies to different levels. Supporters who do not self-identify as ultras often still participate in the performance. Ultimately, the physical dominance and governing mentality of the central ultras group will impact how the group performs and who is welcomed into the space.

What makes ultras distinctive is their hierarchy and organisation. While the core of the ultras may be predominantly young and male, female ultras can hold significant roles within the group (Cere, 2002; Ginhoux, 2018). There are specific roles and decision-making processes. Often decisions on the form and content of the performances are made in small decision-making groups, called *direttivi* in Italian, that are comprised of a capo and others responsible for fundraising, recruitment and creative ideas. While members are free to share ideas, the majority of members follow their leadership. Conflict with leadership either leads to power battles or the formation of new groups.

The contradictions of the literature are partly a result of the complex processes at work within the ultras movement. On the one hand, the ultras are fragmenting and smaller groups are emerging. This is leading to conflict and differentiation within fan bases. On the other, it shows how ultras of different teams are putting aside differences to discuss big issues that affect all groups (Doidge, 2017). Ultras are anything but homogenous. Traditional rivalries and twinning arrangements have broken up and been reconfigured. These relationships are fluid, ebbing and flowing depending on the context. While ultras of the Genoese clubs, Sampdoria and Genoa, are traditional rivals, they joined forces to launch an ultras congress to decide upon shared 'values' in the wake of the murder of a Genoa fan, Vincenzo Spagnolo, by an AC Milan ultra. This murder also reflected the fragmentation of the AC Milan ultras (Podaliri and Balestri, 1998). Spagnolo's murderer was part of the *Barbour Gang* who dressed in 'English' Barbour jackets and sought to emulate English casuals. They acted independently of the main ultras group, the *Brigate Rossonere*, so they could evade police. The Poznan

Pact in Poland drew up a similar set of 'rules of engagement' after an escalation of violence and police repression. The independent, separate and often hostile groups support each other in clashes with the police. In 2011 ultras presented the same slogan against the government at several stadiums: 'the biggest enemy comes close in conflict with the system and the government'.

What is clear is that the ultras are a specific style of fandom, coupled with a willingness to defend this style through violence and political protest. This cultural form is influenced by contact with other fans through physical interaction and social media. While ultras of competing groups are collaborating nationally, they are also sharing ideas and culture across Europe (Doidge, 2017). Many of the foci of protests are against similar trends across the continent. The result is a unique case study on the development of a European cultural and political movement.

Football as public sphere

The cross-cultural nature of football makes it a pertinent space for the development of a public sphere. Habermas (1989) argued a public sphere was created through individuals exchanging ideas in coffee shops. Aside from the bourgeois and masculine focus of Habermas's work, he identifies the importance of discussing ideas in a shared space in the construction of political ideas. In this case, both Guschwan (2013) and Testa and Armstrong (2010) have identified how the stadium is a key site in the creation of political identities. Guschwan (2013: 11) suggests that 'the discourse within the stadium can be unruly and pose a threat to dominant powers, and the stadium is well suited for the fragmented public sphere heavily influenced by media. The stadium is one venue that enables an even broader spectrum of ideas to be expressed.' Roversi and Balestri (2000: 191) identify 'the disintegration of many places of assembly and socialisation outside stadium' as a major factor in the stadium becoming the major expression of politics. Stadiums are a great space for the presentation of cultural performances (Alexander, 2006), gaining importance due to the sizeable audience.

While the stadium is a powerful site in the creation of a public sphere, football is not restricted to ninety minutes on a Saturday or Sunday afternoon. Football is an everyday, mundane practice (Stone, 2007). As Nowell-Smith (1979) has argued, football is debated all week in bars, clubs and workplaces. The discussions that take place often last longer than the match itself. This is particularly true of the media who fill newspaper columns and television airtime with discussions, debates and gossip about football. It is while discussing football that other public matters can be discussed. Supporters' clubs provide similar spaces for the discussion of political matters that help shape public opinion (Doidge, 2015a). Similarly, the political messages that are displayed by the ultras across Europe are not produced solely within the stadium. They are discussed in pubs and meeting places before the match. The banners and chants are devised and produced away from the stadium. In order to prepare their extraordinary choreographies, which can extend to hundreds of metres in length, Polish ultras use old, abandoned buildings or rent factory halls. These spaces of production are kept strictly confidential in fear of 'uninvited guests' from other clubs. These ideas are shaped continuously throughout the week. A significant aspect of Habermas's (1989) theory is that ideas developed in private are shared and debated in public. Significantly, these styles have started to be displayed outside of the stadium in other public spaces. In Algeria young people started creating tifos and displaying them on an abandoned six-storey building to protest against the regime of Abdelaziz Bouteflika (Mezahi, 2019). The ultras style has moved full circle from political protests in the piazzas of Italy to the stadium, and back to political protests.

Football also provides a space to expand social networks away from traditional family, friends and work colleagues. Putnam (*et al.*, 1993; 2000) has suggested that 'bridging social capital' helps to link people from different demographic backgrounds; fans can be 'bridged' thanks to common passion and love for the club. This social capital supports different groups to develop a wider understanding of their community, while sharing and debating political ideas. Areas with stronger 'civic traditions', Putnam *et al.* (1993) argue, help make 'democracy work'. Putnam and his colleagues construct extreme generalisations about Italian society, while overlooking the fact that the two biggest corruption scandals in Italian history originated in the 'civic' north. It can also not be assumed that political ideas will automatically emerge from shared social spaces; members have to want to participate in the debate. Despite this, Putnam identifies the importance of interpersonal networks in sharing and debating ideas. Interpersonal networks are crucial in the case of football fandom as many undertakings and actions are based on an informal and 'guerrilla' level of trust. Consequently, football supporters' federations, supporters' clubs and ultras groups are pertinent sites for the development of ideas and help contribute to a wider engagement with politics.

The political economy of football: the economic transformation of global football

Arguably, football fans constitute one of the biggest social movements, particularly in Europe today. Regular fixtures and social media provide numerous opportunities for fans to interact and share ideas about football, governance and local or national politics. The political identities detailed above explicitly link to modern identities based on nationalism and religion. New political movements and identities are forming around specific changes in football, as the global game has undergone a dramatic economic and social transformation since the 1990s. The pan-European Champions League has led to greater interaction among fans and this has impacted fan identity (King, 2000; 2003). In addition, the economic transformation has affected the relationship between fans and the clubs they support. Fan groups from across the globe have politicised in various ways in response to these commercial changes. They have also initiated campaigns for greater inclusion within football, particularly in relation to racism, sexism, homophobia and disability rights.

The commercial transformation in European football has also had a detrimental effect on numerous clubs. Since 1992 there have been over forty clubs who have entered administration in English football. Meanwhile, Scotland's most successful club, Rangers, was relegated to the lowest professional league in 2012 after financial mismanagement. Even Borussia Dortmund, one of Germany's most successful and popular clubs, went bankrupt in 2005. In the early twenty-first century several Italian clubs experienced financial crisis after their parent companies went bankrupt (Foot, 2006; Doidge, 2015a). This led to Silvio Berlusconi introducing the *salva calcio* ('Save football') law in 2002. Major clubs like Fiorentina and Napoli went under during this period, and were forced to reform and work their way back up from the lower divisions. The response to these financial crises has been varied. In the Balkans, particularly in Bulgaria and Romania, major football clubs have been financially struggling to survive with many smaller clubs already in administration (Chiriac, 2012; Borisov, 2015). The politico-economic modernisation after 1989 has also affected many clubs in Poland. Some of them, who were financed during the communist era by State industries, lost both financial and organisational stability. Many of them have been revived by the most engaged fans, who, metaphorically speaking, changed scarves to ties (Kossakowski, 2017a).

In England supporters' trusts have been formed to raise money to save local clubs (see Brown, 1998; García and Welford, 2015; Dunn, 2017). These supporters' trusts were given political support in 1999 by the New Labour government who assisted with the formation of an umbrella organisation, Supporters' Direct. Active supporter engagement in Germany successfully saved many clubs from crisis (Merkel, 2012). This form of fan engagement has been minimal or delayed in other nations, for example in Italy (Doidge, 2014; 2015a). These fans pursue many different forms and levels of engagement. Some are passive fans (Cleland, 2010), who simply wish to watch the sport and have no other involvement. Many others see their fandom as a significant part of their individual identity and will engage with the sport in a variety of ways. This can include establishing and participating in political movements to preserve this identity or challenge perceived changes to the sport.

Tarrow (1998) suggests that social movements operate in a cycle depending on the efficacy of the political regime. More importantly, social movements take advantage of political opportunity when they perceive that their actions will have an effect. While Tarrow is correct to highlight the importance of the political structure to the growth, sustenance and success of political movements, it is not always due to political weakness. For football fans across Europe, the various campaigns, organisations and protests have centred on specific changes that they perceive to have directly impacted them. In some cases the focus is legislation imposed to combat violence, while in others it is all-seater stadiums and ticket prices which impact the enjoyment of some fans. For example, various disparate fans and ultras united across Italy to challenge the imposition of a fan identity card known as the *tessera del tifoso* (Guschwan, 2013). This was not due to political opportunity, but perceived injustice and frustration at continued draconian legislation aimed at preventing violence.

The transformation of football fandom

Football operates at a unique level. Simultaneously, it helps to reinforce local, national and regional identification. As noted, it is rare for clubs not to be named after a geographical location. Examples include Juventus of Turin, Celtic and Rangers of Glasgow, Go Ahead Eagles based in Deventer in the Netherlands and Millonarios FC from Bogotá. Some names reflect the industrial roots of a club, such as Rayon Sports in Rwanda, Germany's Bayer Leverkusen and most clubs in the Japanese J-League. Others illustrate a broader narrative, such as Al Ahly ('My Family') in Cairo, Vasco da Gama in Rio or Olympiacos in Athens. But generally, in club football teams are invariably named after a locality. This could be a city district (e.g. St Pauli in Hamburg, Sampdoria in Genoa or Beşiktaş in Istanbul), a city (e.g. AEK Athens, Olympique de

Marseilles or Ajax Amsterdam) or a region (e.g. River Plate, Lazio, East Bengal, Bohemians or Notts County). This moniker helps provide a local identity for fans (see Chapter 7). These teams take part in regional or national leagues. Regular interaction among fans within these leagues helps determine the extent of the locale or nation. For example, Trieste was annexed by Italy after the First World War. Mussolini ensured that the city's football team, Triestina, were members of the first Serie A national championships (Foot, 2006). The fans had to be Italian if their club was playing in the Italian championship. Similarly, national football teams help maintain an identification with the nation. International competition provides opportunities to delineate oneself from other nations. Newly established states, like Croatia or Kosovo, often ask for membership in international sport associations as intensively as they demand membership in the United Nations (Menary, 2007; Brentin and Tregoures, 2016). There are also some non-FIFA international competitions, like the CONIFA World Cup or Island Games, that provide additional space for micro-states or unrecognised nations to place themselves on the world stage.

The growth of the European Union, in particular, has provided new opportunities for actors to participate in European political action (Tarrow, 1995; Della Porta and Tarrow, 2005). As Della Porta and Diani (2006: 44) argue, 'the presence of supranational entities tends to change the criteria according to which actors define themselves, as well as their strategies'. UEFA, the European football federation, is a significant supranational institution that impacts the identity and strategies of fans. As a result, UEFA have become a significant target for many ultras groups across Europe. Although UEFA was formed in 1954, it reflected the primacy of the nation in post-war Europe; the interests of national federations were paramount. In 1992, following extensive lobbying from elite European clubs, UEFA reformatted the European Cup competition (King, 2003), creating the Champions League, which ensured more intercontinental matches and enhanced television revenues. It is this commercial focus that ultras criticise the most. The criticisms expressed by the ultras could be regarded as a voice on how the reorganisation of European competitions has focused on the financial interests of owners, clubs and federations, not fans. These criticisms have led to similar patterns of protest being replicated towards clubs, national federations and governments across the globe, as Chapter 7 will highlight.

Football both unites and divides. Regular European matches through UEFA competitions have increased cross-continental interaction. In some cases, this continues to facilitate division on national or ethnic lines. Occasionally, this leads to violence, racism and abuse. For others it encourages cross-cultural exchange. The 'English disease' of hooliganism influenced masculine fan groups across Europe in the 1980s (Giulianotti, 1999; Spaaij, 2006; Tsoukala, 2009). Since the 1990s, the ultras style of fandom has spread from Italy across the Mediterranean and is now the dominant form of fandom in Europe and globally in general. Significantly, both contradictory styles can exist within the same fan group. Supporters of Legia Warsaw in Poland can take the cultural influences of the Italian ultras and English hooligans, while simultaneously exhibiting racism and xenophobia towards non-Poles (Doidge, 2014). These cultural influences do not automatically lead to political agreement, let alone action.

Fans have mobilised in response to the politico-economic transformation of football in the 1990s. These early movements witnessed fans mobilising locally around specific issues affecting their club. The challenge, as King (2003) has argued, is how to sustain these movements without particular national grievances. Despite this, fans have united nationally and across Europe around a specific set of issues, particularly the new forms of consumerism implemented by clubs, ticket prices and, notably, around additional security and policing. National groups like the Football Supporters' Association (FSA) in England and Wales, Association of Active Football Fans (BAFF) in Germany, National Union of Supporters Associations (OZSK) in Poland and Turkey's Taraftar Haklari Derneği continue to form in order to champion fans' rights and issues, and not only those engaged in ultras culture. Alongside these groups and associations, Football Supporters Europe (FSE) has been running since 2008 to support and connect fans. They have held annual congresses in London, Hamburg, Barcelona, Copenhagen and Istanbul, plus numerous networking events across Europe. These fan-led events help provide a physical space for fans from across the continent to meet and share ideas, strategies and issues. Regionalisation of fan-led associations and movements help delineate the continent, while simultaneously bringing fans together within a common cultural space (Cleland *et al.*, 2018).

The emotional performance of the ultras

Much of the academic literature on football fans has followed a fairly consistent focus on political mobilisation or hooliganism (Taylor, 1971a; 1971b; Dunning *et al.*, 1988; Redhead, 1997; King, 1998; 2003; Sandvoss, 2003; Spaaij, 2006; Millward, 2011; Pope, 2012; Dunn, 2014; Doidge, 2015a; Cleland *et al.*, 2018; Numerato, 2018). While these themes exist within this book – after all, they are hard to deny in the canon of activities ultras undertake – this book takes a new approach to understanding football fandom. Through an analysis of the ultras, this book argues that while there are certain common aspects to ultras fandom, notably the choreographies, devotion to the team, predominantly masculine nature and use of violence, many groups are heterogeneous and have different traditions, ideas and approaches. To overcome this, and perhaps unsurprisingly for a book called *Ultras: The Passion and Performance of Contemporary Football Fandom*, it draws on theories of performance and emotions to highlight a more fundamental sociological question: how do groups form? Through the ritualistic performances, ultras produce a collective emotional energy that not only unites them during the match but also sustains their identification to the club between matches. This combination of regular performances and emotional belonging can help us understand the formation of groups around forms of consumption like football.

Consequently, the following two chapters will focus on the performance and emotional aspects of fandom and provide a theoretical structure for the book. Chapter 1 outlines the ultras' performance and how the collective rituals associated with their style of fandom helps produce a wider collective, thus challenging ideas that contemporary social life is individualistic. The act of producing the spectacle within the stadium – before, during and after the match – constitutes the ritual process, within which there is a liminal space that helps establish the collective. These regular rituals help the collective perfect their activities and reinforce themselves as a group. This produces a sense of flow that builds a sense of emotional attachment to the group. The role of emotions is explored further in Chapter 2. These have been under-theorised in football fandom studies, yet they help explain the range of relationships that fans create, as well as the anxiety and euphoria that the game produces. These emotions are externalised as love as fans ontologically identify with the football club. This sustains their involvement until the next game.

Subsequent chapters outline the various key features of the ultras style of fandom. History and tradition are important aspects of social collectives, and the ultras are no exception. Chapter 3 draws on Hobsbawm's notion of invented traditions to highlight how ultras construct their histories through choreographies and entwine them into the histories of their city, region or nation. As well as the stadium, social media is also a space for the performance of the ultras, which will be explored in Chapter 4. Choreographies, stories and stickers are photographed, filmed or recounted online to continue the public presentation of the groups. As noted earlier, the ultras are predominantly masculine fan groups. Chapter 5 provides an analysis of the performance of gender, particularly hegemonic masculinity, through the choreographies and activities of ultras groups. This gendered approach leads into a chapter on violence (Chapter 6), which has become a part of the repertoire of some groups. Again, much of the violence is performative and is designed to assert symbolic dominance over rivals. Once again, choreographies help present this symbolic violence. Ultras are also political in a variety of ways. Chapter 7 will address the ideological and football politics that characterise much of the ultras' activities. Again, these politics are performed through chants, banners, stickers and choreographies to reinforce the groups' conceptions of themselves.

Ultras: The Passion and Performance of Contemporary Football Fandom seeks to make a clear theoretical shift in studies of football fandom. While it sits in the body of literature focused on political mobilisations and hooliganism, it emphasises more fundamental sociological questions about group formation, notably collective performances and emotional relationships. In this way we seek to move away from studies of fans that are restricted to one club, one nation or even one region. Choreographies, stickers and public comments are texts that present these collectives to the outside world. By looking at performances and emotions, we try to take a more universal outlook that permits analysis of groups across the globe. Although the primary focus is Europe, mainly due to this region being the birthplace of the movement and the specialism of the authors, we aspire that the theoretical principles can apply elsewhere. More fundamentally, we hope to present an argument that the ultras, and football fandom more generally, are incredibly important groups to study as they articulate more than would simple customers of a football club.

1

The ultras' performance

Shortly before kick-off at the UEFA Europa League match between Legia Warsaw of Poland and FK Aktobe of Kazakhstan in 2014, the home fans displayed a giant frieze that extended across the height of both tiers of the Zyleta stand of the stadium. The image was a lampoon of the logo of UEFA. In the centre of the UEFA insignia was an illustration of an obese pig, dressed in a shirt bestowed with euro currency symbols. In his trotters, the pig was holding a piece of paper inscribed with '6 < 1'. Underneath this altered UEFA logo was a banner, written in English, stating, 'Because football doesn't matter. Money does'. Pointedly, the word 'football' was written in red and green ink, the colours of the Polish champions. Meanwhile, the colours of the word 'money' were green and white horizontal stripes. Throughout the display the Legia Warsaw fans chanted loudly while rhythmically clapping. After their rendition, they applauded themselves before many members of the stand held aloft red flares to provide a powerful visual display. Once the smoke subsided the match began, while the fans continued to sing loudly in unison.

In one performance, it is possible to encapsulate the phenomenon of the ultras, a particular form of football fandom. Over seven thousand fans occupy the Zyleta stand at the Marshall Józef Piłsudski Municipal Stadium. The fanatical fans, or ultras, also take their name from the moniker of the stand. Predominantly male, they wear white T-shirts over their outerwear to present a uniformed bloc and sing and clap throughout the match. On the occasion of the match against FK Aktobe, these fans were making clear their dislike of football's governing body in Europe. Legia Warsaw had recently beaten Celtic, the Scottish champions, 6–1 over two legs in Europe's premier competition, the Champions League. Despite this victory on the field, a bureaucratic error had resulted in an ineligible player, Bartosz Bereszynski, coming on as a substitute in the eighty-eighth minute of the second leg. Due to the error, Legia Warsaw were expelled from the competition and demoted to the Europa League, while Celtic continued in place of the Polish champions. The *Zyleta* ultras group were displaying their displeasure at being the victims of UEFA's bureaucracy and suggested that money was the real cause of their expulsion. The banner's message, 'Because football doesn't matter. Money does', was unambiguous and written in English to reach a global audience. 'Football' was inscribed in the colours of Legia to reinforce that their team stood for the values of the sport. The colours of Celtic – green and white – were used for the word 'money' to insinuate that their larger fan base and potential television audience was the 'real' reason that Legia Warsaw had been expelled from the Champions League. The central image strengthened the suggestion that UEFA bureaucrats were fat pigs, adorned with money. The ultras' protest was reinforced by the use of hundreds of flares; bearing in mind that pyrotechnics are banned by UEFA, these fans wanted to make their repudiation of UEFA regulations unambiguously clear. In one scene, it was possible to see a public expression of protest against European regulation that drew on a variety of cultural forms taken from across the continent.

There is a diverse range of aspects that make up the identity of the ultras. From choreographies, *striscione* (banners) and chanting, stickers that are exchanged with friends or used to publicise the group, to violence and chaos, there are certain common themes that unite ultras from all teams. Despite this unification and similar culture, there are certain specific features that are unique to fans of each team. Choreographies are one of the distinctive aspects of ultras culture, and the one that distinguishes it from other fan cultures, specifically the 'English style' of hooligans or casuals (Roversi and Balestri, 2000). The choreographies are a vivid, colourful expression of the passion of the ultras in the stands. They range from flags, banners, scarves or coordinated clothing, to vast works of art painted onto colossal pieces of cloth that are stitched together to cover the stand. These images will draw on local history, significant moments from the club's past, or make barbed political statements. Alongside this visual spectacle, fans will also engage in singing, chanting and clapping. The combination of this aural and visual spectacle is designed to present the group to the wider public. As these performances constitute such an important part of the ultras style of fandom, this chapter will draw on theories of performance and group mobilisation. And with the ultras representing one of the largest collectives across contemporary Europe, and expanding into Africa, Asia and North America, this chapter will challenge notions of a growing individualism in society, before addressing how the rituals of football encourage the collective identity of ultras. Finally, it seeks to place the role of emotion centrally in the story. One of the most important ingredients of the fan experience is the atmosphere. This is vital in encouraging the collective effervescence of the group and helps link the individual fan to the wider collective.

Collective identity in an individualistic society

The ultras represent a rare collective culture that manifests itself across geographical boundaries. Consequently, they pose a theoretical puzzle for those commentators that suggest that society is becoming more individualistic and less focused on wider social collectives. The decline in public engagement in civil society has been a central focus of academic, media and political discourse for centuries. Rapid industrialisation and urbanisation during the nineteenth century led to increased academic analysis of transitions from *Gemeinschaft* to *Gesellschaft* and resulted in the birth of sociology as a discipline (Tönnies, 2001). Communities began to move from the rigid mechanical solidarity of small kinship communities to the organic solidarity of larger, fragmented society (Durkheim, 1997). This transition was seen to contribute to a sense of helplessness, or anomie, as members of society lost their traditional purpose and focus of life (Durkheim, 1952).

Taking a social-psychological approach, Riesman (1961) suggested that social actors have moved through various character traits. Society has moved from groups of 'tradition-directed' individuals, who focused on tradition to provide group solidarity and regulation to the more 'inner-directed' individuals of the modern era. These individuals had a moral compass internalised through their education and upbringing and this drove the individual to succeed. These individuals were possessed of a strong work ethic and focused inwards, on themselves and their family. As businesses changed from small family enterprises into large corporations, and as the service sector and bureaucracy grew, individuals became more 'other-directed'; they had to be aware of other people, as they had to rely on them for support. Morality was not internalised, but was done in relation to others, depending on the context and impact.

Public participation has become increasingly privatised throughout modernity. Elias (1978; 2000) suggested that the public body became increasingly privatised as intimate actions, such as eating, bathing and going to the bathroom, were removed from the public gaze. These new manners and morals became internalised by cultural elites that then acted as a marker of distinction for others (or those who Riesman would call 'other-directed') to emulate. As human activities became increasingly specialist with greater division of labour, individuals began to form figurations, or networks of interdependence. As these networks grew, individuals became increasingly disconnected from each other and it became harder for the individual to understand the overall social context (Elias, 2001). As individual personality was asserted, social actors removed themselves from the wider public, a development which has been assisted by the increased range of privatised spaces available to individuals (Elias, 2001). However, this privatisation and individualisation necessitated a paradox. According to Habermas (1989), the 'public' became a space where private individuals utilised the knowledge they had amassed privately to debate wider issues publicly. As the 'public' debated politics and science in associations and coffee houses, there was a greater interest in the wider public life, which led to the State and society becoming entwined. Separation from the 'public' would lead to a less holistic understanding of the world. However, Habermas's conception of the 'public' clearly focused on white, middle-class, masculine discussions of 'public opinion', which also isolated itself from other forms of knowledge. That said, for the ultras, engagement with other fans online, in bars and around the stadium helps to create a broader understanding of themselves as a wider collective of ultras.

Changes to consumption have facilitated the increased individualisation of society. Habermas (1989) argued that the rise of television took individuals away from public discussion by keeping them at home. Consumption was also identified as a key foundation of individualisation by Sennett (1976), a student of Riesman. Sennett argued that other-directed individuals, who became focused on presenting themselves to other people, lost sight of the wider public engagement which built a cohesive society. Other-directed social actors learned to develop themselves in relation to others, but in Sennett's opinion this led to increased narcissism and inward-focus, rather than wider public engagement. Increases in production actively promoted and provided an increased range of commodities for consumption. This permitted individuals to consume commodities that could present their personality and identity to the public gaze (Sennett, 1976).

The decline of community has captured the imagination of politicians, academics and the media. In particular, the term 'social capital' has evolved to reflect this decline and has become a popular academic abstraction. Broadly speaking, social capital refers to the networks of people an individual can call upon in order to navigate their way through life (Bourdieu, 1986; Coleman, 1988; Putnam *et al.*, 1993; Portes, 1998; Putnam, 2000). The current popularity of social capital has enabled it to be seen as the 'missing link' between the anomie of society and the increased individualism and decline of participation in public life. Furthermore, the term has been extended to explain political involvement and democracy. In his analysis of the success and failure of Italian regions, Putnam has suggested that social capital generated in civic associations helps in 'making democracy work' (Putnam et al., 1993). Putnam builds on the observations of Tocqueville, who suggested that lack of associationism led to 'soft despotism', where individuals stop engaging with government in exchange for material needs (Tocqueville, 1969).

The arguments towards individualism negate the social aspects of the self (Mead, 1934). Our sense of identity and self is located through interaction with others and in opposition to conceptions of the 'other' with whom we choose (or not) to interact. This informs our social actions, morals and opinions (Mauss, 1967; Goffman, 1971; Elias, 2001). Modern society has become evermore complicated with wider networks and divisions of labour (Elias, 1978; 2001). 'But the epoch which produces this standpoint,' as Marx (1970: 189) argues, 'namely that of the solitary individual, is precisely the epoch of the (as yet) most highly developed social … relations.' The more complicated the society, the more opportunities there are to articulate one's sense of self. In a global society that has intensified inter-relations between individuals through regular interaction in cultural events like football, there become many opportunities to articulate the self.

Football fandom is an extension of the self. Ontologically, the team becomes an extension of the individual. As Maguire (1999) argues, fans refer to teams in the first-person plural: 'we' won or lost on Saturday or Sunday; friends ask how 'you' did at the weekend. The use of personal pronouns explicitly links the individual with the team. With football fandom, this ontological extension ensures that fans can take changes to 'their' football team very personally. Katz (1999) showed in relation to road rage that an 'attack' on the car becomes an 'attack' on the individual. This can be true of physical violence or abuse by other fans. As demonstrated in relation to hooliganism, indiscriminate policing can help unify the group of fans (Stott and Reicher, 1998; Stott et al., 2001; Doidge, 2015a). Politico-economic changes within the governance of the game can also act as motivation. These 'attacks' elicit an embodied emotional response. Some fans take them personally and this drives their motivation to challenge or resist. As Katz (1999: 24) argues, 'we must understand how becoming "pissed off" is not simply a "release of tension" or some other negatively defined phenomenon but is a positive affect to construct new meaning for the situation'. Likewise, social movements occur from a 'moral shock' which helps mobilise activists who work to build on this moral outrage and anger to focus attention (Jasper, 1997). Fans, and ultras in particular, mobilise in order to assert some control over their club.

The decline of participation in associations underplays the proliferation of new forms of association and new social movements since the 1960s. There has been an increase in single-issue movements in a wide range of fields, from environmentalism to consumer groups (Touraine, 1981; Melucci and Mier, 1989). These groups have also been affected by changes to consumption. While Putnam (2000) identifies this range of social movements, he suggests that they have been reduced to acts of consumption where individuals 'purchase' a social movement through a regular donation. This argument negates the influence of new social movements in transforming consciousness, particularly around the civil rights, feminism, sexuality and environmental issues. While traditional political and social groups are fragmenting, Maffesoli (1996: 81) argues that movements and groups are forming and are often 'tied by culture, communication, leisure or fashion, to a commodity'. It is in this context that we can see how ultras have emerged as a collective force.

The ultras' performance

The ultras provide an opportunity to see how social groups form. They comprise two significant aspects: repetitive performances and conflict. Football provides a regular space where collective identities can be performed; they are a ritual. These performances arise out of conflict with others – be they rival fans, the football authorities or the State. According to Geertz (1983: 29): 'Given the dialectical nature of things, we all need our opponents, and both sorts of approach are essential.' Likewise, Carlson (1996: 5) states: 'Performance is always performance *for* someone, some audience that recognises and validates it as a performance even when, as is occasionally the case, that audience is the self.' This reaffirms that the individual self is socially constructed (Mead, 1934). Riesman (1961) reinforces this with his conception of other-directed individuals: our sense of self, morality and identity is done in relation to the audience we are addressing. Cooley (1902) referred to this as the 'looking-glass self': we build a conception of ourselves by reflecting on the information we receive from our interactions with others.

The importance of the ultras' performance is that it takes into account the audience and presents a stylised impression of the group. Goffman (1959) identified how individuals choose a range of personas depending upon the social context. Although he was specifically referring to an individual's presentation of self within specific settings, we can extend this to the presentation of the group. How we present ourselves in an interview is very different to the self we present down the pub with friends. His dramaturgical model divided the performance into two distinct areas: front- and back-region performances. While performances in the front region, or more public spaces, are more formal and carefully constructed, those in the back region are more relaxed. Yet this public presentation of self is constructed in the back region in negotiation and interaction with others. As Giulianotti (1995) highlighted with the Tartan Army, fans of Scotland's national team, there is a careful negotiation on how fans (and ultras) should present themselves. For the ultras the choreographies are discussed, planned and produced backstage, in private and away from the public gaze. Part of this is to prevent their rivals from knowing what will be performed. Yet these preparations also carefully construct the desired image of the group to their rivals and fellow fans, and crucially, to themselves.

While recognising that a performance is for an audience, within the stadium there are multiple audiences: rival fans, the players, media, the authorities, club officials and the ultras group themselves. As Abercrombie and Longhurst (1998: 68–9) observe,

> The essential feature of this audience-experience is that, in contemporary society everyone becomes an audience all the time. Being a member of an audience is no longer an exceptional event, nor an everyday event. Rather it is constitutive of everyday life.

As individuals and groups are always performers who present themselves in everyday life, they are also audiences. Consequently, everybody becomes members of the audience. It is within the spectacle inside the stadium that the individual becomes part of a collective.

> It is the transformation of this relationship between performer and crowd, from the separation of audience and actors to one in which the spectators acquire the active role of participants in collective processes, that is sometimes cathartic and that may symbolise or even create a community. (Carter, 2008: 86)

The operative word here is 'active'. Many people attend football stadiums and watch the match. Not all of them will feel part of the community in the same way. And not all of them will feel that they are ultras. What distinguishes the ultras is the active engagement in staging the spectacle. Each individual participates in the performance and it is this active participation that creates and recreates the collective.

It is through repetitive social actions that the self is constructed.

MacIntyre (1985: 32) critiqued Goffman by arguing that he 'has liq-
uidated the self into its role-playing, arguing that the self is no more
than "a peg" on which the clothes of the role are hung ... For Goffman,
for whom the social world is all, the self is therefore nothing at all, it
occupies no social space.' But this rests on the notion that there is an
essentialised self, rather than social selves, or a self that is constructed
through action. Butler (1990) argues that identity is not an act or mas-
querade, but a continually repeated performance; 'there need not be
a "doer behind the deed,"' as Butler (1990: 142) argues, 'but that the
"doer" is variably constructed in and through the deed.' Regular repetitive practice helps reinforce the self, and football provides one space for
this. It is this repetition that is key, as '[t]he subject is not *determined*
by the rules through which it is generated because signification is *not
a founding act, but rather a regulated process of repetition* that both
conceals itself and enforces its rules precisely through the production of
substantialising effects' (Butler, 1990: 145, original emphasis).

The performative aspects of football fandom allow the expression
of one's sense of self, replete with notions of politics, locality, race and
gender. Fans are not cultural dupes or non-volitional actors as Goffman
or Butler may suggest. Significantly, fans are active producers *and* consumers of this performance. Reinforcing the repetitive nature of fandom,
Hills (2002: 159, original emphasis) argues that

> Each and every expression of fan identity is hence both a non-volitional
> citation *and* the (consumerist) 'choice' of a volitional fan-subject. The
> performative consumption which characterises media fandom ... is hence
> both an act and an iteration-without-origin.

Consuming football is a resource used by fans for identity production
and social performances. What is significant about ultras is that they
eschew official merchandise from their clubs. They produce their own
scarves, flags, stickers, banners and choreographies. Ultras groups then
consume their own products. They wear the scarves and T-shirts of their
ultras group. Choreographies are recorded and photographed to enjoy
again, as well as posted online to showcase the group to others.

On a more fundamental level, the group breathe together. Although
breathing is a primary biological activity, it is rarely consciously
acknowledged. Yet breathing together helps create the community as
they become embodied through shared cultural activities or rhythmic
activity in unison (Lande, 2007). Singing in groups requires a synchronisation of breathing. Choral singing requires participants to inhale
briefly before long exhalations during the song (Hemakom *et al.*, 2017).
As argued later in the chapter, quality is not important in the ultras'

performance; participation is the only requirement. Consequently, few ultras are expert singers who have learned how to breathe efficiently in order to sing well. Singing as a collective harmonises breathing and helps produce a sense of collective rhythm and synchronisation. This bodily performance incorporates the individual into the wider collective.

Through repetitive practice, members perfect their performance and delineate themselves from others. Chambliss (1989) observed that elite swimmers were different from others through the quality of the work they did when they trained and how they approached it, not just through working harder or for longer. Excellence was 'mundane', not exceptional. Elite swimmers did not just swim more; they enjoyed training, particularly the early starts. More importantly, they repeatedly practised the less enjoyable aspects of their sport: the turns, dives and small elements of technique. It is this attention to detail that elevates the ordinary into the extraordinary. What makes being an ultra a way of life is this attention to detail. It is not just about attending more games. Many fans attend matches home and away, but that does not make them ultras. It is what you do in preparation for the match that matters. And this is not simply a one-off event, but something that is done every week. Acting in the correct manner, wearing the right clothes and working in solidarity with fellow members are acts that have to be demonstrated repeatedly.

The body is the locus of the performance. Carter (2018) argues that physical performances (like running) help us understand what it means to be human through the senses, thoughts and physical activity. The mind, body and environs meld to locate the individual self. Carter misses emotion from his eloquent argument; our senses are stimulated by our experiences, feelings and emotions produced from the activity (as we shall see in the following chapter). Yet Carter makes an important contribution as the environs are vital to understanding the self and one's embodied identity. The other fans, the stadium and the match all tell the fan that they are a living, sensual, emotional, embodied social being. Moreover, it is the social environs that help the individual locate themselves as ultras in the stadium.

The body is an important way of locating the individual within the group. Ultras wear clothing or sport tattoos that inscribe their bodies with the symbols of their fandom. Alongside the scarves and T-shirts of their group, ultras use their bodies to present themselves and their group. Using symbolic clothing is a cultural code that expresses our identity through imitation and repetition. These repetitive performances draw on existing cultural cues and stylistic expressions. The choice of costume helps present our identity to our audiences. For example, at Livorno, a club with many ultras who would identify as communist, their political identity is demonstrated through their clothing (Doidge, 2013). Ultras wear green, military-style jackets and caps, or sport T-shirts and flags adorned with left-wing symbols, like Che Guevara, the red star, or the hammer and sickle. In some cases, these symbols are literally inscribed on the body in the form of tattoos. For Butler (1990), the performance of drag queens both subverts and reinforces gendered identities. Members of *Ultras Dynamo* of Dynamo Dresden have taken the parody aspect of drag further by deliberately dressing as the stereotype of post-unification East Germans (Ziesche, 2018). As Ziesche (2018: 889) highlights, 'these costumes also resemble and imitate the looks of people in the 1990s, arguably the most violent years in Dynamo's history. Thus, the appearance could also be used to reinforce the fan scene's violent image.'

Greater connectivity across the globe is helping expand these cultural cues. Social media, blogs, fanzines, films and other forms of media help present and re-present significant aspects of ultras culture. These cues are taken up and incorporated into the specific culture of the group. Ultras and casuals, as the two dominant football cultures, are drawn upon within specific locales. Certain brands and styles of dress are incorporated, but these need to be understood in relation to the context of the group. In relation to ultras at Dinamo București, Guțu (2017: 920–921) demonstrates that

> If until now the team scarf or t-shirt defined one's belonging to the group, being a rather 'democratic' way to join a supporter's group, today, the scarf in the team's colours is replaced by knowing the symbolic dress code which makes your entrance in the subculture, adherence to which, implicitly, becomes more important than adherence to the team.

Furthermore, the specific brands associated with the casuals subculture, like Stone Island, Fred Perry or The North Face, 'have no symbolic meaning for an individual who does not have access to the cultural codes of the group, and they can be "strong" signs, of recognition and belonging for the members of the movement' (Guțu, 2017: 924). Being part of the group helps reinforce these symbols of fandom.

These brands are incorporated into other symbols of fandom, particularly stickers. These commercial signs of ultras culture become reconfigured as a symbol of the group themselves. The *Ultras Boys* of Maccabi Haifa incorporated The North Face logo in the green and white colours of the club into a sticker stating *North Boys*. Fans of Panathinaikos, another club whose colours are green and white, designed a sticker saying *Ultras Athens* in the Lonsdale font. The *Ben-Side* group from Alkmaar in the Netherlands designed a variety of stickers incorporating the Stone Island logo and the laurel wreath of Fred Perry. The three stripes and trefoil of adidas are integrated into a variety of stickers, always in the colours of the football team. This follows the popularity of adidas shoes among group members. Fans at Malmö redesigned the trefoil to incorporate the skyline of the Swedish city. A sticker created by Freiburg casuals represents probably the best example of incorporating casual brands into the image of the group. The design incorporated the laurel wreath and 'FR' of Fred Perry, the 'e' of Ellesse, the 'i' in adidas, 'BU' from Burberry, 'R' from The North Face, and the 'G' from Peaceful Hooligan, all above the Stone Island logo with the word 'casual' incorporated. The result is a collage reading 'Freiburg Casual'. These stickers represent a form 'performative consumption', where ultras produce and consume their own merchandise (Hills, 2002).

The ultras way of life: a collective ritual

Humans are not isolated individuals, but social creatures. How we account for collective behaviour is the central question for sociology. It is not just the individual self that is a performance; individuals working together as collectives are also performances. Ultras are a clear demonstration of public performances in the contemporary world. Understanding performance as a ritual will help understand how social actors who engage in acts of fandom transform themselves from distinct individuals into part of a wider group. This is not simply a passive engagement with fandom; it is about transforming individual consciousness. These fans see themselves as part of a wider group; their sense of self is collapsed into that of the collective. Ritual and performance theory will help to explain this conflation.

Ultras are the active representation of resistance to the commercialisation of football. The economic transformation of the sport has focused on fans as customers, leading to an active resistance (King, 1998; 2003; Doidge, 2015a; Numerato, 2015; 2018; Cleland *et al.*, 2018; Hodges, 2018; Nuhrat, 2018a; Perasović and Mustapić, 2018). While performance implies theatre, and many fans are actively resisting the pacification and gentrification of football fandom, the theatre analogy is important as it highlights the role of ritual.

> The move from ritual to theatre happens when a participating audience fragments into a collection of people who attend because the show is advertised, who pay admission, who evaluate what they are going to see before, during and after seeing it. The move from theatre to ritual happens when the audience is transformed from a collection of separate individuals into a group or congregation or participants. (Schechner, 2003: 157)

This fracture has occurred within football with greater commercialisation. Many fans are isolated customers, attending the match independently and not engaging in collective behaviour. The ultras, in contrast, actively resist this. They have incorporated the audience and turned theatre back into ritual, which in turn transforms individuals into a collective. The very act of performing is a political act. It is a unified expression of unity in contrast to the behaviour of individual customers. Ultras are actively embodying the Against Modern Football stance by not becoming isolated consumers.

Individual fans still congregate around football and meet with others. Yet coalescing does not come naturally; it takes time and preparation. As Durkheim (1964: 230–231) identified:

> Individual minds cannot come into contact and communicate with each other except by coming out of themselves; but they cannot do this except by movements. So it is the homogeneity of these movements that gives the group consciousness of itself and consequently makes it exist. When this homogeneity is once established and these movements have once taken a stereotyped form, they serve to symbolise the corresponding representations. But they symbolise them only because they have aided in forming them.

Physically moving together helps individuals demonstrate their unity and highlights their feelings regarding that unity. Working together helps synchronise the group's participants as well as symbolising their solidarity. Yet it is the physical act of coming together and moving together that produces this consciousness.

Once a group is formed, teamwork is vital. Goffman (1959) identified the importance of teamwork in carefully presenting the group to others. Friends and acquaintances will collaborate to ensure that the performance is upheld. 'A team', Goffman (1959: 50) highlights, 'has been defined as a set of performers who co-operate in presenting a single performance.' Both inside and outside of the stadium, ultras are expected to present a unified team to others. This includes fellow fans and non-ultras of their own team, rival ultras and police. This can give power to individuals, because 'while a team-performance is in progress, any member of the tram has the power to give the show away or to disrupt it by inappropriate conduct' (Goffman, 1959: 50). This reinforces the importance of solidarity and trust among ultras. Major deviations from the ultras code can bring serious attention from the authorities, or rival groups. For example, when the young Genoa fan Vincenzo Spagnolo was stabbed by an ultra from Milan's *Barbour Gang* in 1992, the ultras of Milan sang that there was 'one fewer' of the Genoa fans (Foot, 2006; Ferreri, 2008; Stefanini, 2009; Doidge, 2015a). Yet this event caused a 'moral shock' (Jasper, 1997) that united rival ultras after undue attention from the media and politicians. Rival groups met to draw up a 'code of conduct' to reiterate how ultras should behave (Ferreri, 2008; Stefanini, 2009; Doidge, 2015a).

As a central part of the ultras style of fandom is the collective spectacle in the stadium, comprised of choreographies, chanting, banners, clapping and jumping, we need to understand the individual performances in a collective sense. As Maffesoli (1996) argues, new social groups form as older forms of solidarity have fragmented. He suggests that the ritual is how emotional communities and solidarity are formed – ritual is not goal-orientated – it is 'repetitive and therefore comforting ... Its sole function is to confirm a group's view of itself' (Maffesoli, 1996: 17). As argued in the previous section, the individual identity is performed through repetitive practice. Football provides a convenient space for the repetitive practice of identity. There are regular matches throughout the season which provide a focus for fans and ultras alike. Football is also an everyday activity; it pervades conversation throughout the week, not just on a matchday (Nowell-Smith, 1979: Stone, 2007). Conversations will take place in pubs, bars, at work and on social media. All of this maintains the intensity of interaction that can be sustained until the next match. The ultras style of fandom can intensify this passion as members of the group will discuss, plan and produce the key parts of the performance: choreographies, chants and banners.

Regular interaction helps engender a sense of belonging to a wider community. In his analysis of the Aboriginal corroberee rituals, Durkheim (1964) demonstrated how a community formed from disparate individuals. Periodic gatherings and ritualistic practices help form a collective emotional energy, a 'collective effervescence' that engenders a sense of belonging to the group. Through the rituals of the festival, specific symbols, or totems, become venerated and come to symbolise the group itself. As the symbol is sacred, a hierarchy emerges that is permitted to handle it. These symbols are produced by the group themselves, and at the same time symbolise the group. This helps to delineate who is a member of the group, and who is an outsider.

The connection to football is important here. Fans regularly congregate in the emotional cauldron of the stadium. They engage in chants, clapping and other actions that help generate the atmosphere, which at the same time produces the collective effervescence of the group. Within this febrile atmosphere, specific symbols become sacred – the club, the colours, the badge, the players. It is no coincidence that players will kiss the badge on their shirt when they want to demonstrate their loyalty to the fans. Likewise, acts of stealing flags, banners and scarves become symbolic triumphs in clashes between rival ultras. Placing stickers in rivals' territory is a symbolic performance, while covering rival clubs' stickers over with those of your group becomes another symbolic victory. At the same time, colours help delineate who is a member of the group and who is a rival. For the ultras, this is taken to another level as they constitute a subgroup within the wider fan base. They will meet regularly away from the match to prepare their choreographies, plan chants and produce banners. As they also produce their own scarves, T-shirts and badges that symbolise their group, these ultras collectives become impassioned communities semi-independent of the football club.

The songs are also practised. The stadium provides the space where the performance is enacted, but the groundwork is done 'backstage' beforehand. Some individual fans will practise the existing repertoire by looking at YouTube clips or even through purchasing ultras songs on CD (Ibraheem, 2015). Songs are simple, repetitive and relatively easy to follow, reinforcing the importance of the collective appealing to a wide cohort. But they are not egalitarian as the lyrics depict the values that members are expected to adhere to (Ibraheem, 2015). They will be about victory, venerating the club's colours and star players, hating the police or denigrating rivals. Often these are depicted in very masculine terms. It is within this audioscape that the individual becomes subsumed within the collective. These are no longer solitary voices, but a collective aural community.

New songs are produced by core ultras members away from the stadium before being brought to the broader collective. Lyrics will be discussed and debated in bars or online. Members will run through the words and actions to bring others along. Sometimes they are practised on the train or coach on the way to the match. At the stadium, there will be clear direction from the capo so as to bring as many people as possible into the chant. There will be one or two practice runs to make sure that the performers know the lyrics and actions before the full chant is performed. Songs are never sung once, but cycled around before the next set of chants is started. This gives the performers the opportunity to practise and perfect each new chant before moving on. Big matches are never used for dry runs; new songs are tested out at smaller matches in preparation for the derbies or big games.

It is within the physical participation of the ritual that the group becomes formed. It is important to note that the rituals do not have to be 'for' something; they are 'neither substantive nor functional' as Rappaport (1999: 26) states. But football rituals are a public performance; it is the performance that gives the ritual its existence. As Rappaport (1999) argues, rituals are performative. They inform the participant about the changes taking place and they guide their response, sometimes precisely. While these conventions are not imposed on performers, the act of participation reinforces them. For Rappaport (1999: 125): 'To establish a convention – a general public understanding, a regular procedure, an institution – is *both* to ascribe existence to it *and* to accept it.' What is powerful about the ultras is that they have regular, repetitive interactions where conventions, rules and ways of carrying oneself are discussed, debated and, more importantly, put into practice in stadiums.

There is a ritual process. A fan or ultra does not just turn up and engage in the spectacle. Turner ([1969] 1997: 95) identifies three phases: 'separation, margin (or limen, signifying "threshold" in Latin), and aggregation'. In the first phase the individuals prepare to detach from everyday life and get themselves ready for the performance. This can include personal rituals, like wearing lucky socks or a specific T-shirt. Such garments, along with scarves, hats and other items, signify that the individual is going to a football event. The second phase is liminal; the individual 'passes through a cultural realm that has few or none of the attributes of the past or coming state' (Turner, [1969] 1997: 95). This is the focus of the ritual and will be addressed in subsequent paragraphs. Once the ritual is over, the individuals may remove themselves from the event, but they are acquainted with the rules and conventions of the ritual. They acquiesce to these conventions and are prepared for subsequent events. Only through repetitive practice does the fan demonstrate their acceptance of these new conventions and in doing so they show their belonging to a broader community.

It is within the liminal space of the stadium that the ultras way of life is shaped. The emotional energy of the spectacle derives from the ritualist acts within this space. These acts help form the sense of community. Turner ([1969] 1997) calls this a *communitas* and refers to the shared experience of the community that forms through ritualistic practice. Once fans have symbolically prepared themselves for the match, they engage in the ritual performance of the spectacle. *Communitas* is the spirit of communion that unites members of these ritualistic rights. It is borne of the collective effervescence (Durkheim, 1964) found within the group's activities. It helps reinforce the conflicts and dialectical aspects of society. 'For individuals and groups', argues Turner ([1969] 1997: 97), 'social life is a type of dialectical process that involves successive experience of high and low, *communitas* and structure, homogeneity and differentiation, equality and inequality.' While Turner reduces social life into a series of binary oppositions, he does highlight the dialectical aspects that help differentiate the emotional energy of the stadium to the more mundane existence of everyday life.

The liminal space of the stadium permits a transgressive atmosphere that fuels the emotional energy of participants. Existing social structures loosen and individuals become more able to make new social relations (Turner, 1974; Bakhtin, 1984). It should be noted that pre-existing social hierarchies are not necessarily abolished (Geertz, 1972). With his conception of the carnivalesque, Bakhtin (1984) observes how spectacle and performance help make a transgressive carnival. The rules and conventions of everyday life are subverted, hierarchies and sacred symbols become degraded and members become united under a 'folk consciousness'. The carnival 'elides different aspects of power relations thereby simultaneously reversing, intensifying, and reinforcing those relations with the same spectacle' (Carter, 2008). But within this liminal space is still an opportunity for a 'folk consciousness' to emerge as new social relationships become available under the temporary unity of the ritual, event or football match. While Bakhtin (1984) argues that the carnival was a temporary inversion of social life, and that the social hierarchies and conventions returned afterwards, this new consciousness can help transform social consciousness and order as well. Rituals are not fixed activities that simply recreate themselves, but are fluid social phenomena. As Turner (1974) highlights, the playful, ludic elements of the liminal space can challenge existing dualisms and boundaries. More importantly, individuals can meet, exchange ideas or simply form new acquaintances and friendships.

The carnivalesque also reinforces the dialectical nature of ultras life. The stadium becomes a sacred space that delimits membership and permits transgression. Ultras take ownership of the space by decorating it with their flags, banners and staging their choreographies. Yet this is only permitted through official sanction. Some ultras groups are specifically named after the part of the stadium where they stand, especially in Greece with *Gate 13* (Panathinaikos), *Original 21* (AEK), *Gate 7* (Olympiacos) and *Gate 4* (PAOK). Police, clubs and football federations have tolerated the ultras because of the spectacle they create (De Biasi and Lanfranchi, 1997; Doidge, 2015a). Without the gaze of the authorities, the liminal space of the stadium is permitted to flourish. It is for this reason that conflict occurs when authorities seek to challenge the folk consciousness of the stadiums.

The importance of the carnivalesque spectacle is that members are actively engaged within it. As Francesco, a Livorno ultra (personal interview, June 2009, cited in Doidge, 2015a), states:

I want to be me. I want to be in the spectacle. I want to cheer on the team.
I want to help them in every possible way, to try and help them.

Ultras are not passive observers, but active participants within the spectacle. They plan, prepare and produce the spectacle, and this reinforces
their sense of belonging to the group and the football club. It builds the
emotional energy and fuels a wider sense of community. According to
Bakhtin (1984: 7):

> Carnival is not a spectacle seen by the people; they live in it, and everyone
> participates because its very idea embraces all the people. While carnival
> lasts, there is no life outside it. During carnival time life is subject only to
> its laws, that is, the laws of its own freedom.

This reinforces the performative aspects of the group. The actor and
performer are entwined. The ultras are both performing in their own
spectacle, while observing others within it (Doidge, 2015a). It is this
sense of 'living in the moment' that fuels the broader collective.

Choreographies help reinforce the sense of community that unites
ultras, and can have a positive force. Choreographies, particularly in
Italy, will draw on specific local images and narratives in order to link
the fans, the club and the city. Others reinforce who is seen as a member
of your community. A good example of a positive ultras display occurred
in December 2007 when Fiorentina faced Inter. The wife of Fiorentina's
manager, Cesare Prandelli, had died of cancer on the Monday before
the match. The Fiorentina ultras displayed *striscione* with a message
that, translated, read: 'The time that passes deadens the sorrow, but if
you need her, raise your eyes to the sky… her star will drive you forever
and carry us far.' Similarly, after a motorway bridge in Genoa collapsed
and killed forty-three people in August 2018, Napoli ultras displayed
a banner commemorating the victims. Ultras also undertake a range of
charity work for their local communities (Testa and Armstrong, 2010;
Doidge, 2015a). While some of these are directed at specifically local
projects, some do extend the imagined community wider. For example,
after an earthquake struck the Central Italian town of L'Aquila in 2009,
Livornese ultras organised a collection for the victims. Many of these
acts will derive from specific conventions and traditions from within the
individual groups. In the UK, for example, ultras from both Clapton
and Whitehawk have organised collections for foodbanks in their local
communities, while during their match against Hannover in April
2019 Hertha Berlin's ultras group, *Harlekins*, collected donations for
Löwenzahn, a Hannover-based charity that helps children deal with the
loss of a loved one. Not all ultras groups will engage in such activities;

it depends on the focus of those active within the groups, as well as how the particular group wants to be seen to others.

The presentation of the ultras is not restricted to the stadium. Visual representations of the groups are displayed outside the stadium through stickers and graffiti. These depict stylised images of the groups and how they seek to portray themselves. Many images present an anonymous ultra, with their face covered in a balaclava, scarf covering the mouth and lower part of the face, or wearing a hoodie (or a combination of all three). This highlights that the individual member is subsumed within a larger collective identity, but also illustrates the group's willing-ness to engage in deviant activity; their obscured individualism means the authorities cannot detect them. This enhances the anti-authority approach of many groups. Graffiti and stickers also represent the politi-cal and historical aspects of the groups. Stickers from Ajax Amsterdam will incorporate three white crosses on a black and red background, which is the symbol of the Dutch city. Others explicitly incorporate political symbols to denote the group's ideology and act as a form of marketing. These include the Celtic crosses used by *Ultras Sur* of Real Madrid and the fist smashing a swastika on St Pauli stickers (widely copied by other left-wing groups). Others incorporate the logo of the group or club (in the obligatory club colours) with slogans like 'ACAB' or 'Against Modern Football'. Each of these pieces of material culture maintain the performance throughout the week and become sites of contest.

Flow: a collective experience

Much of the literature on ritual and performance focus on the meaning or function of the activity. The voices of participants are conspicuous by their absence. Fans and ultras enjoy going to football as an activity in itself. It has meaning for the participants, many of whom are engaging in sociability (Simmel, 1950; Giulianotti, 2005; Doidge, 2015a). Some ultras are engaging for wider political or personal values, but many are simply participating because they enjoy it. It is for this reason that observing and understanding emotion in fandom is important, as will be argued in the following chapter. As we shall see, football fandom is a collective emotional experience. This section introduces the concept of flow (Csikszentmihalyi, 1979; 1992; 2008) into fandom, and looks at how individual engagement can produce a sense of flow, exuberance and pleasure that helps demonstrate how the individual ontologically identifies with the wider collective.

One of the key aspects of football fandom, and the ultras style in particular, is the identification of the individual to the broader collective. This is done through the collective effervescence of the atmosphere. Within these moments, ultras cease to identify as individuals, with their range of identities that exist in everyday life. Within the liminal space of the stadium, the individual identifies as an ultra within the collective. They engage in the collective rituals of the choreography and produce an atmosphere that can be intoxicating, liberating and life-affirming. This feeling can elevate the individual consciousness, and produce intense feelings of euphoria and achievement. For Csikszentmihalyi (2008: 71), flow is about optimal experience, which is

> a sense that one's skills are adequate to cope with the challenges at hand, in a goal-directed, rule-bound action system that provides clear clues as to how one is performing. Concentration is so intense that there is no attention left over to think about anything irrelevant, or to worry about problems. Self-consciousness disappears, and the sense of time becomes distorted. An activity that produces such experiences is so gratifying that people are willing to do it for its own sake, with little concern for what they will get out of it, even when it is difficult, or dangerous.

Therefore, flow is a subjective phenomenon that an individual experiences through successfully engaging in an activity that they enjoy. Ultimately, flow is associated with happiness as it is about personal achievement (Csikszentmihalyi, 1992). Flow is produced by focusing on a clear activity with a defined set of rules or obligations, which pushes the individual, and gives immediate feedback. This feeling transcends consciousness and results in the individual losing track of time and their self-consciousness.

Much of the focus of Csikszentmihalyi's work is on leisure activities, although some has assessed the world of work (Csikszentmihalyi and Csikszentmihalyi, 1988; Csikszentmihalyi, 2008). Specifically addressing flow in sport, Jackson and Csikszentmihalyi (1999: 5) suggest that flow is

> a state of consciousness where one becomes totally absorbed in what one is doing, to the exclusion of all other thoughts and emotions. So flow is about focus. More than just focus, however, flow is harmonious experience where mind and body are working together effortlessly, leaving the person feeling that something special has just occurred. So flow is about enjoyment … Although winning is important, flow does not depend on it, and flow offers something more than just a successful outcome. This is because flow lifts experience from the ordinary to the optimal, and it is in those moments that we feel truly alive and in tune with what we are doing.

The key notion here is that flow is a 'harmonious experience where mind and body are working together effortlessly'. The self is transformed in this moment and the individual experiences something vastly different to their daily routine. Indeed, the person experiencing flow will feel separate from their everyday life. Time will change and their focus will be on the activity, rather than other issues or feelings. There is a mindfulness within the activity that enables the individual to be completely present in their own mind, body and emotions to the exclusion of everything else.

Predominantly, Csikszentmihalyi's focus is on *doing* these activities, as opposed to watching these activities. This chapter argues that the ultras style of fandom is not a passive observation of other people playing sport, but an active involvement in creating the spectacle. For ultras, fandom is an active leisure pursuit that takes time and money. Fandom structures one's social life and provides a wide network of relationships. Most importantly, as will be discussed in the following chapter, it also provides an emotional connection to a wider collective. It is this wider social connection that is missing from Csikszentmihalyi's analysis. Ultras and football fans are heterogeneous; they come from a wide variety of backgrounds and have multitude of motivations for attending football. While there is an important feeling of flow deriving from some football matches, some of this feeling develops from emotional bonds and social relationships. Attending matches is a sociable activity and this can produce feelings of happiness and pleasure (Simmel, 1950; Giulianotti, 2005; Doidge, 2015a).

There is a link between flow and ritual. The liminal space of the ritual temporarily suspends normal social roles or behaviours (Turner, 1974; Bakhtin, 1984). For Turner (1997), this is *communitas*, the emotionally rewarding closeness to others which is fairly free of social responsibilities. This helps cement the social bonds of solidarity. According to Turner (1974: 79), 'it is not teamwork in flow that is quintessential, but *being* together, with being the operative word, not doing'. Yet football fans are not disembodied individuals whose metaphysical essence just descends coincidentally on a football stadium. Fans are humans engaged in physical activity together. As Durkheim (1964: 230–231) argues, individuals have to come out of themselves to connect with others. This is done through movement together, which helps synchronise the bodies, breathing and actions of the participants. It is the physical, embodied act of the ritual that is important. The *doing* is performative and aids in becoming. Most importantly for an analysis of football ultras, it is doing these activities together that helps the group to generate the collective effervescence; just sitting and watching football in the same space does not create the same collective as designing, choreographing and performing as a collective. This helps create that sense of flow, of individuals feeling euphoric (or in despair) as a collective.

The collective release of emotional energy gives a sense of power, control and euphoria. As put forward by Goffman (1961), euphoria is a combined result of the rules of a gathering and a spontaneous engagement. The state of ecstasy can be confirmed by a quote from a Lech Poznan ultra: 'In the second half, we got higher and higher and … it was total madness until the end of the game' (*To My Kibice!*, 2015: 7). In collective flow, ultras can cross borders they never would in 'ordinary' circumstances. Collective flow occurs within the ultras' sections of the stadium due to the liminal aspects of the matchday rituals, as one Lechia Gdańsk ultras member (personal interview, 2017) recounts:

> It makes me feel free when there are so many people. I wouldn't stand up and start jumping at a family dinner at home because I'd look funny, to say the least. But everyone can do it in the stadium. If we really get into cheering, we start jumping; if there's one guy who takes off his shirt, in a second it turns out that half of the crowd has done the same. It's such an overwhelming feeling of freedom; for ninety or a hundred and twenty minutes, I've got my own world and I can do whatever. When we're in the stand and we're this one group, we all do the same and it's an incredible feeling, it turns out I'm not an effing lunatic at all. There are a few thousand people here reacting just like me.

The collective ritual loosens inhibitions and allows the performers to transcend their daily lives. Within this space, the participants become one group, not a collection of individuals.

Flow is about transcending the self and pushing oneself further. There is euphoria in the victory of the team, but there can equally be flow in defeat, of knowing that you have given your all for the team, of being part of the group and experiencing the collective effervescence of the atmosphere. Disjunctures occur when the feeling is not reciprocated. When fans feel that the players have not pushed themselves into a flow state, or that the coach or owners are not committed in the same way as the fans (Portelli, 1993; Klugman, 2008). Fans and ultras can only control so much regarding events on the pitch. Anger at the coaches or players is a way of them retaining control and motivating themselves to return for future games.

Flow is not just about transcending the self, but about (re)creating the self. As Marx (1970) highlighted, the self only becomes actualised when confronted with difference. 'Flow helps to integrate the self because in that state of deep concentration consciousness is unusually well ordered. Thoughts, intentions, feelings and all the senses are focused on the same goal. Experience is harmony. And then the flow episode is over, one feels more "together" than before, not only internally but also with respect to other people and the world in general' (Csikszentmihalyi, 2008: 41). As with Turner's ritual process, there is a disaggregation from one's pre-existing life before connecting with the collective. For Csikszentmihalyi (2008: 41), the self becomes actualised through a paradoxical process of differentiation and integration: 'Differentiation implies a movement toward uniqueness, toward separating oneself from others. Integration refers to the opposite: a union with other people, with ideas and entities beyond the self. A complex self is one that succeeds in combining these opposite tendencies.' The dedicated ultra will engage in the performance with intensity, possibly helping craft new songs, or helping produce the choreography. They have learned new skills and developed themselves as individuals. But at the same time, they have integrated into the group further and embedded their collective identity.

It is within the collective effervescence of the performance that the self and collective become ontologically conflated. It is at this optimal experience that 'people become so involved in what they are doing that the activity becomes spontaneous, almost automatic; they stop being aware of themselves as separate from the actions they are performing' (Csikszentmihalyi, 2008: 53). The performance of the ultras is about participation, flow and being part of it. No one is questioning the vocal ability of the singers, or the quality of the drumming. Individual consciousness becomes merged with the physical activity. The mind, body and emotions clearly become fused and focused on the activity. Through these flow states we can begin to understand why fans ontologically identify with the team through the use of personal pronouns: 'we won' or 'you lost'.

After the ritual performance has subsided, there are opportunities for reflection to help locate the self in the event. As Csikszentmihalyi (2008: 66) argues, 'when the activity is over and self-consciousness has a chance to resume, the self that the person reflects upon is not the same self that existed before the flow experience: it is now enriched by new skills and fresh achievements'. As Numerato (2015) observes, fans engage in self-reflective behaviour in order to present the group to others. This reflection does not always have to be critical. Violent scuffles can be reproduced through the reflection of the event, even if the wider recollection of the event differs among group members (King, 2001). A hooligan who wishes to present themselves as a tough guy will narrate their story to present themselves accordingly.

Ritual and repetitive practice helps the individuals within the group to take control, and thereby achieve a sense of flow. Matchday preparations, particularly around choreographies, not only ensure that the individuals are invested in the match long before kick-off, but that they are taking control of their emotions and bodies. As Chambliss (1989) highlights, regular, repetitive practice enables elite swimmers to perform at the highest level. Enjoying the finer details of choreographies and other matchday preparations ensures that the ultras are motivated to attend, but also helps them take control of their own destiny. As Wacquant (2004) observes in relation to boxers, one does not simply become a boxer by getting in the ring. It takes regular, repetitive practice through a variety of exercises in order to be accepted as a boxer. Becoming an ultra is a similar process. The individual must master the various activities: the chants, actions, emotions and uniform in order to be accepted. These activities, engaged with regularly over time, help to integrate the individual into the group, build relationships and experience feelings of flow.

The rhythm and intensity of the performance do not simply emerge organically from the fans themselves, or events on the pitch. What makes the ultras an important social phenomenon is their social organisation and how this creates and maintains the collective. What differentiates the ultras style of fandom from others is that there is direction; ultras have a capo who acts as a conductor to the crowd. The capo fulfils the role of what Goffman (1959: 61) calls a 'director' who brings 'back into line a member of the team whose performance becomes unsuitable'. Predominantly, capos are male, embodying a hypermasculine attitude; they cajole and encourage the crowd to sing, jump and clap. In the theatre, the conductor faces the performers – the orchestra and the singers or dancers. While most football fans face the pitch, and the players performing on it, the capo faces the ultras; these are the true performers, not the players. Like the conductor, the capo has their back to the audience: for the ultras, the audience in the stadium comprises players, directors and rival fans. As capos face the crowd, not the pitch, rarely does the performance of the ultras synchronise with the performance on the pitch. Often the capos stand on specially constructed scaffolding, others on the edge of stairwells. This reinforces the legitimacy of the ultras within the stadium. In the all-seater stadiums of the UK, individuals would not be allowed to stand or congregate around stairwells for health and safety reasons. Ultimately, this becomes one of the conflicts between ultras and authorities that helps to shape the ultras mentality.

The capos help the feeling of flow as a collective through trying to establish a sense of rhythm among the members. As highlighted earlier, Durkheim (1964) argued that it is the physical act of doing something together that can unite a group. Similarly, Collins (2004: 68) argues that 'rhythmic synchronisation is correlated with solidarity'. Indeed, 'shared rhythm seems to be critical to all joint performances' (King and de Rond, 2011: 566). But rhythm and solidarity do not just occur, they require practice, direction and communication, which reinforces the importance of the role of the capo. 'While rhythm can stimulate a sense of group solidarity,' King and de Rond (2011: 566) contend,

> coordinated collective performance is possible only through the shared discovery of precise rhythmic patterns. Participants in ensemble productions have to synchronise their actions, finding a rhythm of one kind or another, to they would not be able to engage in coherent, sequenced social practice at all. They would interrupt each other, cut across or physically obstruct one another.

Clear communication is vital if collective rhythm is to be achieved. King and de Rond (2011) observe that it is not simply about giving the best physical performance but also about having the emotional intelligence to link the various egos, power blocs and ideas.

Having a shared vision provides a totemic focus for the group (Durkheim, 1964; Chambliss, 1989; Wacquant, 2004; King and de Rond, 2011), uniting the members with a common purpose. This may emerge spontaneously from the group in the shared folk consciousness that arises through the collective performance. But it can also come from the leaders of the group. It has been observed that this can come from the manager or head coach of a formal sports club (Wacquant, 2004; Doidge and Sandri, 2018a), but it can also come from the leaders of less formal ultras groups (Testa and Armstrong, 2010; Doidge, 2015a; Ginhoux, 2018).

The internal politics of the group is an important factor of collective rhythmic performance and group dynamics. Ultras are not a homogenous group, but a varied network of relationships; the liminal space permits a varied demographic to mix and socialise. Some of these individuals are friendly, others are antagonistic. The formal structures of the group, as noted earlier, provide a committee with a capo and directors with other responsibilities like fundraising or designing the choreographies. But they will not necessarily have shared visions and strategies for the group. Most groups encourage the open discussion of viewpoints, but this does not make them democracies as the capo is likely to have the final say. Dissenting members must fall into line, stage a coup or split from the group. Although physicality is one way of asserting this vision (Ginhoux, 2018), having the emotional intelligence to communicate in a way that is appropriate to the members is also important (Katz, 1999;

King and de Rond, 2011). Recognising and respecting authority helps maintain the delicate power balances away from the performance, but also helps generate the necessary solidarity that ensures the performance has the desired impact on matchday.

Conclusion

Although a variety of theoretical frames have been used to study the community of football fans, performance theory has rarely been applied in such research. This is quite surprising considering that in nearly every country, fans make use of performance as a tool of manifesting their identity. Indeed, from the matchday choreographies of ultras groups, through rhythmic clapping and jumping, to stadium chants, the world of football fans abounds in performative and dramatic activity. As illustrated above, the ultras' performances are not only spectacles for the sake of producing a spectacle. They are permeated with a collective spirit, political stances and intensified emotional 'flow'. These performances are of a ritual nature, repeated regularly like the Holy Mass in a church or salat in a mosque. These repetitive acts help the individual become part of the collective as the individual body entrains with the mass of bodies around them. This collective flow controls the emotions of the group and helps maintain and reinforce the collective.

The ultras' performances are also a form of communication with the 'outside' world. In the age of the widespread popularity of social media, enormous choreographies with more or less controversial images swiftly reach a global audience. Preparing the choreographies takes a huge amount of time, money and human resources. In most cases, these choreographies are presented only once – they have to be unique, original and outstanding. This preparation means that the engagement with the match begins weeks or months beforehand and builds the individual connection to the group and football club. Other performances, stickers and graffiti also require engagement away from the match and help maintain the wider presentation of the group outside the stadium. In many cases, these performances manifest the notorious and uncompromising style, the passion and the emotions that ultras experience during the 'show'. And emotions, as introduced in next chapter, play an important role in the field of football fandom.

2

It's only a game? Centralising emotions in football fandom

The hot summer sun is beating down as the rare heatwave continues across Britain. Fans arrive at the small stadium in shorts, T-shirts and sunglasses, ready to enjoy an afternoon's football. It is the first match of the season. The pre-season friendlies have gone well under the new coach who has been working with the young team and now has the opportunity to put that hard work into action. Even though the World Cup in Russia made it feel that football had not gone away, in reality it was three and a half long months since Whitehawk had last played at their home ground in East Brighton. An hour before the match, various fans arrive at the ground and see faces that they have not seen for a quarter of a year. Fans embrace, happy to renew old acquaintances and potentially make some new ones. Conversations focus on the new team, the new coach and prospects for the season. In this moment, minutes before the whistle that will kick off the new season, there is optimism, anticipation and euphoria. At the same moment across the country, and at similar moments across the world, football fans are united in a feeling of enthusiasm and expectation. Each new season provides a new opportunity for potential success. It also provides the opportunity to be sociable, to meet friends, sup a beer and have a laugh. The build up to kick-off continues as the fans gather outside the clubhouse, beers in hand, waiting to see which direction the teams will be attacking before deciding where they will stand to watch the first half (as is the custom in non-league football in the UK). With the home team playing towards the Sea End, the fans proceed to take their place on the terrace. As the new strike force gets the game under way, the fans translate that pre-season euphoria into songs, chants, clapping, rhythmic drumming and jumping up and down. The season has started.

At every match, football fans will experience a range of emotions.

They will experience highs and lows, anger and joy, frustration and release. Most fans will understand the feelings of exhilaration when a goal is scored, the anger at a blatant foul or anxiety before big matches. These feelings will not only be directed at events on the pitch, although they do provide a focus. Some fans will come to the match confident that their team will do well. Others may be harbouring latent frustration at the manager or the board for lack of success on the pitch. Microsociologically, some fans may be happy to be with their friends or family, joyous to be experiencing a shared social activity (Simmel, 1950). In other cases, fans may be having to manage their emotions in response to racism, sexism or homophobia. As Doidge (2015a: 181) observes: 'Football invokes strong emotion in its followers.' According to Cleland *et al.* (2018: 39–40): 'Most football fans will acknowledge that football is an emotional experience. One of the things that draws people to football is the atmosphere. This collective emotional experience links many people under the shared experience of singing, clapping and cheering in unison.' And as Pope (2012: 186) points out: 'Sport can produce extremes in terms of emotional responses, with phrases such as: "bouncing", "upbeat", "euphoria", "buzzing" and "happy" used to describe feelings after a victory, but "foul" or "bad" moods, "depressed", and "down" when defeated, or even being "gutted", "sick" or "devastated", and needing time to "sulk" and "recover".'

The significance of emotions has come to prominence since 2018 when the International Football Association Board first wrote the use of a video assistant referee (VAR) into the laws of the game and introduced it at high-profile matches. Bayern Munich ultras displayed a banner at their Champions League match against Liverpool that declared (in English) 'Modern football kills emotion. Fuck VAR. Fuck UEFA' (Maltby, 2019). Here ultras recognise that emotion is a significant part of their enjoyment of the match. Pausing the match to check a video screen leaves the fans (and atmosphere) in limbo, effectively muting the emotions in the stadium. Yet, as will be argued later, rarely are these emotional aspects taken into account by academics. Occasionally, the writer may allude to an atmosphere, or specific feelings at an event, but rarely are emotions used as an analytical tool.

This chapter argues that, as emotions are an important component of social life, researchers of football should engage with the sociological literature on emotion to fully understand the collective character of fans. Marx (1970) argued that social praxis is a 'sensuous human activity', which infers an emotional and physical action, rather than being something overtly cognitive. Similarly, Durkheim (1964) identified that the emotional 'collective effervescence', which derives from periodic congregation, is instrumental in building solidarity among disparate individuals. As will be argued, later theorists such as Randall Collins (1975; 1990; 2008) and Arlie Hochschild ([1983] 2003) can help us understand the collectives that coalesce around football. As Collins (1990: 28) argues, '[e]motions are the "glue" of solidarity – and what mobilises conflict', and there is much conflict in football fandom. Yet it is the regular (ritualistic) practice of fandom that facilitates these emotional identities. As Carter (2008: 67) observes: 'Sport is only truly effective at emoting collective identities when performed in front of a crowd on a regular basis.' The football season provides games every week that present a space for collective emotions to be articulated. More fundamentally, Denzin (2007: 1) states: 'People are their emotions. To understand who a person is, it is necessary to understand emotion.' In the emotionally saturated football stadium, we can draw on analyses of emotions to truly understand these popular social collectives.

By arguing that emotions are central to the understanding of football, this book not only seeks to make a contribution to the literature on emotional sociology but also, innovatively, it seeks to centralise the importance of football as an essential way of understanding how groups form. It highlights how football provides a space where social relationships can form through regular interaction, and these relationships and practices are infused with emotion. After identifying the emotional gap in the literature, this chapter will outline the broader literature on the sociology of emotion. In order to argue that emotion is an important analytical tool with which to study football, it will illustrate how emotion can be incorporated methodologically. It will then address the role of emotion in forming the collective, how this is performed and how this translates to symbols and space.

Centralising the role of emotions

In the midst of the Balkans wars in the 1990s, Meštrović (1997) questioned why the rest of the world was not repulsed by the various atrocities and mobilised accordingly. He suggested that the West had become a 'postemotional society' where individuals no longer emotionally connected with suffering around the globe. Meštrović (1997) generalised that individuals place their own needs and feelings at the forefront of their lives, rather than concern themselves with humanitarian emergencies in distant lands. As outlined in the previous chapter, other theorists have similarly argued that Western society is becoming more individualistic and focused on individual goals and identity (Giddens, 1990; 1991; 1992; Beck, 1992; Putnam *et al.*, 1993; Putnam,

2000). This book argues that new groups can still emerge, with the ultras being a notable new social collective. Even though he generalises and overlooks groups mobilising in new ways, in particular around humanitarian issues (Doidge and Sandri, 2018b), Meštrović (1997) identifies the significance of emotions in how individuals build relationships and mobilise collectively.

There is a strange relationship between emotions and Western culture. For Meštrović (1997) to suggest that we live in a postemotional society suggests that we used to live in an emotional society. Yet emotions have been relatively absent from public discussion or academic thought. Being emotional was invariably seen as animalistic, uncivilised or feminine. Since the Enlightenment, the quality of 'rationality' has been prized for human action (Abu-Lughod, 1986; Lutz, 1986; Lutz and White, 1986; Solomon, 1993; Elster, 1999; 2008; Reddy, 2001; Dixon, 2003; Denzin 2007). Weber (1978) took this rational approach further and made it central to his social ontology. He thought it was 'convenient to treat all irrational, affectually determined elements of behaviour as factors of deviation from a conceptually pure type of rational action' (Weber, 1978: 6).

Rationality is tied to the notion of 'reason', which is seen as the apotheosis of humanity and differentiates humans from other animals. In contrast, emotion has been viewed negatively and radically distinct from reason (Lutz, 1986; Damasio, 1994; Barbalet, 1998; Shilling, 2002). Western thinkers have negated the role of the body (Shilling, 1991; Solomon, 1993), yet the body can retain historical memories of emotional trauma (van der Kolk, 2014). In Europe there was a transition in the early nineteenth century to a secular vernacular describing 'emotions', rather than the more religious 'passions' (Solomon, 1993; Dixon, 2003). This was not simply substituting a new word for an old meaning (Dixon, 2003); it reflected the shift from a theological framework linking passions to the soul and morality, to a more scientific expression used to understand the workings of the mind. Consequently, we should be careful of conflating passions with emotions.

One consequence of this transition was an overly positivistic approach to the study of emotions. Psychology observed specific patterns in the body and concluded that emotions were subjective and followed earlier Western traditions of linear and dualistic notions of cognition that discounted emotion (Reddy, 2001). There are no tidy divisions between conscious and unconscious, subliminal or involuntary actions. There are many triggers for thought, including emotional ones, and these require variable amounts of suppression or enhancement. Moreover, the specific focus on the brain as the centre of cognition minimises the role of the neurological system and emotion (Damasio, 1994; 1999). Rather than reduce the individual to the two separate parts of the mind and the body, as suggested by Descartes, in reality the body and mind work together symbiotically. Feeling and reason are 'an interaction of the systems underlying the normal processes of emotion, feeling, reason, and decision making' (Damasio, 1994: 54). Accordingly, there is no purely 'rational' action devoid of emotion. 'Reason unguided by appropriate emotion', Barbalet (1998: 31) argues, 'leads to a disjointedness of purpose.' Indeed, emotion is a way for the individual to make sense of the world (Katz, 1999). As Solomon (1993: 15, original emphasis) states, '*emotions are judgements*, not blind or irrational forces that victimise us ... emotions create our interests and purpose'.

The philosophical, psychological and neurological approaches have overly focused on the subjective experience of emotions. By looking at groups like the ultras, we can challenge some of the epistemological and normative assumptions around emotions. As highlighted earlier, emotions are seen in the West as phenomena to suppress or ignore. How emotions are expressed is socially learned and based on cultural norms. Eastern philosophical ideas based on meditation and being present in the body note that emotions are neither good nor bad, just warning systems. In reality, the emotions themselves are not unwarranted; the issue is whether they are expressed in socially appropriate ways. Anger is neither good nor bad; it can motivate an individual to fight injustice or it can lead to violence. The same is true of joy; cheering joyously at a funeral is unsuitable, but at a football stadium after your team scores a goal it is appropriate. Individuals learn these manners, either through internalising a moral code or by reflecting upon the appropriate behaviours through interaction with others (Riesman, 1961). Humans are social, as well as emotional, creatures (Immordino-Yang and Damasio, 2007). Engaging with other people helps us to locate ourselves as individuals through understanding different ways of acting, behaving and feeling.

The focus on individual emotions and how they are expressed in Western daily society led to a refinement and suppression of emotion. Elias's (2000) meta-analysis of Western civilisation centred on the refinement of bodily habits, and about control of the emotions in particular. Expressing self-control was seen as civilised and the actions of a higher class of individual. Yet the 'art of human observation ... is never concerned with the individual in isolation ... the individual is always seen in his social context, as a human being in his relation to others, as an individual in a social situation' (Elias, 2000: 419). Culturally accepted forms of emotional expression are learned in relation to others. As noted in Chapter 1, Riesman (1961) identified the 'other-directed' personality type who learned to present themselves in relation to others.

Despite the implicit absence of emotions within academic literature, there has been a substantial shift in focus since the 1980s. Some of this literature has been found, possibly expectedly, in psychology (Ekman and Davidson, 1994; Lazarus, 1994) and neurology (Damasio, 1994; 1999; Ledoux, 1999), but there has also been a development of interest in anthropology (Abu-Lughod, 1986; Lutz, 1986; Lutz and White, 1986; Abu-Lughod and Lutz, 1990), cultural studies (Ahmed, 2004), history (Stearns and Stearns, 1985; 1986; Reddy, 2001; Dixon, 2003) and philosophy (Solomon, 1993; Elster, 1999; 2008). As intellectual knowledge does not operate in isolation, there has also been an 'emotional turn' in sociology (Gould, 2010; Lemmings and Brooks, 2014). This can be traced back to the work of Randall Collins (1975; 1990; 2008) and Arlie Hochschild ([1983] 2003), but includes Thomas Kemper (1978; 1990), Norman Denzin (2007) and Jack Barbalet (2002), although it could be argued that emotions and the control of emotions were evident much earlier in the sociological canon in the work of Emile Durkheim (1964) and Norbert Elias (2000).

There has also been a 'turn to affect' (Clough and Halley, 2007), which has introduced the concept of affect into the social science literature, particularly around cultural studies and geography. This has primarily been influenced by Deleuzian post-structuralism (e.g. Deleuze, 1988; Massumi, 2002; Deleuze and Guattari, 2013), although critical theorists have also theorised on affect (e.g. Ahmed, 2004; Ngai, 2007). A book on football fandom is not the place to conduct an in-depth analysis of affect and how it varies from emotion; these debates have been well covered elsewhere (see Probyn, 2005; Greco and Stenner, 2008; Gould, 2010; Wetherell, 2012). But it should acknowledge the importance of the term, and how it has informed the debate, even if that debate is extremely complicated with little convergence on definitions.

Briefly, emotions are seen to be properties of a person, whereas affect is something that induces that emotion. As Probyn (2005: 20; original emphasis) observes, it is the difference between '*being* affected and *having* an emotion'. This has roots in the narrow definition used by psychologists and neuroscientists, who have seen emotion as physical reactions in the body or brain. With this argument, emotion is seen as subjective rather than social. But the same argument can operate in reverse, with affect being something that exists external to the body. Gregg and Seigworth (2010: 2) describe affect as a 'force', while Gould (2010: 20) suggests that affect is 'unbound: it has no fixed object, no prior aim; rather it is unattached, free-floating, mobile energy'. The metaphor of an external energy is reinforced by Wetherell (2012: 12), who suggests affect is a flow, it 'is always "turned on", and "simmering", moving along, since social action is continually embodied'. While Wetherell is correct to highlight the practised, embodied aspects of emotional experiences, the concept of flow suggests that it is an observable phenomenon. As with the concept of force, energy or flow, Wetherell's theorisation suggests that affect influences the body unconsciously and from outside the body. If affect exists outside the body, then where does it reside? Someone who hates football will not simply pick up on the exuberance in the stadium.

A clearer way of understanding affect is that it is those feelings that are difficult to describe – 'bodily, sensory, inarticulate, nonconscious experience' (Gould, 2010: 20). In this case affect is somatic and not cognitive. It is for this reason that individuals who have suffered a trauma may experience unconscious flashbacks (van der Kolk, 2014). Yet the distinction between emotion, feelings and affect is still not clear. If affect is nonconscious, then how does this translate to emotion? Psychologists and neurologists return to biological determinism and suggest that there are certain hardwired emotions (Ekman, 1972; 2003; Damasio, 1994; 1999; Ekman and Davidson, 1994; Panskepp, 1998). Often these arguments suggest there are six primary emotions: anger, fear, surprise, happiness, sadness and disgust (with love absent) (Turner, 2000). If these are hardwired, then how does an individual learn to stop being angry? Furthermore, if these emotions are seen as distinct, and studied as such, then they become reified. In reality, we are confronted with a range of feelings and emotions. A football fan confronted by a baton-wielding policeman will feel anger, fear, maybe surprise, or even enjoyment; it is possible to feel a range of emotions in any given situation (Doidge and Sandri, 2018b).

So, if affect is nonconscious, how is this different from emotion? Wetherell (2012: 4, original emphasis) describes affect as '*embodied meaning-making*. Mostly, this will be something that could be understood as *human emotion*.' This begs the question: why do academics differentiate? What is required is a clear theorisation of emotion so that we can understand people's lived experiences. For the average fan in the stadium, they will not use terms like 'affect' or engage in Deleuzian poststructuralism. So, engaging the wider public with terms like 'emotion' is preferable. Even if affect is a nonconscious, embodied response, how someone responds and articulates it is through the language of feelings and emotion. Feelings are subjective, bodily experiences (Gould, 2010) which are understood based on the individual's lived experience and social influences. Meanwhile, emotion is the socially understood expression of those feelings (or affects). This expression is still embodied as it takes habitual practice to manage, suppress or perform emotion appropriately for the social context (Wetherell, 2012).

The issue with focusing on affect, as something external to the individual, rather than emotion, is that it misses the emotions and feelings the individual can summon themselves. Despite Heidegger's (1962) assertion that emotions cannot be turned off and on, they can be suppressed or invoked depending on the wishes of the individual. The joy of anticipation, anxiety or fear of confrontation can all be summoned independently. These can be conscious thoughts that nurture the physical response within the body. Worrying about the next match or looking forward to the long away trip with friends are feelings that are developed away from social interaction but are built on sustained social relationships. As Denzin (2007: 52) argued: 'All emotions are relational phenomena. They are learned in social relationships, initially the primary group of the family.' The feelings one consciously summons are reminisces of past interaction. Anxiety derives from memories of social difficulty or past frustration or sadness at yet another failure by the team. Once again, the team is seen as ontologically an extension of the self. Fear of failure of the team feels as real as the trepidation of social awkwardness.

Here, phenomenology can help our understanding. Phenomenology seeks to describe how the individual experiences phenomena. Centralising the body in the analysis, we can interrogate the sum total of experiences, feelings, traumas and desires within the individual. Emotion is a central part of this analysis as it is an embodied response. Emotion is our way of understanding and engaging with the world, as Merleau-Ponty (1971: 52, original emphasis) states:

> We must reject the prejudice which makes 'inner realities' out of love, hate, or anger, leaving them accessible to one single witness: the person who feels them. Anger, shame, hate, and love are not psychic facts hidden at the bottom of another's consciousness: they are types of behavior or styles of conduct which are visible from the outside. They exist *on* this face or *in* those gestures, not hidden behind them.

Our bodies physically display the emotions of social actors. It is clear when fans are happy or sad. Their posture can demonstrate whether they are confident striding towards the match (or hooligan confrontation), or worried or anxious.

By suggesting that emotion is something that happens in the body, and affect happens outside, academics negate the social influence on emotions. The anthropological and sociological approaches to emotions have reiterated the importance of social and cultural influences. It was anthropologists like Abu-Lughod (1986) and Lutz (1986) who dramatically expanded our understanding of emotions through observing the difference between different cultures, as well as the difference between public and private displays of emotion. It is for this reason that suppression of emotion is such an important aspect of our daily lives (Scheff, 1992; Elias, 2000). The act of presenting oneself in public is not simply about wearing the right clothes or performing the right actions; it is about exhibiting emotion in the correct way. As Goffman (1959: 75, original emphasis) states: 'To *be* a given kind of a person … is not merely to possess the required attributes, but also to sustain the standards of conduct and appearance that one's social group attaches thereto.'

Emotions are unquestionably social. They may be felt subjectively, but emotions are felt and understood in relation to others. Emotions are also what bind us to others. Durkheim (1964) argued that the euphoria of the collective ritual dramatically contrasted with the mundane life of the disparate hunter-gatherers. Coming together for the ritual and actively engaging in the collective performance produced a 'collective effervescence' that bound the members. Durkheim (1964: 217) spoke of 'transports of enthusiasm' and a 'sort of electricity' among those physically co-present which 'launches them to an extraordinary height of exaltation'. The ritual not only provides the focal point for the members to attend, but also provides the collective social interaction and physical action that builds flow, solidarity and rhythm among members.

Rituals can also help us to understand how emotions translate from the individual to the wider collective. Goffman (1967) took a micro-sociological approach to human behaviour and posited that social relations were built on repetitive 'interaction rituals'; from handshakes to facial expressions, how we interact on a daily basis is based on socially determined rules and norms. Collins (1975; 1981; 1990; 2004; 2008) develops Goffman's interaction rituals to incorporate Durkheim's analysis of ritual. When individuals meet and engage in these interaction rituals, a collective effervescence can ensue. Social actors, Collins (1981: 994) argues, 'rely on tacit assumptions and organisational routine … these negotiations are carried out implicitly, on a different level than the use of conscious manipulated verbal symbols … This is emotional rather than cognitive.' As individuals meet and interact, emotions are triggered and developed. Some lead to firm friendships, others to animosity. Like Durkheim, Collins (1981) suggests that emotions can be contagious. Yet one cannot 'catch' happiness or anger: they are embodied responses that have developed over time through social interaction. Football provides that social space where these interactions can take place and social relationships form.

When interacting with others, we are fed a multitude of emotional cues. We do not simply learn about emotions; they provide vital feedback. It is for this reason that academics should take emotions seriously, as tuning into emotions can help us understand the emotional space of fandom more fully. Emotions help people make some sense of the world (Collins, 1981; Katz, 1999; TenHouten, 2007). The feelings we experience when we enter the stadium, see our friends or celebrate that goal being scored are not simply the product of biological hardwiring; they are produced through regular social interaction. When the fan is in a crowd, there are many emotional stimuli such as the capo directing the chants, chatting with one's friends or the events on the pitch. Add to this the paraphernalia of the choreography and pyrotechnics, plus external factors like the police, rival fans and media stories, and you have a multitude of motivations and feelings. All of these combine to create a collective experience. Football fandom is one area where people make a sustained emotional investment. The practice of fandom helps fans manage and control their own emotions (Gabler, 2013). Yet they are also the architects of their own feelings. Emotions are produced from the very rituals the fans enact and they nourish the fans' emotional desires.

The absence of emotions in the study of fans

While there is some acknowledgement that fans have emotions, there has been little systematic investigation of the full range of emotions experienced at football. What analysis there has been falls into two broad categories: love and anger. Perhaps it is no surprise that scholars focus on the more extreme emotions. As mentioned earlier, emotions are invariably seen as irrational. Those who are emotional are invariably out of control, or acting negatively and unreasonably. Many of these adverbs describe a popular image of fandom, as being crazy, feverish or obsessive. In those moments of euphoria and despair at the end of a match, the more extreme emotions are displayed. Yet humans have a wide range of emotions, some of which can be conflictual (Doidge and Sandri, 2018b). Within the cauldron of the football stadium, there is a whole range of emotions on display. Fans and ultras can produce their own moments of ecstasy even when their team is losing. There can be concern for an injured star player even when winning, or frustration at a coach substituting a player that an individual fan sees as vital to the team. Even with hooliganism, anger may not be the motivating factor; there can be fun in transgression of social norms (King, 1997a).

The early focus on hooliganism and violence led to a focus on anger. Elias's (2000) 'civilising process' argued that Western society was becoming more emotionally controlled. Public expressions of emotion, notably anger and its link to physical violence, became increasingly viewed as unacceptable. The 'Leicester School' of hooliganism suggested that football violence was linked to this social norm of controlled emotion elsewhere in society (Dunning *et al.*, 1988). As we shall see in Chapter 6 on violence, and in particular with the work of Randall Collins, emotion is a key determining factor for violence. For the figurationalists, like Elias and Dunning, sport is seen as a 'quest for excitement' and becomes a mimetic activity where emotions that are normally suppressed can find expression. In industrial societies sport was not just an activity for amusement and physical exercise, it was also an emotional outlet. Elias and Dunning (1986: 24) argue that

> In such societies, there is only a comparatively limited scope for the show of strong feelings, of strong antipathies towards and dislike of people, let alone of hot anger, wild hatred or the urge to hit someone over the head. People strongly agitated, in the grip of feelings they cannot control, are cases for hospital or prison. Conditions of high excitement are regarded as abnormal in a person, as a dangerous prelude to violence in a crowd. However, to contain strong feelings, to preserve an even control of drives, affects and emotions steadily throughout one's life is likely to raise tensions.

Elsewhere they also argue that 'in advanced industrial societies, leisure activities form an enclave for the socially approved arousal of moderate excitement behaviour in public' (Elias and Dunning, 1986: 46).

Elias and Dunning (1986) take a functional approach to sport. It is mimetic and helps to dissipate or control emotions. Elias and Dunning focus on sport providing the ritual focus, but negate other rituals of sociality, such as going to the pub, chatting at work or reading social media. Each of these evokes different emotions and feelings away from the sport itself. To suggest that the reason for sport's existence is purely to minimise violence is teleological. Where is the tension when friends meet or when fan groups engage in community activities, such as working with refugees or the homeless? A diverse range of feelings and emotions are at work, and to reduce sport to one of emotional control minimises a wide field of enquiry. This is not to deny that sport can be emotionally cathartic (Stone, 2013; Doidge and Sandri, 2018a), or that it provides emotional ritual focus, but these are not the only ways that emotions underpin football fandom.

Pleasure is a primary aspect of Spaaij's (2008) analysis of hooliganism. Recognising the importance of Dunning and Elias's 'quest for excitement', Spaaij observes that fighting at football matches contrasts sharply with the boredom participants experience in other aspects of their lives. Fighting provides an important sense of self and group identity that produces emotional arousal. Significantly, Spaaij identifies the sense of control that hooligans acquire. He also recognises that emotions are not compartmentalised. In order to derive pleasure from the fights, participants have to master their own fear. Courage, therefore, is exhibited by continuing to engage, even though the individual is scared. While it is important to recognise the pleasurable and fearful aspects of hooliganism, this is only one part of fan culture. Other emotions are exhibited, many of which help create the buzz of attending matches. As mentioned previously, the sociability of meeting your friends in a pub is also an aspect of the solidarity and pleasure derived from football.

In contrast to the expressive performances of anger, other writers have observed the frequency with which fans talk of their love of their team (King, 1997b; Farred, 2002; Klugman, 2008; 2009; Pope, 2012; Doidge, 2013; 2015a). Often the understanding of love is implicitly assumed. Yet there are different types of love, maybe up to fourteen (Lomas, 2018), and different cultures use diverse terms to describe them. Is the love of a football club like the romantic love towards a partner, or like the Greek verb *meraki*, relating to the love of experiences? Or is it like the Sanskrit work *bhakti*, meaning devotional love? Rather than centralising love as the predominant emotion experienced by football fans, theoretical clarity is required. Academics should be drawing on all the emotions experienced by fans and recognising that it is not simply love that unites the group and provides solidarity, but the whole breadth of emotions. Sharing in collective despair, for example, unites members as much as the euphoria following a victory.

In his analysis of fans of Australian Rules football, Klugman (2008) asserts that love is the central emotion for fans. He argues that the word 'love' is frequently invoked by fans and therefore important to study and theorise. Love is important, he contends, because it extends to devotion, despair and other acts that may seem obsessive. Like Elias, Klugman draws on the work of Freud ([1921] 2001) and his study of group psychology, in which Freud argues that love is the distinct force that unites people in groups. A group identifies with a leader (or an abstract idea or object) and they love this leader in the belief the leader loves them back. Freud drew on the work of Le Bon (1896), who argued that collectives become governed by a 'group mind' which consequently overpowers individual members. This denies the agency of individual members and also the multitude of reasons participants engage in an activity (for more, see, e.g., Stott and Reicher [1998] on social identity theory). Likewise, Freud's focus on the love of the leader also denies the agency of members of the group. As argued earlier, it is the physical participation in the ritual that imbues a totem with symbolism, not blind devotion. By focusing on the fans' love of the club, Klugman discounts the impact of the fans' interactions with other fans, both within the club or external to the group. Humans are social animals and have wide networks of relationships, some of which are not connected to their fandom. Feelings and emotions connected to friendship, family or acquaintances are many and varied, and not all associated with love.

The rituals of fandom help fans demonstrate the love they feel towards their club. Varela (2014) provides an account of the hard-drinking, masculine fans of a *barras* in Mexico.[1] Through deliberately going against rational everyday life in the football carnival through the performance of the *colorido* (choreography), these masculine fans unite as a group and demonstrate their love of the club. Particularly through alcohol consumption, they engage in the practice of *aguante* (meaning endurance or patience). Varela (2014: 442) argues:

> Social practices of the RK [*barras*] fans are a constellation of "passionate" elements and representations of the 'love for the club', which fall into the logic of sentimental exacerbation. This exacerbation of sentimental behavior is linked to a masculine body and moral performance: *aguantar* is to love. To love is to suffer. To suffer is to cause harm. To harm is to fight, to drink, to venture in an endless party-style martyrdom.

This practice of *aguante* is a way of enduring pain and suffering, which demonstrates the love they have for the club. As with Klugman above, Varela assumes that these fans love their club as they would love another human. However, ritual is important in bringing the group together and developing the social relationships where feelings of love can emerge.

Linguistic variations of emotional terms like 'love' not only help to provide nuance and subtlety to our understanding of fandom but also reflect how fans adapt to the commercialisation of football. Nuhrat's (2018a) exposition illustrates not only how fans in Turkey express their love of their club, but also how this is incorporated into narratives of accommodation and resistance to commercialisation. Like Varela's (2014) *aguante* in Mexican Spanish, there are words in Turkish that describe the love relating to sacrifice (*sevda*), as well as the love that seems irrational, like a sickness (*aşk*). As clubs recognise the feelings fans have for their team, they want to capitalise on this love to sell more products. Fans can either purchase official products in order to demonstrate their love, or resist through the self-sacrifice of not purchasing official merchandise. Fans identify and distinguish themselves from others through their presentation of self, which symbolises the emotion and devotion they have in respect of their club, based on the rules that they construct.

Love and negotiating commodification occur in King's (1997b) nuanced analysis. He highlights the emotional elements of love, pride and solidarity within a particular masculine fan group. Pride at the financial power over their rivals is one symbol of the love of their club, but King highlights how this love is generated and manifested. Drawing on Durkheim, King highlights the collective effervescence of the group and how it becomes symbolised in the football club. This emotion is described as love, and this encourages a certain amount of compliance regarding how the club is run as it translates as success, reflecting their masculine pride. As King (1997b: 333) argues,

> The ecstasy of the lads' support and the love they have for the club are symbiotic ... this love which the lads feel for their team is simultaneously also a love for the feeling of solidarity which they experience every time they attend a game and participate in the communal practice of drinking and singing ... The team, and the love invested in it, is a symbol of the values and friendships that exist between the lads.

As Durkheim (1964) argues, the groups collectively worship the totem, but this represents the group, so effectively they are worshipping themselves and the solidarity they feel. Yet King's focus on the solidarity of the collective minimises other feelings, both within the group and in relation to others, as well as providing a stable image of group solidarity. Group dynamics are never uniform and consistent; there are disagreements, moments of close interpersonal joy within a smaller group, plus moments of individual tragedy. Recognising these variable, inconsistent and sometimes contradictory emotions will help us understand the dynamics of football fan groups like the ultras.

The importance of relationships was emphasised by Pope (2012) in her analysis of football fans. The emotional investment made by these fans was enough to structure who they were likely to have an intimate relationship with, and even when family events should be organised. Pope highlights how rugby fans distinguish themselves as feeling less emotional than their football counterparts. Again, the assumption is that feeling emotional is excessive or irrational. This does not mean that rugby fans do not feel any emotions when their team loses, they may just not feel them to the same degree, or express them in the same way. As with other practices of group formation, distinguishing oneself from another group can be important. In this case, the contrast between 'emotional' football fans and 'cool' rugby fans is more about the narrative of distinction, rather than an interrogation of the emotions experienced by fans in the moment. Either way, emotion is a clear way of demarcating group identity.

When writers highlight emotions, they invariably assume that emotions are excessive and focus on the performative elements of fandom. Ashmore (2017) critiques football studies that have invariably focused on loud, expressive emotions, as performed through chants and choreographies. As Ashmore highlights, fans of non-league football in the UK will see atmosphere in a variety of phenomena at a stadium, including visiting the club bar, chatting with friends or enjoying new surroundings. While he is correct to say that many scholars focus on these aspects, there are other emotions at play when fans congregate, particularly as they socialise (Doidge, 2015a). Ashmore (2017: 30) draws on work around affect as he seeks to 'move beyond the human-centric focus of existing work to consider a whole number of things and flows that make up atmospheres at football matches'. He suggests that stadium architecture or the geographical location contribute to the atmosphere of non-league football. Yet he fails to explain how a stadium generates an atmosphere without humans involved. Emotions or affect are not free-floating, waiting for humans to pluck them from their environs, but are constituted within the body in interaction with others.

The lack of bodily analysis of emotions is also exhibited in Doidge's (2015a) exploration of Italian football and the ultras. He frequently alludes to emotion, but does not use it as a central tool of analysis. He describes the emotional presentation of football on Italian television but fails to analyse how emotion contributes to the commercial and political manipulation of the sport. Doidge also highlights the various emotional aspects of the ultras in Italy, particularly linked to stadium security, policing and violence. He identifies how aggressive policing and stadium regulations can increase tension around matches, which can provoke violence and heightened confusion and anger. Similarly, he refers to the emotional attachments fans (and ultras in particular) have to their clubs, and how the rituals of the game generate this collective solidarity that manifests in the performance of choreographies, chants and abuse (Doidge, 2015a; 2015b). Yet he does not locate it in the bodily actions of the fans and ultras. As with others, there is no systematic theorising of emotion within the analysis; there is simply a recognition that emotions are there.

Referencing the German ultras scene, Gabler (2013: 81) argues that 'emotions undoubtedly play a decisive role in football'. Gabler contends that the ultras style of fandom is a way of structuring emotions within norms permitted by the clubs, authorities and media. Consequently, ultras adapt their approach 'just far enough so as not to be forbidden, but also [display] a certain degree of (at least symbolic) non-conformity through specific forms of deviant behaviour' (Gabler, 2013: 83). Ultras do not have free rein on their emotions within the stadium, or associated spaces. The process of producing choreographies is a way of organising and controlling emotions. Significantly, Gabler highlights the internal dynamics of the various ultras groups and how these also influence the responses of the group. The simultaneous fragmentation and unity of ultras (Gabler, 2013; Doidge, 2015a; 2017) has created many internal dynamics within the ultras scene and leaders are constantly negotiating, often through fear or threats of violence. When combined with the wider resentment and anger that some groups feel towards changes within football, recognising the emotional dynamics of the groups will help academics to understand fan mobilisation more clearly.

As outlined in the Introduction, emotions are the clearest demarcation of groups of fans. At the precise moment the net ripples with the impact of the ball when a goal is scored, or the referee blows the final whistle, there are two clear groups of fans: there is no clearer distinction than that between the euphoria of the winning fans and the despair of the losers. This is magnified as the importance of the match is increased, particularly in cup competitions, as the image of the Ajax players prostrate on the turf after Lucas Moura scored the winning goal for Tottenham Hotspur in the 2019 Champions League semi-final testifies. Fans rely on rivalries to articulate their own sense of self (Carter, 2008; Gabler, 2013; Doidge, 2015a; Nuhrat, 2018a). Archetti (2001: 154) argues that 'no identity can ever exist by itself and without an array of opposites, negatives and contradictions'. While it is important that fans have a symbolic other, a rival with which to contest one's identity, the emotional dimension is fundamental to understanding group formation.

Emotions are used to differentiate rival fans within the stadium. Songs will valorise the group and use the language of emotions to exalt the team, the fans or the city. Similarly emotive language will also demonise the other team. In this way the group performs their emotions. Participating in the performance is one way of enacting an emotional sense of self within the collective, and can produce a sense of flow or collective effervescence. Chants such as 'We love you Whitehawk, we do' or 'Stand up if you hate the scum' help to establish the participants as a collective. Significantly, the use of emotional language helps differentiate the groups. It is for this reason that banners declare that the club is in the fans' hearts or that the fans love the club, like when Roma fans unfurled an enormous one reading simply *TI AMO* (I love you) to the team before the Rome derby in 1983. Ultras at FC Nürnberg have a song *Eine Liebe die ein Leben hält* (A love that holds a life).

Many studies of football have highlighted how fans differentiate themselves from others. Racism has become one of the clear areas of focus, yet emotion is strangely absent from analysis of racism in football (Back *et al.*, 1999; King, 2004; Burdsey, 2011; Ratna, 2014; Doidge, 2015a). Discrimination and abuse can provoke strong feelings, such as anger, shame and disgust. While it is rare to witness such violent responses, incidents such as Eric Cantona's kung fu kick aimed at a Crystal Palace supporter in 1995 illustrate the emotion work that is required from victims of abuse. Football continues to be presented as a white, masculine sport, and those who are considered racialised 'others' have to supress feelings in order to be accepted (Burdsey, 2007; Müller *et al.*, 2007; Ratna, 2014; Mauro, 2016). The language used in analysis often downplays the emotion. For example, Ratna (2014: 298, 301) uses terms such as 'aggrieved' or 'disturbed' to describe the feelings her respondents had when feeling excluded, marginalised or othered. This reflects the racialisation of emotion and how players and academics suppress or downplay emotive terms so as not to appear overly confrontational.

When emotion is discussed, the focus is always on the emotion of the victim, never on the emotion of the perpetrator. The victim tries to describe the 'feeling' they have when being watched (Ratna, 2014), or when trying to account for someone's racist abuse (Müller *et al.*, 2007). Yet these emotions are also vital signs of significant interactions. Social interactions do not need to be animated or grandiose to hold significant meaning for someone. Silence when entering a pub or a furtive glance can convey important messages. For example, Back *et al.* (2001: 301) recount a black England fan's 'weird' feeling when white Combat 18 activists walked past before an England match against Scotland. Eye contact and a nod communicated that 'Any other day it'd be different, but today it's about the fucking Jocks' (Back *et al.*, 2001: 301). The feelings one has in relation to these micro-interactions are important signs. Shared feelings can be unspoken; there is a phenomenological aspect to emotional belonging. Recognising that a fan has shared the same trials and tribulations can be recognised in a look in the eyes or a nod of the head (Klugman, 2009). A whole sense of belonging can be communicated with minimal gestures, yet it does not mean that emotions are not there.

The central absence of emotion within the study of football fandom is conspicuous considering the etymology of the words used to describe followers of football. The word 'fan' is shortened from 'fanatic', denoting zealous and devoted followers. Formerly, this referred to religious devotees, but the term has become associated with sports fans since the nineteenth century. The Italian word for 'fan', *tifoso*, infers a similar irrational and uncontrollable condition as its roots are alleged to derive from 'typhus'; fans are inflicted with a malady that produces frenzied fever in its sufferers (Foot, 2006). This is magnified with the ultras, who take this passion to another level (Testa and Armstrong, 2010; Doidge, 2015a). All of these monikers suggest that the person displaying such fever is irrational and not in control of their emotions. Yet it is not irrational to have emotions. This artificial binary implies that humans are either rational or emotional.

The absence of emotions in academic analysis is due to emotions being seen as female and/or irrational. Sport was identified by Elias and Dunning (1986) as a way of controlling emotion, particularly in men. Too often, emotions are used to minimise or exclude participants, particularly women, from sport. More often, the term 'emotional' is used negatively to describe people, usually women, who do not conform to a hegemonic ideal (Lutz, 1986). These emotions are hysteria, crying, and sadness. Despite this, emotions like anger and frustration are seen as perfectly rational male responses. Yet for Goodwin *et al.* (2001: 9): 'Emotions can be seen as an aspect of all social action and social relations. They accompany rational acts as fully as irrational ones.' Moreover, emotions are not always irrational. As Crossley (2002: 49) argues,

> It is perfectly understandable that a person who is mistreated will become angry, for example, just as it is perfectly understandable that an individual who loses a loved one will become upset. We would not deem an individual who reacted in these ways irrational and would probably think it odd if they did not react in these ways.

This becomes much more apparent in football fandom. Non-fans will often see the emotional responses of fans as irrational. A comment such as 'it's only a game' accentuates this lack of understanding. Acting on the basis of emotion is not irrational. The families of the victims of the 1989 Hillsborough disaster, for instance, were motivated to continue to fight for justice based on the grief, anger and frustration resulting from the systematic failings of the police, government and football authorities. Ultimately, humans are emotional beings. To ignore or minimise the role of emotion, particularly within the emotionally saturated world of football, is to ignore a significant aspect of the social phenomenon.

Emotions in collective action

The absence of emotion in studies of fandom is surprising due to the study of collective action being one area where the study of emotions has influenced analysis. Le Bon (1896) saw the crowd inflecting emotions of anger, fear and anxiety onto the individual. He argued that this emotional response would lead to irrationality – the bedrock of Enlightenment thinking. Le Bon (1896: 32) argued that '[i]solated, he may be a cultivated individual; in a crowd, he is a barbarian – this is a creature acting by instinct'. He felt that emotions were contagious and being in crowds would result in people becoming uncivilised and emotional. This has been clearly critiqued by social psychologists such as Clifford Stott, John Drury and Steve Reicher (e.g. Stott and Reicher, 1998; Stott *et al.*, 2001). Yet the emotional element remains a popular criticism of protestors, particularly from politicians and sections of the media. As Gould (2004: 161–162) argues,

> Importantly, this characterisation of protesters as less-than-rational and as hysterical, uninformed, naive, unreasonable and so on – although disputed by contemporary social movement scholars and discredited by recent research – is still popular today among politicians, in the media, and in public discourse more generally.

Clearly, there is a political dimension to characterising protestors as uncivilised as it justifies any repercussions. But what is significant about understanding the role of emotions is that external commentators are not coming from the same emotional perspective.

As Katz (1999) observes, emotions are a subjective response. It can be very difficult to explain to others how one is feeling. After a contentious incident on the pitch, talk to the fans of a rival club, or observe their interactions on social media. They may be adamant that a player should not have been sent off, or a penalty was incorrectly awarded. Yet to the less emotionally invested fan, it does not seem so obvious, the referee made the correct decisions or the fans' reactions may seem irrational. It is for this reason that it is difficult to write about a fan group without emotional involvement as the outsider does not see the experiences in the same way. Failing to identify the emotional dimension, let alone not understanding it, will mean a significant element has been excluded and any analysis weakened.

By the 1960s, particularly among the non-violent civil rights movements, emotions had to be controlled. This was magnified as social science researchers, many of whom sympathised with the movements they studied, sought to emotionally distance themselves from the groups and focused on the strategies and politics of social movements (Goodwin *et al.*, 2001). The same can be argued of football scholarship; academics do not seem to study their own teams. Yet in order to authenticate themselves, many either uncritically try to prove their (white, working-class, male) credentials as a football fan, or distance themselves emotionally from their fandom and engage in 'rational' social scientific research. As Bairner (2012) argues, there are rarely discussions about sport at sociology of sport conferences.

Football is an interesting social phenomenon. Fandom is not a mere commercial activity; it is an ongoing sensual process. There is an intertwining of the self with the club. It becomes a Durkheimian totem that symbolises the self within a community. As one of the many football cliches goes, no one wants to have their ashes scattered in a supermarket, yet millions of fans have done something similar at their team's football ground. The revered Liverpool manager Bill Shankly clarified this feeling when he said: 'Some people think football is a matter of life and death. I assure you, it's much more serious than that.' Emotion is one of the enticing and intoxicating aspects of watching and playing football. The despair of a loss or relegation is balanced by the joy of scoring and winning. In these moments, fans and players alike are united or divided.

Emotions are 'the "glue" of solidarity – and what mobilises conflict' (Collins, 1990). It is the emotional attachment to clubs that keep fans coming back regularly, as well as mobilising politically.

> Emotions pervade all social life, social movements included. The most prosaic daily routines, seemingly neutral, can provoke violent emotional responses when interrupted. Unusual actions probably involve even more, and more complex, feelings. Not only are emotions part of our responses to events, but they also – in the form of deep affective attachments – shape the goals of our actions. (Jasper, 1998, 398)

There has been an emotional turn in sociology in the twenty-first century. Goodwin *et al.* (2001) and Goodwin and Jasper (2004), for example, attempt to bring emotion back into the study of social movements. Yet sport is conspicuous by its absence. Few social activities command such a great range of emotional engagement in a public space: the ecstasy of victory; the despair of relegation; the joy of being among similar people. When there is already an intense emotional engagement from a group, then it is no surprise that conflict, both political and violent, can ensue. As Crossley (2002: 137) suggests: 'Emotions are very often a crucial source of the energy which fuels movement activism and engagement.'

Understanding emotions in relation to power is an important consideration when studying collective mobilisations. Power dynamics within the group, and between the group and others, all have an emotional dimension. As Kemper (1978: 371) observes: 'A very large class of human emotions results from real, anticipated, recollected, or imagine outcomes of power and status relations.' This can include distress, anger, guilt shame, pride, security and happiness. Challenges to one's status can produce a wealth of intense emotions (Kemper, 1978). As Jasper (1998) and Collins (1990) state, even minor changes to one's position can stimulate heightened emotional responses. Football has undergone a significant politico-economic transformation that has shifted the power, status and wealth of certain clubs and marginalised many others. This has provoked intense emotions, and fans have mobilised accordingly.

The presentation of the 'correct' emotion is also sanctioned through power structures. Moreover, 'power is exercised through and reproduced in our feelings, and it is forceful and effective precisely because of that' (Gould, 2010: 39). Who can use emotional responses, and when, are exercised through power relations. Reinforcing the social construction element of emotions, this can range from socially appropriate spaces to show one's feelings (Abu-Lughod, 1986) to how to produce 'emotional labour' and manage and manufacture emotions for the workplace (Hochschild, 1983). Nuhrat (2018a) observes that the commercialisation of Turkish football has seen clubs commodify the fans' 'love' for their club. Yet love is varied and has many potential outcomes (sex, crimes of passion, suffering or romance). Clubs permit the love of the club that can be demonstrated through purchasing official merchandise, but not the type that would provoke an attack on a rival fan group. There is a discourse around emotions that underlines the power dynamics associated with them (Abu-Lughod and Lutz, 1990). This does not have to come from clubs or authorities but can be established through the group or social norms, particularly around gender and who can express what type of emotion (Lutz, 1988).

The importance of emotions to the ultras

The spectacle of football (and sport in general) helps fans and ultras to make sense of their emotions and the social world around them. As Carter (2008: 66) observes in relation to Cuban baseball,

> The fans' jubilation at the end of the baseball game reflects their perspective of being involved and their emotional involvement in such spectacles. As an audience they are not separate from the spectacle; they are an integral part of it … Fans' use of nostalgic, sometimes painful memories, posits a 'once was' with a 'now' in a collective emotional reaction that dramatizes the uncertainties of contemporary everyday life.

The rituals of fandom enable ultras to feel emotionally connected to a wider collective. They do this through the construction of narratives that link the past to the present and locate themselves, both as an individual and as a group, into this wider narrative. Their emotional sense of belonging is developed and located through these narratives within the spectacle of the match.

Emotions do not simply create the bonds of attachment to the football club, but they help unify the wider community of fans. As shown in the previous section, Durkheim (1964) argued that one of the key aspects of group formation was the collective effervescence that emerges from rituals. The intense emotional energy that these rites engender contrast with the mundane everyday existence of the individual members. Simmel (1950) showed that meeting with people who were like you was enjoyable. These feelings of sociability were an end in themselves. Fans regularly go to stadiums to meet friends and be sociable, and through the repetitive acts of the crowd, they help produce the emotional energy that underpins the atmosphere. This is intoxicating and produces feelings towards the football club and their fellow fans. Through emotional attachment, the individual feels part of a wider collective.

Not only does emotion underpin the solidarity of the group, it has to be carefully managed in order to maintain this solidarity and present the correct image of the group. Hochschild (1983) showed that people working in the service sector have to 'undertake emotional labour' to manage their emotions in order to make their customers feel special and engaged. Emotional labour, according to Hochschild (1983: 7),

> requires one to induce or suppress feeling in order to sustain the outward countenance that produces the proper state of mind in others – in this case, the sense of being cared for in a convivial and safe place. This kind of labor calls for a coordination of mind and feeling, and it sometimes draws on a source of self that we honor as deep and integral to our individuality.

Despite the emotions permeating football, these have to be carefully controlled. In this way, football fandom is a form of emotional labour. Fan groups have 'emotion cultures' (Gordon, 1989). Within these groups, '[f]eeling "rules" demarcate how much of a given feeling, held in a given way, is crazy, unusual but understandable, normal, inappropriate, or almost inappropriate for a given social context' (Hochschild, 1983: 122). These rules determine how fans and ultras should present, manage and express their emotions and feelings.

The correct control and management of emotion helps determine hierarchies within ultras groups. Collins (2008) has shown how control of emotion is vital in violent confrontations. This will be explored in more depth in Chapter 6. This helps determine the successful fighters and those who will attain a reputation. Emotional control also helps determine significant figures within the ultras group. Collins (2004) highlighted how the firefighters became the symbols after the 9/11 terrorist attack on New York. Amidst the confusion and chaos of the attack, the firefighters resorted to their training and commanded the emotional space of the event; they took control and coordinated the rescue and cleanup.

In a similar manner, the capos dominate the emotional space at the front of the football crowd. They have to be able to manage their emotions, and with them, the emotions of the fans in the stands. As King and de Rond (2011) identified with key individuals in the Cambridge rowing team for the Boat Race, knowing when and how to communicate was a key skill in getting the group to achieve rhythm. The role of the capo becomes crucial in managing this emotional rhythm. In their role as conductor, they are not just directing the chants and movements, they also need to know when to get angry, when to express joy and when to cajole. The 'conductor' of the ultras from one Polish club (personal interview, 2017) summarises his 'emotional labour':

> In most cases, this is psychology. You don't see situation on the pitch, so it is very important to read it from the facial expressions of people what is happening on the pitch. You must feel what you may allow to. This is primarily the observation of people. Sometimes just one quick look at the pitch. ... These are emotions. A lot of people are at the stadium. You cannot control everyone. You have a derby match, for example, you see an outbreak between people and it is spreading out. And it's difficult to control it. You can try to do it, say something, scream that it is not a good moment, but you can also give it a chance to spread.

Being able to read the crowd and manage their emotions is an important part of leading and organising groups. Without this ability, the capo would be superseded by someone who can manage their emotional labour correctly. The importance of emotions in understanding the ultras style of fandom is not restricted to motivation or management of emotions. Emotions are not simply psychological or physiological reactions; the group produces emotions themselves. 'More than *manage* emotions – a term that implies a preexisting emotional state that then is amplified or dampened – the emotion work of movements *generates* feelings' (Gould, 2010: 213, original emphasis).

Emotional investment by the ultras is an embodied experience. It is not simply a cognitive process; it entails using the body within the performance. Chanting, clapping and jumping are all physical activities that physiologically arouse the body. Sinclair *et al.* (1994) observed that those who were shown emotionally laden phrases after doing physical exercise exhibited heightened emotion. These respondents interpreted their increased physical arousal through exercise as increased emotional arousal. The physical activity of ultras fandom increases physical arousal. When combined with an activity that has been invested with a lot of emotion, respondents are likely to feel even more emotionally aroused. This in turn becomes a motivating factor for subsequent performances. Emotionally charged victories and defeats are the ones that remain in the memory. Events with high emotion are ones that leave a lasting imprint on the group, and are more likely to be continually discussed and reminisced (King, 2001; McGaugh, 2006). Ultras typify their style of fandom through a greater intensity of engagement with the various activities associated with being a fan. They imbue their relationship with the club with more emotion, the intensity of the emotions generated through their rituals and bodily co-presence, and the heightened physical arousal all contribute to an amplified emotional engagement with the match.

Conclusion

The fundamentals of the discipline of sociology are to understand how groups form. The ultras provide a clear example of regular collective behaviour through an act of consumption. Yet these fans are not merely customers; they are active emotional participants in the spectacle. Ultras and many football fans ontologically identify with the club. They simultaneously feel that the club is an extension of themselves, and express an unwavering devotion to the club. This can be seen in how fans say 'we won at the weekend' or 'I love the club'. Understanding of this relationship between the fans and the club is fundamental in explaining the continued participation of the ultras. It is this emotional engagement with the game of football and fellow fans that generates and maintains the passion in the stadium.

Despite this, studies of football fans have relatively neglected the importance of emotions. Understanding emotions is about understanding what it means to be human. And the emotional cauldron of a football stadium provides us with a rare space in contemporary society to interrogate the meaning of being human. The liminal space of the match permits emotional expression that is deemed unacceptable in everyday society, particularly for men. As Katz (1999) identifies, emotions are a way of taking control of a situation. The tension that exists within the match requires careful management. The fans invest time, money and emotion in their clubs. This can lead to anxiety frustration and anger but equally the team's victories can lead to euphoria and extreme happiness. In the unpredictable world of football, generating emotional energy through collective singing, clapping and choreography helps the ultras to manage their own feelings and emotions while at the same time demonstrating their love for their club. The rituals of football enable these emotions to be continually managed, either by ramping up the excitement or dissipating tension. It is in those moments of victory and defeat that the rival fans are distinct. It is these emotional experiences that help build a history and tradition of ultras fandom.

Note

1 In colloquial Spanish from the River Plate region, *barras* means an informal gorup of people, or more usually, a gang.

3

The formation of the ultras

One of the most important banners displayed by the group Ultras Lechia Gdańsk is the one which proudly declared *My tworzymy historię* ('We create history'). Either side of the slogan were two representations of the city of Gdańsk. To the right was an image of Neptune holding aloft his trident. The image was taken from the historic Neptune's Fountain that symbolises the seafaring importance of the city. To the left was a representation of the giant cranes of the Gdańsk shipyard and the port's importance to the politics and economy of the city. The shipyard was the birthplace of Poland's *Solidarność* (Solidarity) movement that was the first non-communist trade union in the Soviet Bloc. Led by Lech Wałęsa, the future Polish president, it marked one of the first successful steps in challenging communism in Eastern Europe (Touraine, 1983). The banner was green, and the lettering white. Running underneath were two stripes: one white, one red. The prominence of the green and white reflected the colours of the team. The white and red stripes underneath were a nod to the Polish flag that, along with the cranes of the shipyard, illustrate how the fans see the club as situated in the local city and the wider nation. The banner also had another literal meaning: the fans themselves rebuilt the football club after financial and organisational collapse in 2001. The fans took care of the players, cleaned the stadium, collected money for day-to-day operations and laid the foundation for a new, better history for the club (Kossakowski, 2017a). By writing their own chapter in the history of the club, the fans have helped create their own memories and legends.

Through a simple banner it is possible to see multiple and interlacing histories. We can discern the history of the ultras as they helped the club rise from its knees. But we can also see how the fan group locates themselves in a broader history of their city and their nation. C.L.R.

James (1963) observed that former colonies could not refer back to a history in the same way as their colonial masters. 'Underdeveloped countries have to go back centuries to rebuild one. We of the West Indies have none at all, none that we know of. To such people the three W's, Ram and Val wrecking English batting, help to fill a huge gap in their consciousness and in their needs' (James, 1963: 225).[1] New groups, not just nations, feel the need to locate themselves in history and sport becomes an important social space for them to situate themselves in the locality, nation and sport.

Interwoven with these histories is that of the club, as the ultras' history is almost always written in the colours of the football team they support. Through an analysis of the ultras we do not simply see the development of a fan phenomenon, but also how history is woven into the performances of the groups and symbolises the love they have for their club, locality, nation, politics or religion. Nobody verifies the 'rightness' of the fans' stories, or checks whether the ultras' performances correspond to historically verifiable facts. As Tonkin (1995: 2) highlights: 'In more than one language, the same word – in English it is "history" – has to stand both for "the past", history-as-lived, and "representations of pastness", history-as-recorded.' The etymology derives from the Greek *istoría* which leads to *storia* (Italian), *historia* (Spanish and Polish), *histoire* (French), *istórija* (Bulgarian), *istórija* (Russian), *hìstōrija* (Serbo-Croat), *história* (Hebrew). Likewise, in Turkish (*geshikhte*), Arabic (*tarikh*) and German (*geschichte*), the word means both history and story. While many languages, like English, separate out the meanings, the root is both an academic discipline and a narrative.

The ultras permit the interrogation of alternative stories and histories. Within the football world there are many competing viewpoints. Journalists present their own narratives that feed a particular media storyline. The clubs themselves frequently have official histories that recount matches, achievements and despair. Yet these histories are adapted as clubs acclimatise to the conditions of contemporary commercial football. Football histories can be commodified and sold as 'official' to fans around the globe. Separately, ultras groups will have their own stories and histories. When analysing a history of a movement, it is important to ask: 'In whose interest is it to try to achieve an authentic representation of a historic past or of a distinctive culture?' (Barthel-Bouchier, 2001: 222). An analysis of ultras history (like a wider history of football) must also address the question of power in the production of historical discourse. This is not just an awareness of the power between the football authorities and fans, but also power within fan groups themselves. Who has the power to narrate a story relates to positions of power within the group (King, 2001).

Although the development of the historical identity of ultras groups in different countries is important, ultras culture should be looked at as one responding to social changes. The history of ultras in different countries must therefore take into account the socio-economic and cultural heritage of particular regions, as well as the current state of football in the country, the impact of commercialisation and legal restrictions. Ultras terraces tend to be a filter through which external political and cultural influences permeate. The filter, however, is not a passive structure, but a living tissue which creates history on the basis of relations with the outside world.

This book is a sociological analysis of the ultras phenomenon. It is not a history of the ultras, nor does it prioritise historical methods. It is also not possible to provide an in-depth insight into ultras across the globe in one small chapter. Instead, this chapter seeks to present a thematic outline of significant events that have helped shape ultras in their brief but colourful history. We do not analyse each country, nor go in-depth into specific groups, and the presented cases are not ranked in order of importance. We attempt to pull out some of the common features of ultras globally, yet it is important to analyse that these frames of interpretation do not have the same meaning in every country; sometimes, due to local specificities, completely different aspects gain importance. We highlight some basic distinguishing features while recognising that many ultras groups are not mentioned here.

This chapter starts with the work of Hobsbawm's (1983) 'invented traditions' and how it links to Anderson's (1983) work on nations as 'imagined communities'. These concepts illustrate how practices that are seen as traditional and existing since time immemorial are often recent inventions that appeal to history. Through ritual and repetitive practice, individual members of the social group not only identify with each other in the present, but also draw upon historical roots to legitimise and justify actions and identities. Yet oral history is socially constructed (Tonkin, 1995). It is related by individuals within groups and transmitted through stories, banners, conversations and choreographies. The question of whose history it is should always be asked, and we are presenting just one interpretation.

Following this illustration of the epistemological aspects of history, we outline the fan traditions of England and Italy in the 1970s to distinguish between the difference styles. This will be followed with a presentation of the roots of ultras in Italy before demonstrating how this style has influenced ultras groups in other continents. There are two important aspects of the cultural diffusion of the ultras style, namely physical interaction at matches or tournaments, or viewing images on social media. Broadly, the ultras movement adopts a certain style of performance (banners, flags, pyrotechnics), often with a political link. Passionate devotion to the team, and the immediate locality are over-riding features of these groups as they seek to differentiate themselves from rivals. Violence becomes more prominent for some groups and this leads to repression by State authorities (and is covered in more detail in Chapter 6). This coincides with the politico-economic transformation of football in the 1990s, and the twenty-first century has seen ultras uniting around football politics as they try to resist 'modern football'.

The invention of the ultras tradition

As illustrated in the opening paragraph, ultras present their own history. Global, national and local events impact the shape and development of the group, their histories and members' memories. The history of groups is constantly performed and reimagined. As outlined in Chapter 1, football is a popular social activity where individuals and groups enact their identity. The ritualistic nature of the sport provides a regular space where groups can meet and interact, and this helps sustain the group over time, providing continuity and tradition. Yet these practices have not existed forever; football as we know it only became codified in the nineteenth century and established as a popular sport across the world since the turn of the twentieth century. The ultras style of fandom can trace its roots back to the late 1960s in Italy, making its traditions considerably younger than the sport itself. It is for this reason that Hobsbawm's use of 'invented tradition' is apposite in this case. 'Invented tradition', Hobsbawm (1983: 1) outlines, 'is taken to mean a set of practices, normally governed by overtly or tacitly accepted rules and of a ritual or symbolic nature, which seek to inculcate certain values and norms of behaviour by repetition, which automatically implies continu-ity with the past.' The ritual and symbolic nature of fandom is important here; it is the regular practice of fandom that ensures continuity over time. This can mean that the paraphernalia used (like flags and banners) becomes a tradition, but so too do the narratives that become reified in the stories of the group. Although Hobsbawm (1983) overwhelmingly focuses on national traditions, the ritual process of invented traditions can work within localised groups. Each group instigates and habitualises certain practices which over time become ossified as traditions.

As Durkheim showed, the symbols of the group are both venerated by the group and created by them through regular practice. In effect, the invented traditions of the group become the ritual focus and ensure their survival. But it is through these ritual practices that the group is unified. Anderson (1983) extrapolated that the regular practice of daily rituals was what helped unify individuals as a nation, or 'imagined community'. Through the daily ritual of reading a newspaper or watching the weather forecast, a group of people are unified in a shared practice. They are linked through language, geography and history. Similarly, Smith (1986) argued that shared 'myths, symbols, memories and values' helped underpin nationalism. As illustrated in the previous two chapters, the symbols and memories of ultras are regularly enacted at matches. Indeed, Hobsbawm (1990: 143) explicitly linked this to football by arguing that an 'imagined community of millions seems more real as a team of eleven named people'.

These invented traditions socialise members into what to remember (and what to forget). Effectively, the imagined community of the ultras group is also a mnemonic community (Zerubavel, 1996). Certain events are commemorated and memorialised and become part of the collective memory of the group. 'The notion of a "collective memory"', Zerubavel (1996: 294, original emphasis) argues, 'implies a past that is not only commonly shared but also jointly remembered ... By helping ensure that an entire mnemonic community will come to remember its past *together*, as a group, society affects not only what and who we remember but also when we remember it!' Ultras groups will memorialise certain events in local history or specific players and this helps to recreate the collective memory of the group and continue the traditions of the ultras.

History and memory are intertwined in the present. According to Collard (1989: 101): 'In looking at the ways in which a particular history is experienced, thought about, and used in the present, it is clear that memory is profoundly influenced by discourses and experiences in the present ... This makes it a very complicated construction as well as a very active process.' The process requires continuous repetition, but adapts to discourses in the present. When ultras of the Czech side Jablonec displayed a banner of a blonde woman (holding a shield inscribed with 'Europa') kicking an anthropomorphic representation of a pig-faced man wearing traditional 'Muslim' dress towards Turkey, they were drawing on traditional and historic representations of 'Europe' and 'Islam' but in the contemporary context of the 2015 'refugee crisis' in Europe (*Ultras-Tifo*, 2015). As with other areas of group representation, individuals build their understandings on pre-existing knowledge (Goffman, 1959; Butler, 1990). These 'pre-existing systems of schematised knowledge not only influence the ways in which people categorize, but also the ways in which they make inferences' (Rydgren, 2007: 228).

As with other aspects of the ultras style of fandom, history is also a performance. The choreographies, banners and stories recounted to other members all help present the group to themselves and to others. 'Narrators are, in more than one sense, formed by their own narrations. Their reputations, and thus their self-identity, can be made by the skill of their performance' (Tonkin, 1995: 50). As Goffman and Butler demonstrated in previous chapters, individual identities are repetitive performances. Likewise, the group is constantly performed and the narrative of their history helps establish the group and how they are seen.

Emotions are a key feature of the collective memories and histories of groups. Habitualised, mundane behaviour is often internalised and forgotten. Emotionally charged events are more likely to leave a lasting impression on the group (McGaugh, 2006; Rydgren, 2007). This is not just because the emotion of the situation leaves a traumatic memory, but the emotion means that it gets repeated regularly, either in the media or within the group (King, 2001; Rydgren, 2007). These emotionally charged events are woven into the narrative of the group and transmitted to new members. This helps account 'for the sense of pride, pain, or shame we sometimes experience with regard to events that had happened to groups and communities to which we belong long before we had joined them' (Zerubavel, 1996: 290). These emotions help socialise new members into the collective. This oral tradition continues with ultras and is bolstered by the proliferation of images that are captured and circulated on social media.

The origins of the ultras

Although football fans come in many shapes and sizes, there are two broad traditions: English and Italian. One evolved into hooliganism and the 'casuals' style and the other into ultras. A book about ultras is not the place to enter into a detailed synopsis of hooliganism and the hooligan and casual subcultures, as this has been outlined much better elsewhere (Taylor, 1971a; Marsh et al., 1978; Williams et al., 1989; Murphy et al., 1990; Giulianotti, 1994; Armstrong, 1998; Perryman, 2002; Frosdick and Marsh, 2005; Spaaij, 2006; Stott and Pearson, 2007; Collins, 2008; Tsoukala, 2009). It is useful, however, to highlight the British style as this becomes a continuous counterpoint for how the ultras style is either differentiated from hooliganism, or how it incorporates aspects of it. Hooligans were predominantly masculine in composition, fairly organic in structure, and rather than having a clear leader they were headed by a collection of dominant older men. Fights ranged from spontaneous encounters with rival fans, usually in relation to masculine notions of taking territory like rival terraces or pubs. Later they evolved to less public spaces, in car parks and waste ground away from the stadium so as to avoid detection by the police. It was this aspect that contributed to the development of the casuals style, where fans did not wear team colours so there was less chance of them being identified by the authorities.

Unlike hooligans, the ultras style is about conspicuous performances. Colours, flags and banners are used to make a prominent display, both within and on the approach to the stadium. Ultras are also more structured and, as noted in Chapter 1, have a leader (the capo) who heads a small decision-making group with individuals responsible for fundraising, recruitment and creative ideas. This structure evolved from formalised fan groups from Southern Europe in the 1950s. The group *Torcida* from Hajduk Split, for instance, can trace its history back to 1950, when some sailors witnessed the passionate fans at the World Cup in Brazil and decided to form a group of their own; consequently, they adopted the Portuguese term for supporters as the name of their group. Although they adopted a passionate type of support, they did not introduce the other performative aspects of the ultras style; this originated in Italy. The same is true of Spain where masculine fan groups called *peñas* formed around bars (Llopis-Goig, 2015). Similar organised fan groups, like Inter's *I Moschettieri* (The Musketeers), emerged in Italy in the 1950s (Guerra *et al.*, 2010). In the absence of professionalised football administration, these fan clubs, like the *peñas*, organised travel to matches and distributed tickets (Doidge, 2015a; Llopis-Goig, 2015). By the late 1960s the political milieu in Italy witnessed a transformation of fandom in stadiums across the peninsular. The first ultras group was AC Milan's *Fossa dei Leoni* (Lions' Den) in 1968 and was quickly followed by *The Boys* at Inter. However, the collective name came from the Sampdoria group called *Ultras*, who formed in 1970. Even though many of the names of ultras groups were written in Italian, the status of English fans across Europe can be witnessed in the use of English monikers, like *Boys* at Inter and Roma, Sampdoria's *Rude Boys and Girls* or even the later *Barbour Gang* at Milan. As will be shown, the influence of English fan culture and language also spread globally.

Each group and league have their own forms of development and change. In Italy it is possible to discern four phases of development (Podaliri and Balestri, 1998; Doidge, 2015a) that shift from the political in the 1970s with the emergence of violence as a significant part of ultras mentality in the 1980s. From here there is a growth of violence, racism and localism. Yet despite this fragmentation, ultras are starting to unite over growing repression from State authorities and police. Similarly,

Spaaij and Viñas (2005) distinguish four phases of the development of the ultras movement in Spain: the origins of the ultras phenomenon in Spain in the early 1980s; the diffusion and expansion of the Spanish ultras movement in the second half of the 1980s; the radicalisation, politicisation and fragmentation of the ultras groups in the late 1980s and 1990s; and the current situation marked by further fragmentation and decline. It is interesting that while in Italy the traditional divisions based on politics and localism are beginning to be eroded, in Poland the second decade of the twenty-first century has been characterised by a growing importance of politics, nationalism and regional identity in ultras' performances (Kossakowski *et al.*, 2018). Something similar has occurred in Greece with Zaimakis (2018) outlining four phases of the politicisation of fans in the 1970s, through greater organisation in the 1980s, before nationalism took hold in the 1990s, which has continued into the 2000s alongside resistance to State regulation. It seems to be characteristic of the countries of Eastern and South-eastern Europe that political identity, expressed primarily through nationalism, still has an important place in ultras culture. Each geographical location has its own specific social and political context that affects if and when the ultras style is adopted.

As well as distinguishing ultras from hooligans and casuals, it is important to differentiate them from the Latin American style of fandom. Even though there are some visual similarities with the use of flags, chants and devotion to club colours, and they emerged from organised fan groups as in Southern Europe, they operate in subtly different ways. In Argentina the first organised groups of supporters – called *barra bravas* – were formed in the second half of the 1960s and also had a 'militant' and political character with a strongly hierarchical structure (Duke and Crolley, 1996). They have a different relationship with the club presidency, which seeks support from the *barra bravas* to influence elections (Giulianotti, 1999). Today, these groups are more strongly associated with illegal and criminal activities (Grabia, 2011). In Brazil, meanwhile, organised fan groups, called *charanga*, started to emerge in the 1940s. By the end of the 1960s a new style of group – called *torcidas* – was developed, primarily by young men. *Torcidas* resemble the visual and aural style of ultras and have introduced musical instruments though Brazil's carnival tradition (Vimieiro, 2015), although the performative aspects are organised differently to ultras.

English hooligans and Italian ultras

Face-to-face interaction was the predominant way that new ultras groups emerged, particularly across Southern Europe. Before the 1970s few fans travelled away to matches. The midweek European Cup, UEFA Cup and Cup Winners' Cup matches were difficult to attend for those working, and air travel was expensive. Despite this, English fans had started to travel more frequently to away matches, particularly as hooligan firms sought to assert their dominance in rival towns and cities. Away travel also shifted considerably in the 1980s for international tournaments. With a World Cup in Spain and European Championships in France, a new space opened up for the young masculine fan groups of Europe – most notably English hooligans and Italian ultras.

The English style was dominant in Northern Europe as English fans travelled to easy-to-reach matches in the Netherlands and Germany. The first hooligan fight in the Netherlands occurred when Spurs fans clashed with Feyenoord fans during the 1974 UEFA Cup match in Rotterdam (Spaaij, 2006). In Spain, young male fans began to organise smaller groups within *peñas* (Llopis-Goig, 2015). *Boixos Nois* at Barcelona was formed in 1981 and is inspired by the English style. The name means 'Boxwood Boys' and took the bulldog as its symbol. They began as a politically left-leaning group supporting Catalan independence. At Real Madrid, the fans of West Ham United that visited the city for a European Cup Winners' Cup match inspired a group called *Las Banderas* in 1980. They were expelled in the 1981–82 season and replaced by *Ultras Sur*. It was a visit of the Inter Milan ultras in 1981 that had a great impact on the fate of this group, as stressed by one member of *Ultras Sur*: 'We spent the night talking about football, hooliganism and the organization of *ultra* groups with these experienced Italian ultras, and it was decided to denominate ourselves exactly that: ULTRAS' (Spaaij and Viñas, 2005: 83). In contrast to *Boixos Nois*, who were left wing at the time, *Ultras Sur* supported Spanish nationalism. Echoing the importance of the 1982 World Cup, the first ultras group flourished in the host cities, like *Frente Atlético Ultras* of Atlético Madrid, Espanyol's *Brigadas Blanquiazules* in Barcelona and the *Ultra Boys* at Sporting Gijón. From here, ultras groups emerged in other cities across Spain.

The 1982 World Cup also helped launch the ultras in Portugal. One of the earliest organised fan groups was Sporting Lisbon's *Juve Leo*, founded in 1976. The first inspiration for its actions was provided by Brazilian *torcidas* with large banners, before they later adopted the Italian style of choreography and pyrotechnics. The mix of Brazilian and Italian style was reflected in the names of the groups. *Torcida Verde* was formed at Sporting in 1982, while fans of their city rivals Benfica established *Diabos Vermelhos* the same year. From the outset, the group opted for the Italian style. Despite these origins, a new group called *No Name Boys* evolved from its ranks in the early 1990s to cultivate an English, hooligan style.

The English style was the precursor to the ultras in France, and was particularly evident at Paris St Germain (PSG). The formation of PSG as a new club in 1970 necessitated a new way of attracting supporters (Ranc, 2009). The owners introduced a youth card to attract young fans, and also reserved one stand at the stadium for passionate fans and named it the Kop of Boulogne to mimic Liverpool, the pre-eminent team in Europe at the time. The English style was entrenched in 1984 following clashes with England fans in Paris before a warm-up game for the 1984 European Champions. The physical confrontation between local fans and the 'English Disease' reinforced their hooligan style. Despite these origins, the ultras style came to dominate with the formation of the *Boulogne Boys* in 1985. They launched against Olympique de Marseille (l'OM) by unfurling a precursor to the Lechia Gdańsk banner described in the Introduction that simply declared '*notre histoire deviendra legend*' ('our history becomes legend'). This invented tradition not only reflected the formation of a new group at PSG, but it also highlights the ontological conflation between the fans and the club. As a new club, PSG also had to create a history.

Unlike many other countries, France does not have major intra- or inter-city rivalries. As De Biasi and Lanfranchi (1997) argue, the 'importance of difference' is what helps shape and sharpen fan identities. The one that has emerged since the formation of PSG is their rivalry with l'OM. In contrast to the English style emerging in Paris, at Marseille the ultras style became dominant (Hourcade, 2002: 108). Amado (2008) believes that there are at least two reasons for the appearance of an ultras culture in France: the development of true rivalries and the international success of French football. The first ultras group at l'OM was *Commando Ultra*, which developed after the 1984 European Championships in France. The developing rivalry between PSG and l'OM stimulated the differences between each set of fans. In contrast to the more right-wing group at PSG, ultras at l'OM lean to the left, symbolised by Che Guevara flags in the *curva*. These politics continue in *South Winners*, a later ultras group formed in 1987. The situation at l'OM also illustrates the fragmentation of ultras groups as there are at least seven who support the Provençal club, each with their own area in the Stade Velodrome.

Rivalries and friendships among ultras groups in France are informed by localism and regionalism. These groups draw on their own local histories to reinforce and present their group's identity. Through localism and politics, French ultras follow the Italian tradition of *gemellaggio*, which sees groups form friendships with fans of other clubs and share the same rivals (Doidge, 2015a). The *South Side* ultras formed in Bordeaux after a European Cup match against Juventus in 1985, evolving into the *Ultramarines* in 1987. Echoing the fragmentation that has occurred elsewhere, the *Blue Devils* formed in 1990, before the two groups merged. This group is friends with the *Green Angels* at St Etienne. The *Green Angels* draw on the working-class roots of the football club and cultivate a regionalist image of the group through the use of the local dialect (Ginhoux, 2012). Cultural dissemination and appropriation are drawn upon to present the group. The legendary chief of the Apaches, Cochise, is presented in the green and white colours of St Etienne and used as the group's symbol. This Native American is seen to correspond with the mentality of ultras: their insubordination, fighting spirit and savagery. In this way they draw on the physical and violent aspects of masculine fan culture, incorporated into a racialised image.

Hooliganism and the English style were also predominant in Germany. They grew out of the *kutten* fans of the 1970s, named after the denim sleeveless jackets covered in badges (Gabler, 2010). As Merkel (2007: 69) observes: 'From the 1980s to the mid 1990s the subcultural style of young German football fans was largely a mirror image of their English counterparts. Many of their first chants were translations of English songs and the first mass-produced scarves that were sold in Germany were manufactured in Britain.' The transition to a new style was associated with a generational change on German terraces, the collapse of the British culture of supporting and the influence of TV broadcasts of the Italian league. Ultras culture has developed so that now almost every club in Germany has an ultras group among its fans (Gabler, 2010). There are common values linking the German ultras regardless of any animosities: 'true and solely love for one club, strong critical engagement to club related topics and the awareness to be the only true supporters of the club' (Brandt and Hertel, 2015: 66). Wider ultras tropes, such as being against the police, protesting against commercialisation (like the wider fan protests against the existence of RB Leipzig due to their connections to the Red Bull corporation) and not supporting the national team have also been incorporated into various German groups (Gabler, 2010).

Although the ultras style grew and developed across Southern Europe through face-to-face meetings at tournaments and cup matches, elsewhere it took off through the visual aspects seen on television. The growth of deregulated cable and satellite television channels in the late 1980s facilitated a growth in televised football across Europe (King, 2003). The *Mad Boyz* at Bayer Leverkusen supported their club in a way inspired by the Italian and Balkan style (Ultras Leverkusen, n.d.). In those days, when ultras culture in Germany was only just beginning to form, inspiration from other countries was acquired during the few trips abroad and from recordings on VHS tapes. *Mad Boyz* also adopted the St Etienne image of Cochise, changing his colours to those of Leverkusen.

Even though they would have had different football and media influences before unification, fan groups from both the former West and East Germany adopted the ultras style. It could be argued that football is one of the few social activities that has linked the two parts of Germany under an imagined community of ultras fandom. Throughout the 1990s ultras groups flourished in Germany, as demonstrated through the incorporation of their foundation dates in their names, mimicking the nomenclature of some football clubs (Hesse, 2013). Examples include *Desperados Dortmund 99* and *The Unity 01* at Borussia Dortmund, *Commando Canstatt 1997* at VfB Stuttgart and *Ultras Nürnberg 1994*. Invented traditions need a formation date and these are memorialised on banners, flags and clothing.

The spread across the Mediterranean

The geographical location of Italy ensured that the ultras style of fandom was more readily accessible than the English style in Southern Europe. As the English style spread into Northern France, the Netherlands and Germany, and then into Central Europe and Poland, fans across Southern Europe began following the Italian fashion for waving flags, displaying banners and using pyrotechnics. Outside of Italy, the ultras began to take off in Yugoslavia. *Torcida* at Hajduk Split in Croatia can rightfully claim to be the oldest continuous fan group in Europe. Like the ultras in Italy, *Torcida* began utilising flags and banners in the 1970s. Even though *Torcida* can lay claim to a longer history than the ultras, and performed in a similar manner to their Italian counterparts, the relative isolation of the former Yugoslavia ensured that the term 'ultras' was widely adopted, rather than the Portuguese/Croatian term *torcida*. Despite political crackdowns when it was first established, *Torcida* grew in the 1970s (Perasović and Mustapić, 2018). Under Tito, Yugoslavia charted a distinct course from the Leninist-Stalinist Soviet Bloc. In the 1970s there was a slight liberalisation of society and it was in this period that the ultras subculture began to develop. As demonstrated elsewhere,

ultras frequently flourish in turbulent political periods of history, especially just after the liberalisation of authoritarian regimes.

The former Yugoslav context is also important as it reinforces the
importance of identity (particularly ethno-nationalist identity) in the
construction and presentation of fandom. This aspect became quickly
apparent during the Balkan wars of the 1990s, with many soldiers
being recruited from the ranks of ultras groups. As Mills (2013) argues,
football was not just an opportunity for distraction and a boost in
morale for soldiers; the creation of distinct league and cup competitions
helped create the imagined communities of each individual ethnically
homogenous state. Yet this ethnic division occurred earlier than the
wars. During the 1980s the inter-ethnic divisions began to be played out
through football. As Djordjević and Pekić (2018: 357) observe: 'Newly
formed fan groups of Serbian and Croatian teams, established mostly
during this decade, quickly forgot about simple club rivalry. Their new
focus became the national issue, therefore transforming themselves into
spokesmen of nationalist elites coming to power in most of the Yugoslav
republics.'

Throughout this chapter, and this book, the importance of rivalry
retains an important significance for ultras fandom. As the emotional
identity of fan groups gets produced and reproduced through the rituals
of football, each imagined community of fans lives on. In the former
Yugoslavia ethnic identity was paramount and football became the space
where this was played out. This famously occurred at Maksimir Stadium
in Zagreb in 1990 when clashes occurred between fans and players of
Dinamo Zagreb and Red Star Belgrade, as well as with the police (Mills,
2009; Djordjević, 2012; Djordjević and Pekić, 2018). These ethnic
divisions, as expressed through fandom, reinforce the importance of
studying ultras, but also illustrate how deep footballing identities run.
These can exist in the pro-Albanian (and anti-Serbian) attitude of *Plisat*
at FC Pristina in Kosovo or the rivalry in North Macedonia between
the nationalist attitude of *Komiti Zapad* of FC Vardar Skopje and their
conflicts with the mainly Muslim Albanians of Sverceri Skopje. These
differences were clearly pronounced at the Maksimir riots in 1990 as the
protagonists were *Delije* of Red Star Belgrade and the *Bad Blue Boys*
of Dynamo Zagreb. Members of *Delije* formed the majority of General
'Tiger' Arkan's Serbian Volunteer Guard, while the *Bad Blue Boys* and
Torcida joined the ranks of the Croatian army (Djordjević, 2012; Mills,
2013).

Since their inception, these groups in Yugoslavia have regularly
engaged in violence and have drawn comparisons with hooligan groups
in England. Alongside the violence, they engaged in visual choreographies

in the stadium and have a long history of using pyrotechnics as part of their displays (Vukušić and Miošić, 2018). A group of fans of Radnički Kragujevac in Serbia were given the name *Crveni Djavoli* (Red Devils) as their atmosphere was reminiscent of that generated by Manchester United fans at Old Trafford. This group became more organised in 1989 as they started devoting their focus to basketball matches, and this practice has extended across the Mediterranean. Furthermore, *Crveni Djavoli* has incorporated the historical image of the *Hajduk* into their logo. During the eighteenth century, these Robin Hood-type figures were prevalent as bandits against the Ottomans. These historical folk symbols help reinforce the ultras group as rebellious and subversive.

The specifics of the political history of the Balkans have also informed how ultras groups present themselves and interact with each other. The story of *Horde Zla* (Hordes of Evil) from FK Sarajevo and *The Maniacs* at their city rivals FK Zeljeznicar is indicative of this history. Both were formed in 1987, but after the Balkans war they agreed an unusual 'non-aggression pact' because they had been brothers in arms in the army fighting for the independence of Bosnia and Herzegovina. Although rivalries and conflict are important, how each group operates is highly dependent on the individuals and the relationships within each group. Sometimes broader political issues can override club rivalries.

Rivalry is key in Greece. Reinforcing the 'importance of difference', De Biasi and Lanfranchi (1997) argue, putting on bigger and more impressive choreographies helps distinguish between ultras groups. There has been a long-running rivalry between Panathinaikos and Olympiacos, with violence occurring as far back as the 1930s (Newman, 2014). Panathinaikos' *Gate 13* formed in 1966 from a collection of fans who congregated near the eponymous entrance to organise tickets and away travel. As in Italy, Spain and Croatia, these early forms of organisation gave birth to a more active fan group. As detailed elsewhere in this chapter, the wider political situation also impacts heavily on fan mobilisation. The military junta in Greece from 1967 to 1974 prohibited seditious mobilisations, even around football. When the groups re-formed in the mid-1970s, they quickly adopted the ultras and *torcida* style of collective choreographies and rhythmic chanting and clapping. Notably, the Greek groups excelled in the use of pyrotechnics at matches to create intimidating visual spectacles.

Greek groups are noted for being structured through a network of relationships that form friendships or 'brotherhoods'. Like in Italy, *gemellaggi* or twinning arrangements take place between Greek fan groups with a shared political outlook or rival. A similar situation has developed across national borders with Greek clubs. Members of AEK

Athens' *Gate 21* formed a pan-European friendship network with the *Brigate Autonome Livornesi* and the AEK flag is still proudly waved at Livorno matches despite the Tuscan ultras group having long since disbanded (Doidge, 2013). Fans of Olympiacos and Red Star Belgrade formed a friendship in the early 1980s. Shortly afterwards, *Grobari* of Partizan Belgrade and *Gate 4* of PAOK Thessaloniki developed a *bratstvo*, or 'brotherhood', based around a shared enemy and the same club colours (Djordjević and Pekić, 2018). The relationship between the two sets of fans developed after 2006 as groups made more frequent visits to each other's stadiums. The two groups have chosen to focus on their similarities – notably shared colours, and in some cases, Orthodox Christianity – rather than their differences. Indeed, *Gate 4* have a noted anti-fascist and anarchist outlook, which contrasts sharply with the nationalist views of *Grobari*. The desire to keep their politics out of their brotherhood means that the potential for political activism is diminished, even though greater movement of fans provides more opportunities for interaction. Simply meeting people with different political opinions does not automatically mean that activism takes place (Doidge, 2015a; Djordjević and Pekić, 2018)

Like in Greece, Turkish football is dominated by three teams from one city. Consequently, local rivalries are intense as face-to-face meetings are more regular. Active fandom can be traced back to 1963 when Beşiktaş fans called *The Amigos* protested the sale of Birol Peker to Fenerbahçe. This was the first time the fans organised and incorporated protests into their matchday rituals (Battani, 2012). Fan groups were quickly incorporated into the patrimonial structures of the clubs, as in Italy (Doidge, 2015a), which gave them access to tickets and the opportunities to stage choreographies. As elsewhere, a military dictatorship severely restricted fan activities, but democracy and economic and social liberalisation in the 1980s and 1990s in Turkey allowed fans to interact more intensively with fans from other countries, thanks to which the Italian ultras style began to be incorporated into the performance of Turkish groups (Nuhrat, 2018b). Interestingly, supporters in Turkey more often use terms such as 'fans', 'fanatics', 'tribuners' or 'hooligans' rather than 'ultras' (Nuhrat, 2018b). There are few self-styled ultras groups, like Galatasaray's *ultrAslan*. Indeed, Topal (2010) argues that fan groups in Turkey cannot really be called ultras as they are frequently bought off by clubs, but this has also occurred in Italy (Doidge, 2015a). There are difficult compromises as clubs recognise the colour and spectacle these groups bring to the stadium, but seek to tame the aspects they see as extreme in order to present the right commodity to television audiences.

Ultras groups in Turkey have had to engage in a series of negotiations with their clubs in order to continue to operate (Nuhrat, 2018b).

Ultras are not a fixed cultural entity but operate through a complex network of relationships. As has occurred in other countries, early solidarity and uniformity in group identities started to fragment as competing groups tried to assert influence. Following fragmentation, however, many groups seek to unify again. *ultrAslan* of Galatasaray are a good example of this. They formed in 2000 in a merger of sixty-four different groups, and actively sought to identify with the Italian model by incorporating the word 'ultra' with the Turkish word *'aslan'*, meaning 'lion', which symbolised the football club (Battani, 2012). They launched in 2001 with one of their first choreographies being a giant flag covering their stand. Since then, many other groups, such as *Çarşı* of Beşiktaş, Fenerbahçe's *Genç Fenerbahçeliler*, and *Yalı* and *Çarşı* of the Izmir clubs Göztepe and Karşıyaka, respectively, have adopted Italian practice. Some, such as *Tekas* at Bursaspor, have explicitly used Italian words in their names, like *Ultras Green Boys* and *Curva Sud*, in homage to the traditions of the movement (Battani, 2012).

Even though intense rivalries can exist between football fans, extraordinary factors can lead to friendships or the temporary formation of alliances. As has occurred with some left-leaning groups, friendships can be formed on ideological lines (Doidge, 2013). This was spectacularly highlighted in 2013 during the Gezi Park protests in the Beşiktaş neighbourhood of Istanbul. Members of Beşiktaş' *Çarşı* group attended the protests, and were soon joined by members of *Tek Yumruk* of Galatasaray and *Vamos Bien* of Fenerbahçe, both of whom expressed leftist tendencies. Under the banner of 'Istanbul United', these fan groups sought to mobilise around political interests that were not confined to football. In so doing, they sought to make history in different ways.

Ultras groups uniting in the face of wider politics had a more significant impact in Egypt. The Italian language influenced the early passionate fans in Egypt. Until the 1990s, such supporters were called the *terso*, a name deriving from the Italian word *terzo* meaning 'three' and denoting the fans who sat in area of the stadium reserved for third-class tickets (El-Zatmah, 2012). The composition of these fan groups changed from the 1970s, particularly thanks to a growing Islamification within Egyptian society, and fewer women attending matches. By the 2000s groups of young men were identifying as ultras and including pyrotechnics in their matchday displays. The first organised ultras groups were established in 2007 by the fans of the two Cairo giants, Al Ahly (*Ultras Ahlawy*) and Zamalek (*Ultras White Knights*). This was quickly followed by the formation of groups at clubs elsewhere in the country, like the *Green Eagle Ultras* in Port Said and the *Blue Devils Ultras* of Ghazl El Mahalla. It is clear that these groups follow the tradition of incorporating the team's colours into their name, while also including strong or graceful animals or mythical beasts. Each symbolises the strength and power of the (masculine) fan groups.

What characterises the Egyptian ultras is how they emerged and grew under an authoritarian regime. As shown elsewhere in this chapter, ultras as a more political and rebellious force tend to have developed under democratic political systems, especially just after the collapse of dictatorships. In contrast, ultras in Egypt precipitated the fall of an authoritarian regime. For El-Zatmah (2012: 802): 'It is no coincidence that the rise of the Ultras' fan movements in Egypt came at a time when political activist groups, especially youth activists taking advantage of digital technology, had started to organise themselves into political and social movements in opposition to [President] Mubarak's regime.' The broader ultras ideology, as expressed through the mantra of Against Modern Football, manifests in an anti-police, anti-media, anti-football federation, anti-corporate stance (El-Zatmah, 2012; Doidge, 2015a; Perasović and Mustapić, 2018). This approach dovetailed neatly with a wider disenchantment with Egyptian politics and society.

Similar to the case in Istanbul two years later, the ultras of rival football teams united in a square hosting the protests against the Mubarak regime. They were particularly important on 29 January 2011 during the decisive 'Camel Battle' on the Qasr al-Nile bridge, the main entrance to Tahrir Square (El-Zatmah, 2012; Raab, 2012). Supporters of Mubarak armed with swords and chains rode on horses and camels into the protestors in an attempt to disperse them. Years of engaging with the police had taught the ultras about police tactics and teamwork. 'It was the Ultras', El-Zatmah (2012: 808) argues, 'that broke through the lines of police forces that attempted to close the bridge to stop the demonstrators from reaching the Tahrir Square.' Dozens were killed and many more injured. This clash gave confidence to those taking part and many more joined the protests. Mubarak resigned eleven days later. This incident, like the Gezi Park protests in Istanbul, demonstrated that in exceptional circumstances rival groups can join forces to great effect. Their role has not gone unnoticed, as the new El-Sisi regime has banned ultras from football stadiums, effectively neutering their power. Putatively, this was due to the deaths of seventy-four Al Ahly fans in clashes at Port Said in 2012 and twenty-two Zamalek fans who died in a stampede at the Air Defence Stadium after police opened fire.

A similar crackdown has occurred in Morocco. The fertile political climate across North Africa that precipitated the Arab Spring also helped the ultras to grow. Although not as dramatically affected by the Arab Spring as their North African neighbours, Morocco also recognised the power of the ultras. In 2016 the authorities prohibited the use of label 'ultras', as well as bringing flags, banners and drums into stadiums or making choreographies. In Morocco the first ultras groups formed in 2005 with the *Green Boys* at Raja Casablanca, *Winners* at Wydad Casablanca and *Ultras Askary* at FAR Rabat. Despite attempts to crack down on the ultras, the passion and intensity of the emotions in Moroccan stadiums is supplemented with spectacular choreographies, as well as the use of smoke bombs and pyrotechnics. A significant development has occurred in neighbouring Algeria, where choreographies by ultras have influenced political protests away from the stadium as protestors created large tifos on buildings in public spaces (Mezahi, 2019). As elsewhere in the world, the ultras represent one of the rare opportunities to see significant numbers of people organise large-scale public activities. It is for this reason that many authorities have sought to regulate or prohibit their conduct.

Ultras in post-communist countries

The ultras movement also developed in former Soviet Bloc countries in the 1990s. The fall of the Iron Curtain opened up Eastern European countries to new social and cultural influences. It reflects the Yugoslavic exceptionalism in the Soviet Bloc that the Balkans style did not spread to other parts of Eastern Europe. In Central Europe it is possible to see the combined influence of English and Italian styles. After the Velvet Revolution in Czechoslovakia, for example, a group of ultras from Spartak Trnava, *Alkyfans*, was established in the early 1990s, inspired by the behaviour of fans from other countries. The name of the group inferred an English desire to drink heavily and their support was accompanied by '"loud chants" and "clenched fists" from England, enthusiasm for cheering and entertainment on the terraces using flags on pole, scarves, etc. from Italy, and fashion to wear club colours from the Western Europe and the Balkan' (Kušnierová, 2014: 65). Since the dissolution of Czechoslovakia, ultras groups have functioned mainly at the big clubs and with many only starting this century (Carnogurská, 2012).

The mix of English and Italian styles can also be seen in Hungary. The first group of ultras in the country was *Ultra Red Boys Kispest* of the club Kispest Honvéd (who are now called Budapest Honvéd). They were established in 1991 at the start of that culturally and politically fertile time after the collapse of the Soviet Bloc. In their name they use the Italian term 'ultra' as well as the English 'red boys'. This cultural mix can also be seen with the well-known Hungarian group *Ultra Viola Bulldogs* who were established at Ujpest, another Budapest club, in 1992. Not only did they utilise the seemingly ubiquitous symbol of the British bulldog, but they also took influence from the Italian ultras scene. They adopted the Italian term *viola*, as used by ultras and fans of Fiorentina, a club who share the same colours. Fans of Ujpest visited Naples when their team played Napoli in the European Cup in 1990, where they experienced the climate of the ultras world and bought copies of the *Supertifo* fanzine. After another visit to Italy two years later for a match against Parma in the Cup Winners' Cup, they decided to form their own group based on the Italian model. The same mix of influences can also be seen in Bulgaria where groups like the *Izgrev Boys* formed at Botev Plovdiv while their rivals Lokomotiv Plovdiv inaugurated the group *Napoletani*. As elsewhere, fans do not simply adopt others' approaches, but reflexively adapt certain practices into their fandom (Numerato, 2015).

What makes the ultras stand out in post-communist countries is the speed with which organised fandom has taken off. In Poland it was not possible to develop any anti-system movements due to the restrictions of the Communist authorities. Although *Solidarność* emerged in Gdańsk, it was quickly banned. In the communist era, Polish fans were equipped with hand-made scarves and flags; they were unable, however, to act in an organised manner (Kossakowski, 2017b; 2017c). The ultras movement, including performances concerning issues of identity and political life, was only born after democracy. Shortly after the fall of communism, football stadiums were initially overrun by hooligans 'in the British style', although the Poles seemed to be even more savage, destroying everything they came across. At the start, a fan of Miedź Legnica (personal interview, 2017) recalls: 'The fan movement looked like this: there was no division between ultras and hooligans. You were at the same time an ultra and a hooligan. If there was an opportunity to fight, there was a fight and one was looking for it, too.' It was not until the second half of the 1990s that the supporters of the biggest clubs began to display large, hand-made flags and use pyrotechnic devices. The first official group of ultras in Poland was called *Cyberf@ni* (Cyberf@ns), established in 1999 by Legia Warsaw supporters. Other groups were formed very quickly, including *e-Widzew* (Widzew Lódź), *Ultras Lech'01* (Lech Poznan), *Netf@ns Gieksa'01* (GKS Katowice), *IFC Poloni@ '01* (Polonia Warsaw), *Wisła@cy'01* (Wisła Kraców), the names of which highlighted the influence of the newly emerging Internet. In 2002 the number of groups increased; they were formed not only at the biggest clubs but also in smaller centres.

An almost identical story occurred in Romania. Under the Ceausescu regime, ultras groups would not have found favourable conditions to develop. After 1989, however, new-found freedoms exposed fans to new cultural influences. The linguistic and geographic proximity to Italy witnessed a predominantly Italian style emerge, as can be seen in the names of the groups. The first to emerge during the political thaw was *Ultras Farul* from Farul Constanta, which was founded in 1992. Three years later, two very influential groups were formed: *Armata Ultra* of Steaua Bucaresti and *Commando Ultra Curva Sud* from Politehnica Timisoara. It was in the latter case that the clear influences of Italian culture were displayed, as they were the first group to perform choreographies. By the end of the 1990s, the leading clubs had ultras groups with *Nuova Guardia* at Dinamo Bucaresti and *Vecchia Guardia* at Universitatea Cluj in 1996, followed by Rapid Bucaresti's *Ultras Unione* and the *Lupii Galbeni* (Yellow Wolves) at Petrolul Ploiesti two years later. In each case, these groups tended to be influenced by the Italians.

Despite the Italianate origins of the Romanian groups, slowly they began to adopt British influences. As Guțu (2017: 920) observes:

> Gradually, the behaviour cultural monopoly shifts from the Italian style to the British, this being enabled ... by pop culture [movies like *Green Street* and *Football Factory*]. The first British influences in Romanian supporters' groups are embraced by youth of the second generation of ultras, under 30-year olds, probably with a higher appetite for consumption than the first and more interested in cultural differentiation and recognition, through borrowing and effectively creating a dress code.

As with ultras groups elsewhere, the initial groups underwent a process of fragmentation as a new generation of ultras entered the movement and brought with them a new set of influences. Supporters from the former communist countries were isolated from foreign influence for decades, but after the political transformations they eagerly drew on Italian and British patterns. Over time, they began to create their own traditions and aesthetics.

As mentioned earlier, the ultras only took off in Germany in the 1990s, after reunification. Despite the shared practice of fandom, and the ultras style, the process in the former German Democratic Republic (GDR) followed similar patterns to other post-communist nations. Under the Communist regime, political protest was restricted; this would have inhibited the possibilities an Italian-style ultras group had of flourishing. Fans tried to manifest their political identity in whatever ways possible. For supporters of 1. FC Magdeburg, for example, they did so by wearing badges with the names of Western clubs embroidered on their jackets.

On a symbolic level, this shows how the political situation may lead to types of behaviour many fans perceive as going against their fandom. The tacit rule of football fandom, and the ultras in particular, is that one only supports one club: your local club. Wearing the badges of clubs from the West was thus a symbolic act of protest (*To My Kibice Plus*, 2013: 38). This stands in stark contrast to the large physical and conspicuous displays of identity and protest employed by the ultras.

Like Poland, whose initial influence was British hooliganism, the former GDR took its initial cues from Britain (via West Germany) and then Italy. Although early groups did engage in hooliganism, ultras groups began to be established at the end of the 1990s. 1. FC Magdeburg is the oldest football club in the GDR and was established by the authorities who had a policy of separating football from other sports. Magdeburg fans established the first ultras group, *Commando East Side*, in 1999. A year later fans of Dynamo Dresden, the most successful GDR team, established *Ultras Dynamo* and they have set the tone for the size and scale of choreographies in Eastern Germany. Even though the club has not achieved the same heights as it did in the communist period, the ultras have sought to emphasise their passion. In the 2015–16 season the club was playing in the 3. Liga, the third tier of German football, yet the ultras produced the largest choreography in Europe, at a match against 1. FC Magdeburg. The ultras dedicated nearly two and half years of work to preparing the colossal display, spending €25,000 and using 70 km of material and eight sewing machines. The process of preparation and presentation was coordinated by 150 people and the choreography covered every stand in the stadium.

As ultras groups develop, they periodically reassess their history and traditions. Many ultras groups around the world emphasise that they are ultras by naming their group after the movement, like *Ultras Dynamo*, l'OM's *Commando Ultra* or *Ultra Viola Bulldogs* at Ujpest. As the groups emerge, fragment and reform, the cultural process adapts and changes depending on the prevailing views, internal power and awareness of other groups and histories. For example, *Horde Azzuro*, the group supporting German lower-division club Carl Zeiss Jena, explicitly chose to use an Italian phrase meaning 'Blue Horde', without the word 'ultras' in the name. They recognised that Italian groups do not generally include the term in their names, and they wanted to honour and pay tribute to Italian ultras culture.

Political history has left a distinct mark on the countries of the former Soviet Bloc. As Eastern Europe was liberated from Soviet rule, the economic and political systems, as well as sport, had to build their structures and identities from scratch. This is equally true of those who used to be members of the USSR. The ultras movement in these countries took off after a much longer delay than in Poland, Eastern Germany, Bulgaria and Hungary. It is difficult to determine the reasons for this, but certainly the low level of domestic football competition and the popularity of other disciplines, such as basketball in Lithuania and ice hockey in Belarus, seem to be crucial. This does not mean, however, that the ultras movement in the region has not developed.

Interestingly, it was as early as 1985 that a group called *Pietų IV* (South IV) was founded by Zalgiris Vilnius fans. They supported their team in their native language despite Soviet restrictions. Over time, they put more and more emphasis on the ultras' activities. What is particularly interesting about *Pietų IV* is that they have taken the rare step of moving beyond creating choreographies and supporting the team, and actually helped refinance the club in 2009 after Zalgiris Vilnius experienced financial collapse and was expelled from the country's top tier, the A Lyga (Zalgiris, n.d.). In neighbouring Latvia, one group – *H-Side* from Skonto Riga – decides practically everything about the image of ultras culture. *H-Side* is not only responsible for the ultras movement but also organises the season's closing ceremony, where the player of the year is selected (H-Side, n.d.). The ultras movement in Belarus was also established quite late. The first group, *Ultras Dynamo Brest Group*, was founded in 2007. Belarus is a country in which there are two dominant football teams: Dinamo Minsk and BATE Borisov. Both clubs have strong ultras groups, as well as hooligans. Dinamo fans grouped themselves under one name, *Blue-White Devils*. The development of ultras at Borisov gained momentum in 2008 when the team qualified for the Champions League. Seeing other fans and their choreographies helped spur their fans on to engage in ultras activities.

The situation in Russia is quite specific and reinforces how local political and social conditions structure how ultras operate. In Russia the word 'ultras' has a different meaning from in Italy and how it has been adopted across Europe. Generally speaking, ultras in many countries put emphasis on visual displays and expressions of identity and are less likely to engage in hooliganism (although they do not dissociate completely from it). In Russia, however, 'ultras' merge with 'hooligans'; the term 'Russian Ultras' appearing on websites relates primarily to the fighting groups. Here, the emphasis is on violence and hooliganism. In this way, rival groups gain physical and symbolic superiority over their rivals. During Euro 2016 in France the media frequently referred to groups of Russian hooligans as 'Russian ultras'.[2] There are periodic moral panics around ultras (Marchi, 2005; Doidge, 2015a). When the media and politicians conflate hooliganism with ultras, as occurred with

'Russian ultras' in 2016, this has helped label ultras as predominantly violent. This feeds into a broader narrative of State regulation across Europe, as will be outlined in Chapter 7.

The merger of ultras and hooligan styles does not mean that Russian stadiums are devoid of ultras culture. For example, the organisation *Fratria* (Brotherhood) brings together fans of Spartak Moscow, including those who are responsible for the tifos. *Fratria* formally began its activities in 2005, which marked an important turning point in ultras activity in the country. Even though groups do not identify as ultras, fans still display some of the paraphernalia of the ultras style of fandom. This can be traced back to 1980 when fans of Zenit St Petersburg displayed the first flags and scarves, and wrote the group's hymn. The authoritarian system constrained open expressions of identity, especially any signs of political commitment. In common with groups who identify as ultras around the world, the Russian context reinforces the importance of rivalries in fandom, and with ultras and hooliganism in particular. The largest groups operate primarily at Zenit and the Moscow clubs. In each of these cases they have not only the fan base but also the regular opportunities to meet rivals and sharpen their identities through conflict.

The global spread of ultras

The global spread of televised football and thus the visual spectacles of the ultras has facilitated the spread of ultras culture across the world. When the J-League was formed in the 1990s, the Japanese authorities had to develop a fan culture from scratch, effectively having to invent a tradition of fandom. The core principle of its foundation was to build bonds between local community and football club (Doidge and Lieser, 2013). This was to differentiate football fandom from that of the predominant sport of baseball, which had explicit links to businesses. The names of the football clubs were chosen to emphasise the regional character. The visual elements of the Italian style were readily adopted as fans sought to be rebellious and different to their baseball counterparts. As their encounters were through visual displays rather than face-to-face contact, the style as enacted by Japanese ultras was more superficial. As Doidge and Lieser (2013: 11) state: 'Japanese localised fan groups adopted the visual form of ultras fandom, rather than deeper local, political and violent aspects of the ultras.' Unlike in Italy, Japanese ultras do not perform political protests, nor is their history based on oppositions and antagonisms, so choreographies and banners are mostly supportive of the local club and players.

In the United States, Major League Soccer has encountered a similar challenge to the J-League. Not only did they have to create a fan base for each football franchise, they had to compete with the existing major sports, namely baseball, American football, basketball and ice hockey. This is complicated by the relationship supporters in the US have with watching sport. As Gerke (2018: 936) observes: 'US sports entertainment has generally (and increasingly) treated fans at sporting events exclusively as spectators who are to be entertained; fans are encouraged to consume both the game as well as the merchandise, food and drinks that are readily available at major sports stadiums.' US football fans' adoption of chanting, singing and displaying flags and banners thus significantly contrasts with 'consumers' at matches in other sports. Like the Japanese fans, Americans have taken inspiration from the European ultras style (most of all Italian), as well as South American groups of *barra bravas* and *torcidas* (Gerke, 2018). This resulted not only from the fact that fans in the US have little tradition in creating organised forms of support, but also from the fact that many fans have family roots in other countries in which the ultras movement developed earlier. The Italian and English influences can be seen in the labels used by groups, like 'ultras', 'hooligans', 'companies', 'casuals', 'boys', 'army', 'brigade'. Despite the lack of an indigenous football fan culture, US groups are beginning to form organisations, partly to coordinate tickets and transport (replicating how the ultras started in Italy, Spain and Croatia), but also to plan choreographies and discuss new chants.

The global appeal of Italian football in the 1990s significantly impacted on the growth of ultras fandom globally. This is certainly the case in Indonesia where supporters of AC Milan and Juventus became 'the main reference point' (Fuller and Junaedi, 2018), although Fiorentina, Roma, Lazio and Parma also have Indonesian fan clubs. From these initial roots, the availability of content on the Internet, and the popularity of YouTube, has facilitated the knowledge of the ultras' rituals and modes of behaviour. At Indonesian domestic football matches, the terraces are full of flags, banners and pyrotechnics. This is not restricted to the highest division; it permeates throughout the leagues. The case of Indonesia shows the role of the mediatisation process, particularly in places where direct contact is difficult.

The Indonesian context also highlights, as with Italy, Germany and Eastern Europe before, that the wider political and social context has a dramatic influence on the development of ultras culture. Under the authoritarian 'New Order' presidency of Suharto, censorship and ideological conformism was enforced. After the revolution in 1998, new political and cultural freedoms opened up. The punk and hip-hop scenes flourished and the ultras emerged out of this cultural milieu.

Fans during these politically turbulent times look to football to root themselves locally, while locating themselves in history, particularly in a place where those in power controlled what was memorialised and what history was forgotten. For fans, Fuller and Junaedi (2018: 923) argue, football 'becomes not only a means for accessing, interacting with and borrowing from global subcultures, but is also a means into the history of one's own city as a part of strengthening the sense of one's local identity'.

Despite the references to English and Italian styles, cultural forms should not be reified. Culture is a fluid and dynamic part of social life. This can be reflected in the way in which the ultras style of fandom is starting to emerge in the United Kingdom. It is a kind of paradox that ultras culture, flourishing in all geographical locations, has developed only to a modest extent in England (and in the British Isles generally), the homeland of modern football. Although some groups emerged calling themselves ultras, like *Swindon Ultras* in the 1990s and *Toon Ultras* at Newcastle, among the very few groups that follow the ultras style and mentality are the fans of Crystal Palace and their ultras group, *Holmesdale Fanatics*. They were established in 2005 in response to the changing atmosphere of all-seater grounds in the English league: 'The Holmesdale Fanatics bang their drum, wave flags and lead the chants behind one of the goals throughout. The atmosphere they create is a throwback and, since Palace were promoted to the Premier League in 2013, their vociferous support has become widely accepted as one of the best in British football' (Muro, 2015).

The shifting response to changes to football in the early twenty-first century has also facilitated the emergence of an ultras scene in non-league football in England. As fans adapt to the expensive ticket prices, all-seater stadiums and greater surveillance forced upon them, some fans have explicitly stepped away from the elite men's leagues and started following semi-professional football instead (Cleland *et al.*, 2018). Groups at a few clubs, notably Whitehawk in Brighton, and both Clapton and Dulwich Hamlet in London, have referred to themselves as ultras and began to adopt certain aspects of the Italian style. Notably, these three clubs are all based in cities with large migratory populations and fans from different parts of the UK and abroad who have adopted these clubs as regular fans. In each of these cases the groups have embraced a political dimension to their fandom, notably anti-discriminatory and community-focused approaches that seek to advocate social justice, like holding collections for food banks or refugees (Cleland *et al.*, 2018). Here, the explicit resistance to the changes to modern football are combined with an outlet for a more apolitical English style of fandom.

It is in Scotland where the ultras style has had more traction in the UK. Scottish football has been through a period of sustained crisis in the twenty-first century, with the national team failing to qualify for a major tournament since 1998, and the leading club sides struggling to succeed in European competitions. This was compounded by the financial collapse of Rangers in 2012. Although attendances have fallen, fans adopting the ultras style have added some much-needed colour and noise to the stadiums. Although they disbanded in 2010, the first ultras group in Scotland was Aberdeen's *Red Ultras*. This has been followed by others like *Well Bois* at Motherwell and *Sect 43* at Hibernian. The Old Firm clubs have also followed suit with *Blue Order* and *Union Bears* at Rangers, while the *Green Brigade* at Celtic has adopted a broadly left-wing outlook. Alongside banners welcoming refugees, they have also successfully campaigned to have a standing section returned to Parkhead, and this was installed in 2015. However, the *Green Brigade* have also been accused of sectarianism through chants and pro-IRA banners (BBC, 2017). In contrast, the logo of Rangers' *Union Bears* incorporates the Union Flag, rather than a Scottish flag. As with the chosen moniker, it denotes that the group see themselves as part of the union of Great Britain and Northern Ireland. Ultras culture always adapts to local customs and traditions. History does not start anew when a new group emerges – they adapt and build on existing cultural practices.

Conclusion

Rather than detail a history of the ultras through their specific activities and approaches, this chapter has sought to illustrate some of the threads that are common to the formation of many ultras groups around the world. As highlighted at the start of this chapter, history is socially constructed and contested. Who decides on the official narratives are usually those with power; as the old maxim goes, history is written by the winners. Alternatively, the collective memory of members is fostered in the emotional cauldron of the stadium, in the coaches on the way to matches, in bars after games and, in some cases, in political protests in public squares. Traditions are invented, ritualised and institutionalised, and these help create a wider imagined community of participants who are all taking part in the same regular activity.

In this way we can begin to see the ultras as a global movement. Yet, as Kennedy (2013: 133) observes: 'An ultra movement can be legitimately talked about, but it is a loosely based framework marked by local adaptation of the concept.' As has been argued, the ultras have developed locally in relation to local specificities, national political contexts and global changes (notably television and social media). One of the most significant aspects has been how the Italian and English styles have come to dominate. Even though organised fandom existed through *peñas* in Spain, *torcidas* in Brazil (and then Croatia) and *terso* in Egypt, hooliganism and ultras have captured fans imaginations more resolutely. Many groups of supporters in Europe were inspired by British hooligan culture in the 1970s and 1980s. In particular, this influence spread through face-to-face confrontations across Northern Europe, into Northern France, the Netherlands and Germany before shifting to Poland and Russia. Hooliganism influenced the ultras even though violence was always part of the ultras subculture (Roversi, 1991; Roversi and Balestri, 2000; Foot, 2006; Stefanini, 2009; Testa, 2009; Doidge, 2015a). Unlike fans in other countries who adopted the hooligan style, Italians simply incorporated it into the ultras way of life. Consequently, as other groups around the world adopted ultras fandom, they incorporated the violent aspects. In fact, the two footballing styles have come full circle. Some Italian ultras have adopted English casual style, such as the *Barbour Gang* at AC Milan, while the skinhead style has taken off in many groups across the peninsular. Meanwhile, new English groups have followed the ultras approach, often to inject some atmosphere into increasingly sanitised stadiums.

The wider political context is also a key feature of the history of the ultras. Across the globe, ultras have appeared in nascent democratic political climates. In Italy the ultras formed during the 1970s, a decade which was characterised by political terrorism. The political banners that were used in the protests in the streets and piazzas were taken into the stadiums. In Spain, Yugoslavia and Greece, meanwhile, organised fandom started when social life became liberalised, either towards the end of or just after a dictatorship. In the post-communist countries of the Soviet Bloc, as well as Indonesia, the newly found democratic freedoms resulted in new forms of football fandom as they became open to the dominant English and Italian styles. In each case, the localised groups have adapted the influences to their own fan culture. And we come full circle again in situations where the ultras are politicising and taking their strategies and tactics back into the squares, most notably with the Against Modern Football movement (as will be explored in Chapter 7), but also in Gezi Square in Istanbul and Tahrir Square in Cairo.

Despite local differences, it remains prudent to think about the 'common' spirit of ultras culture. This has established itself as invented traditions of resolute support of the football club and the glorification of group identity. This is achieved through emphasis on the local community, history and values, particularly through a specific cult of traditional forms of manhood. This identity is performed through spectacular choreographies or through violence. It is also performed through adopting specific types of dress and avoiding the commodified forms of involvement in football. In many ultras groups around the world, members desire freedom and the opportunity for spontaneous expression of their emotion. In this way, we return to the importance of emotion in the formation of ultras groups. The collective emotional experiences find a clear expression of identity in the stadium and this motivates members to keep returning to renew their acquaintances and friendships.

Notes

1 The 'three Ws' were three cricketers from Barbados – Clyde Walcott, Everton Weekes and Frank Worrell – who were known for their prowess with the bat. Ram and Val were two bowlers, Sonny Ramadhin from Trinidad and Tobago, and Alf Valentine from Jamaica.

2 www.marca.com/en/football/national-teams/2016/07/01/5776a567268e3e507 48b4615.html; http://europe.newsweek.com/euro-2016-why-russian-footballs-ultras-wont-stop-fighting-471641?rm=eu; www.bbc.co.uk/newsbeat/article/3652 8506/who-are-the-russian-ultras-and-how-are-they-different-to-other-football-fans (all accessed 7 May 2019).

4

Social media as a space of continuous performance

Throughout the season fans everywhere are filled with excitement and anticipation as their teams battle and compete for glory and to avoid disappointment. The success and failure of football clubs becomes a symbolic representation of individuals, cities, regions and nations across the globe. Yet the competition is not limited to what takes place on the field. For ultras, status and solidarity is reflected in their spectacular choreographies, and the new season provides more opportunities for creative dominance of their rivals. The technological revolution in smartphones and social media provides numerous platforms for ultras to present their collective performances to a global audience. YouTube and Instagram especially provide visual opportunities to present the groups socially. Spectacular images grab the public's attention and can go viral. In February 2019, prior to their must-win Europa League match against Fenerbahçe, ultras of Zenit St Petersburg lined the road leading up to the Gazprom Arena. As the team bus drove past, each fan lit a flare to provide an illuminating guard of honour (Church, 2019). The spectacular sight of the long street lit up with the orange glow and smoke of the pyrotechnics demonstrated the passion of the fans and the importance of the match. Ultras are no longer just competing with their rivals in the stadium, but now have a variety of global platforms to compare themselves to others. This competition is bolstered with online channels like *Ultras World* or *Ultras-Tifo* ranking performances globally. Like music in the Billboard charts, groups are ranked in order of the best choreographies of the year. The quality of the tifo can be quantified in the number of views for each video. Rivalry and competition thus intensify away from the match.

Football fandom has long been enacted away from the match, from watching on television to conversations in bars and at work. This has only intensified with social media. Within this basic linguistic framework, the rituals of football can be played out online, ensuring the emotional attachment to football club and friends continues long after the game has finished. Platforms like Twitter and Facebook provide semi-permanent networks where fans can meet online, discuss ideas, or plan chants and banners. In some cases, social media is used for 'spying' on rival groups in order to find information about where ultras gather, where they collect flags or the designs of their choreographies. The 'spies' mimic the nicknames of rival group or gain trust to get access to secure chat sessions. Other social media channels, like YouTube and Instagram, seem tailor-made for the ultras style of fandom as they provide a ready platform for posting photos and videos for the presentation of the group to themselves and others. This can also intensify rivalries as ultras groups strive to compete for more exposure or commendation for their tifos. On a deeper level, the images and discussions that take place on social media can become a focal point for each group. As outlined in earlier chapters, the emotion and solidarity of the collective is a powerful motivating force, as Collins (2004: 49) argues, 'whoever has experienced this kind of moment wants to repeat it'. The images reify the memories and emotional experiences of the group. The images become totemic symbols representing the collective and the feelings of love and solidarity produced. Collins (2004) uses the metaphor of the battery to suggest that symbols act as a source of emotional energy for the group. The photos and videos of significant choreographies and collective fan experiences become aides-memoire; they represent the collective to the group themselves.

This book argues that the ultras style of fandom highlights the important role of emotion and performance in mobilising, motivating and continuing group solidarity. This chapter argues that social media provides an important platform for these collective performances through continued interaction away from the match. It outlines the role social media has in the commercial transformation of football as clubs seek to maximise their market. Official websites and social media present a stylised representation of the club. Like fanzines before it, social media has democratised fandom somewhat and enables all fans (with access to the Internet) to contribute to debates and voice their opinions. Despite this supposed democratisation, certain (predominantly masculine) voices are still privileged and the visual presentation of the ultras is tailor-made for social media. The result is that the ultras ensure their hegemonic position as 'authentic', passionate and dedicated fans through their presentation on social media. After presenting the role social media has in facilitating debate among fans, this chapter proceeds to highlight how social media is used by ultras and the important role that it has in the ultras' performance.

Fans and social media

Football has undergone a significant economic transformation since the 1990s (King, 1998; 2003; Giulianotti, 1999; Sugden and Tomlinson, 1999; Millward, 2011; Doidge, 2015a; Cleland *et al.*, 2018; Numerato, 2018). While print media has a long history with sport, television revolutionised the commercial running of the game. It has contributed to changes in the rules and procedures of games, increased the financial success of sports organisations, made possible astonishing increases in athletes' salaries and led to both professionalisation and glamorisation of sport. The growth in media interest in football has continued with social media. Websites, fan forums, Twitter, Facebook, Instagram and YouTube all provide opportunities for clubs to engage with fans, or fans to interact directly with other fans. These platforms further enable users to create and maintain social networks and help individuals connect with others based on common interests (Boyd and Ellison, 2007).

As with television, football clubs are developing social media in order to market their clubs and build relationships with their fans. For the sports business literature, this is about building their 'brands' with their 'customers' to strengthen team identification and increase consumption (Trail *et al.*, 2003; Foster and Hyatt, 2007; Araújo *et al.*, 2014; Meng *et al.*, 2015). As social media provides clubs (and their media and commercial partners) with an additional point of engagement with their fans, it is important to understand the social media audience. For Sandvoss (2004), this took a functional approach though the assessment of fans looking for information, such as scores, watching games or purchasing merchandise. Similarly, Henderson and D'Cruz (2004: 359) state that websites have been developed 'as a mechanism for reaching fans, accessing fan reaction and selling club merchandise'. Many clubs treated social media as an information conduit, passing on team news or sharing competitions (Meng *et al.*, 2015). In some cases, direct, personal communication can arise as fans direct specific queries at the club. In this way, fans are kept permanently in the consumer universe (Kawohl, 2016). Clubs run their own channels on YouTube and broadcast live streams of training or press conferences with the aim of keeping the emotions from the stadium permanently present.

Yet this is actually a passive approach to fandom (Gibbons and Dixon, 2010), in that it treats the fan as a passive consumer of information, rather than an active agent who can interact with other actors online. More than simply spectators, fans are 'prosumers' (producers and consumers) who have the potential to affect the experience of other fans, athletes and officials (Smith and Lord, 2017). Ultras undertake what Hills (2002) calls 'performative consumption'. They produce and consume their own markers of fandom, from stickers and T-shirts to graffiti and choreographies. Ideas that are expressed online can find their way into the choreographies and chants in the stadium. Fundamentally, ultras do not see themselves as customers. They resist this aspect of modern football and produce their own sense of collective self through autonomous performances, choreographies and chants. However, they constantly have to be aware of how the club will market the ultras' activities for commercial gain (Nuhrat, 2018a).

Like football clubs, ultras also utilise social media for public relations and commercial activity. The collective site *Ultras-Tifo*, for instance, operates an online shop with a wide range of ultras merchandise, from jackets and sweatshirts to accessories like balaclavas and flags branded with slogans such as 'Against Modern Football' or 'Anti Uefa Mafia'. In this way, social media acts as a revenue stream for ultras groups and brands. Likewise, ultras groups issue press releases to detail their perspective on key issues; for instance, after allegations that they had directed racist chants at Mario Balotelli, Juventus ultras group *Drughi* issued a press release to explain why it was not racism (Doidge, 2015b). Lazio and Roma ultras produce their own radio shows (Testa and Armstrong, 2010), and many fan groups have their own YouTube channels and podcasts. During protests against their wealthy American owner, James Pallotta, Roma ultras from the *Curva Sud* outlined that they were 'tired' and 'could no longer tolerate this situation after years of lies, proclamations of victories … promises never kept by this "President"' (Lengua, 2018). The ultras accompanied this with a number of banners across the city outlining Pallotta's empty promises, and declared that at the next match against Genoa, there would be a ten-minute silence at the start of the game. In this way social media both communicates the protest to fellow fans and details the motives for it.

Social media and the democratisation of fandom

Fans have long engaged with various aspects of their fandom, yet clubs are reluctant to permit fans to participate in decision-making processes (Taylor, 1992). Access to media helped transform the role of fans and provide a different voice. Fanzines in particular were the driving force for a more democratic voice among football fans (Duke, 1991; Jary *et al.*, 1991; Haynes, 1995). Technological advances in media production have made significant changes to social life. Access to photocopiers from the 1970s made the production of home-produced fanzines a possibility for fans. Most fanzines were club specific, and were often satirical or humorous in nature. While the fanzine movement opened up space for fans' voices within the football world, some indicate that a number of producers were engaged in a broadly left-wing form of cultural resistance (Haynes, 1995; Back *et al.*, 1999), with many leading the way in anti-discrimination activities and the supporters' trust movement. The technological development and spread of the Internet led to the decline of fanzines as fans could engage in real time with other fans, without going through an editor. While many fanzines stopped production, there remain in the UK some longstanding printed publications, such as *United We Stand* and *Dial M for Merthyr*. The 2010s has seen a brief revival of printed fanzines, partly as fans access new design software, but also thanks to the pull of nostalgia. In reality, the fanzine was reborn online, through fan forums (Millward, 2008). Like fanzines before them, these spaces offer insights into how fans air, discuss and negotiate their concerns (Nash, 2000; Ruddock, 2005; Millward, 2008).

The alleged democratisation of the Internet has witnessed analyses of online social and political activism. Wilson (2007: 462) argues that 'there is a dearth of research investigating links between the Internet and sport-related activism'. Since the 1990s there has been a focus on political activism among football fans (Redhead, 1997; King, 1998; 2003; Giulianotti, 1999; Nash, 2000; Millward, 2009; 2011; 2012; Cleland, 2010; Millward and Poulton, 2014; Cleland *et al.*, 2018; Numerato, 2018). While similar analyses of the ultras also highlight the political outlook of some groups (Testa and Armstrong, 2010; Doidge, 2013; 2015a; Ibraheem, 2015; Doidge and Lieser, 2018; Ha-Ilan, 2018; Nuhrat, 2018b; Perasović and Mustapić, 2018), football fandom is not always about political expression. While part of the ultras' identity is about being transgressive, challenging authority and resisting modern football, it is not the only aspect. For some fans, ultras included, there is a sociability associated with fandom (Giulianotti, 2005; Doidge, 2015a). Some fans just want to socialise with other fans like them; not everything has to have an explicit political motivation.

Social media and Internet forums can act as community spaces and develop their own norms of behaviour (Millward, 2008; Gibbons and Dixon, 2010). As Wilson (2007: 395) observes, 'the development and availability of information technologies such as the Internet … certainly will facilitate the building of virtual communities of fans who want to follow specific teams and leagues'. Yet this falls into the trap of assuming fans only support teams or leagues. In the example of ultras (and other football subcultures like casuals and hooligans) the performance of fandom extends beyond specific teams or competitions. Being an ultra is explicitly linked to a football team, but it is also tied to a broader collective identity. Consequently, websites like *Ultras-Tifo* or *TIFO-net* exist to share the ultras style of fandom. In particular, the performative aspects of ultras fandom – the choreographies and banners – can be easily shared globally. Ultras seem to exemplify cultural hybridity, in which translocal beliefs and practices are mutually influential, rather than determined by a hegemonic power (Haenfler, 2014: 131). Therefore, while football fans and ultras in England, Italy, Germany and Belgium may be distinct, they share common symbols. A continuum of different forms of being and acting together is constantly emerging online where 'virtual togetherness', thinking in terms of the boundedness and emotional exchange of communities are experienced (Lindgren, 2017: 104).

Football fandom is a mundane, everyday activity (Nowell-Smith, 1979; Stone, 2007). Football is not just played over ninety minutes on a Saturday or Sunday afternoon; it is played out through repetitive conversations throughout the week. Social media provides an easy and (relatively) accessible space to articulate these banal interactions. Gibbons and Dixon (2010: 606) argue that Internet behaviours should not be considered separately from other aspects of the multifaceted lives of English soccer fans and that 'involvement with Internet sites for English soccer fan interactions would demonstrate a heightened level of fandom more generally – making fans located on the Internet a valuable resource for researchers'. In arguing this, they unwittingly make a similar argument to the one they argue against, which is about certain fans being authentic or unauthentic. If those fans interacting online are similar to those actively engaging in the stadium, we are still privileging certain forms of fandom by only engaging with the outspoken, expressive or dominant voices. Those without access to social media, or those who choose not to engage due to racism or sexism continue to be marginalised (van Dijk, 2005; Servon, 2008).

Many writers have created taxonomies or binaries that attempt to place fans into certain camps of 'participatory', 'active' and 'passive', or 'direct' and 'indirect' (Redhead, 1993; 1997; Giulianotti, 2002; Cleland, 2010; Wann *et al.*, 2001). Crawford (2004) argues that fandom is a career which individuals navigate through, yet this still suggests there is a spectrum that privileges experience or length of service. Both Crawford (2004) and King (1998; 2003) critique the implicit arguments for authenticity and the suggestion that there ever was a 'golden age' of fandom. Fans construct their own identities based on shared notions of how they see football fandom (King, 1997a), and these can be unifying for the group. As Chapter 3 argued, ultras groups draw on an imagined history of their city and themselves. Ultras actively recreate an imagined (and gendered) 'golden age' through tropes such as 'From Father to Son' and 'Support your local team' (Doidge, 2015a). This 'wilful nostalgia' (Maguire, 1999) helps recreate the image of the ideal type of ultra, which is invariably young and male.

Ultras, and fans in general, are active producers of their own identity. Academics arguing for the use of social media and forums as a data source overwhelmingly focus on the textual aspects (Millward, 2008; Gibbons and Dixon, 2010). Duke (1991: 637) made a similar argument in relation to fanzines when he asserted that they 'provide a rich archaeology of texts that are representative of the collective identities of traditional football fans'. Again, Duke suggests the existence of a 'traditional fan' that has never changed over time. Yet the focus on the text misses the performative aspects of fandom. As argued in Chapter 1, fandom is continuously performed and for this reason can change over time. Social media provides a space in which to continue the conversations, ideas and discussions about fandom and football throughout the week. As McLuhan (1964) argued, 'the medium is the message'. But football fandom is not restricted to just one medium. It is performed in many different spaces, from public transport, pubs and stadiums to social media. Focus has to be on the ways that identities are articulated and presented, rather than just analyses of the discourse that takes place online.

Social media as a public sphere

Fan forums and social media are a key area of debate, discussion and expressions of fandom. Digitally networked social media resources – whether social network sites, social apps, forums or blogs – are about sociality (Lindgren, 2017). In a sociological sense they are about what Georg Simmel (1950: 10) called 'sociation'; that is, they enable processes of mediation by which individuals become 'connected by interaction' to form groups and, by extension, build society (Lindgren, 2017: 32). Habermas (1989) argued that debate undertaken in public helped create a 'public sphere'. This, he claimed, helped with the formation of liberal democracy. Yet Habermas's analyses were focused on bourgeois middle-class men, which ensured a narrowly defined definition of the public sphere. Within the ultras, this becomes entrenched, in that specific (white) masculine viewpoints get constantly reaffirmed as 'tradition' and 'the way it is'. While social media may lead to the development of a public sphere, it also recreates inequalities as the power and privilege of specific members can crowd out dissent or alternative views. Despite this, social media as a site for contestation is important in its own right (Nash, 2000; Ruddock, 2005; Millward, 2008). Debate and disagreements are frequent. Football fans are heterogeneous, and they bring their own cultural and moral approaches into these discussions (Smith and Lord, 2017). Even within a tight collective like an ultras group you will not necessarily find uniformity of outlook and strategy. Online, Millward (2008: 304) observed two approaches to differences:

> When two opposing viewpoints are made, two possible outcomes emerge: First, the most common result is that comments are reinterpreted to create group consensus. When this is not possible, an opportunity is given to the supporter to retract his or her statement before the issue is forgotten. On the other hand, the fan may not so easily be forgiven, and his or her comments may be criticized, mocked, politely tolerated, or completely shunned.

Thus, there are both dialectic and dialogic outcomes from discussion online. Discussion does not automatically bring about consensus. This is not automatically democratic, as Ruddock (2005) argues. These discussions take place within the groups' understanding of what is an 'authentic' fan, and redefining the boundaries of who they feel belong. The hegemonic masculinity of ultras fandom remains. Ultimately, fans construct what they see as political on their own terms (Sandvoss, 2003).

While social media can provide a forum for political debate, it does not mean that this is what ultras will use it for. According to Jenkins (2008: 239): 'One way that popular culture can enable a more engaged citizenry is by allowing people to play with power on a microlevel … popular culture may be preparing the way for a more meaningful public culture.' Jenkins does not determine what he means by 'meaningful public culture', but it infers that participation is automatically seen as a positive act. Likewise, Putnam (2000) equates participation in social life with positive social and political virtues. These arguments assume a simple causal relationship between wider social interaction and more democratic values. Similarly, Miller (2008: 213) asks if fans can 'be said to engage with labor exploitation, patriarchy, racism, and neo-imperialism, or in some specifiable way make a difference to politics beyond their own selves, when they interpret texts unusually or chat about romantic frustrations'. This assumes that the only political participation is around progressive politics. Some groups do get involved in such movements, but many others also engage online with nationalistic and exclusionary politics, particularly around gender and race. As

Sandoval and Fuchs (2010) posit, participatory culture is not automatically democratic and inclusive. The inequalities of contemporary society are simply mediated through these new forms of media.

For those like Habermas (1989) and Putnam (2000) who argue that social life has fragmented and civic engagement has declined, participation is key. They argue that participation in public life develops a strong sense of communality and contributes to democracy. They make the false equivalence of participation and democratic outcomes without recognising the structural inequalities that exist to prevent participation from some groups. Within the masculine world of football fandom and ultras, for instance, it is harder for women and ethnic minorities to be accepted into dominant groups (Back *et al.*, 1999; Burdsey, 2007; Williams, 2007; Caudwell, 2011; Dunn, 2014). Arguments of participation being positive assume that everyone enters the discussions equally. Within ultras groups there are internal power dynamics, and while members may have a free voice, that does not mean there is some form of dialectic where there is a synthesis of views. Leading members, such as capos, will always assert their power to make decisions. Therefore, engagement on alternative forms of media is not automatically positive and progressive (Sandoval and Fuchs, 2010). Interactions on social media can support existing political structures, or engage in what Robson (2000) calls the 'dark sense of the carnival' that can see some football fans actively engaging in racism and other forms of abuse and discrimination. Furthermore, for many ultras groups and fan sites, participation is also exclusionary, with members only speaking to fans who hold similar views. So, debate is not necessarily coming from a plurality of viewpoints.

Collective action online is limited by the rivalries that exist within football. Hardt and Negri (2005) suggest that the way to overcome the fragmented and proliferated political collectives is for the multitude of networked organisations to work in cooperation to counter global forces. Ultras in particular reify rivalries and often refuse to work with members of rival groups, even within the same fan base. While there is some evidence of some groups from different (and rival) clubs discussing key issues affecting the ultras movement (Doidge, 2015a; 2017; Brandt *et al.*, 2017), this often takes place only in relation to significant events such as the death of Vincenzo Spagnolo in Genoa in 1995, or the pacts in Poland such as the Gdynia Pact (not to fight at national team matches) and the Poznan Pact (not to use weapons). While Hill *et al.* (2016) argue that *StandAMF* in the UK represents a good example of a grassroots movement that brings together diverse fans from different clubs, these fans would not consider themselves ultras and may not feel the same intense belief precluding cooperation with rival clubs.

Social media and the Internet can help nurture these cooperative networks. Castells (2012) argues that social movements are 'rhizomatic', grassroots in their emergence and grow through connecting groups and individuals through shared emotions over wide networks. Mathers (2014: 1064) criticises Castells' focus on the emotional motivations and on the 'expressive above the instrumental element of the movement', particularly over the 'relative lack of success in delivering radical economic and social reforms'. This assumes that every movement must have instrumental and achievable goals. Collective action, even performative action, can give participants meaning and a feeling of control in difficult circumstances. As Katz (1999) argues, emotions are an embodied way of taking control of a situation. The emotions brought about by a 'moral shock' affecting an individual can spur them into action (Jasper, 1997). Connecting across social media with individuals who have been similarly affected by a moral shock helps the collective form and find focus. Showing solidarity with fellow ultras is also important. For example, AEK Athens group *Original 21* participated in a protest against ticket prices by Bayern Munich ultras at a Champions League game between the two clubs. This show of solidarity reinforced the Against Modern Football mentality, as well as supporting the politics of the ultras, while being rivals on the pitch. These groups connect through shared feelings of disempowerment or outrage, taking control of those emotions. Material goals are secondary to collective solidarity and engagement.

Care should be taken to not reify the role of social media; it is merely a platform for social actors to interact. In arguing that networks are a primary foundation of contemporary society, Castells (1996) suggests that the Internet lays the foundation. Leaderless groups connect through a transnational 'space of flows' where power is congregated around nodes within the network. The Internet becomes this 'space of flows' and social media potentially acts as the specific space where groups meet and debate. As Fuchs (2012) argues, Castells overlooks the networks that existed before these new 'rhizomatic' movements. Ultras have been in existence since the 1960s and have many wide-ranging relationships, not all of which are debated online. Similarly, key individuals, notably the capos, act as nodes within the network. These are not necessarily the 'soft leaders' that Hill *et al.* (2016) identify with *StandAMF*, as capos exert significant formal power within their groups.

Social media as a space of ultras performance

Social media has rapidly become a significant part of social life. Facebook, Twitter, YouTube and Instagram have become important sites for individual self-expression. Ultras groups, as has been discussed, also make extensive use of these tools of communication. As noted in Chapter 3, the first ultras group in Poland was Legia Warsaw's *Cyberf@ ni*, established in 1999 and named after the online forum that the members used. One of the characteristic features of their name and those of several other of the earliest groups in Poland was the inclusion of the '@' symbol in their moniker. This underlined the significance of Internet resources for the ultras' activities. A similar situation occurred in the US with the fan group *The Sons of Ben*, who existed online first to campaign for a Major League Soccer team in Philadelphia. Their primary community space was their own website and sites like MySpace and YouTube (Gibbons and Dixon, 2010).

Many ultras groups have their own websites or Facebook pages. The *Drughi* group at Juventus, for example, has a page followed by over 140,000 people. This becomes a key space not only to share images of important individuals, banners and choreographies, but also to share comments or photos displaying phrases such as '*Toro merda*' (shit Torino) or '*Inter merda*' (shit Inter), or other derogatory comments directed at their rivals. Most ultras groups' pages present similar content. They are not concentrating on match reports or the tactics of the team, but on reinforcing rivalries – the 'importance of difference' (De Biasi and Lanfranchi, 1997) – or presenting the group's banners and choreographies. The importance of social media to the ultras is that it permits their visual style to be circulated across linguistic boundaries. Raja Casablanca's *Green Boys* have over 400,000 followers. The posts are written in Arabic, but the videos and photos transmit more than the linguistic text. They demonstrate the coordination, organisation and passion of the group towards their team.

The translinguistic aspects of choreographies ensure that the ultras style of fandom has global appeal. Sites like *Ultras-Tifo* (which has more than 900,000 followers) provide reports of choreographies, banners and other aspects of ultras actions. The actual game of football is peripheral. Likewise, the *Ultras World* Facebook page (which has nearly one million followers) takes it one step further and promotes the site owners' compilations of 'Top 5 Ultras of the Week', or 'Top 10 Ultras of the Year'. For example, among the ten choreographies chosen for 2017 there were ultras performances from Argentina, Algeria, Denmark, Serbia and Greece. While these 'charts' are not the primary source of motivation for ultras groups, many will be aware that social media has become a powerful tool for presenting identity and mentality. They allow the presentation of the group, the team and the locale, to a global audience.

Early analyses of online social behaviour, such as work by Turkle

(1995), focused on identity becoming fragmented online as individuals anonymously explored different identities. Turkle (1995) highlights the anonymity of the online world where marginalised identities become obscured, opening up opportunities for self-expression. Yet anonymity is not automatically democratic; 'markers of difference' are identified and discriminated against (Schmitz, 1997). In the football world, 'the importance of difference' is a central part of rivalry (De Biasi and Lanfranchi, 1997). These differences get expressed online and this helps to sustain and fuel offline identity (Kennedy, 2006; Boyd, 2007). This is particularly true for the ultras who have a dedicated physical space for their identity performance, which is then articulated online. Furthermore, they do not hide behind the anonymity of online registration to make controversial comments. As outlined elsewhere in this book, many ultras groups revel in their counter-cultural, anti-establishment identity and deliberately transgress social norms in stadiums. Any articulation of similar statements online is simply taking their cues from existing norms offline. As Butler (1993: 225) argues, when an individual 'utters or speaks and thereby produces an effect in discourse, there is first a discourse which precedes and enables that "I" and forms in language the constraining trajectory of its will'. Social media users draw on existing social cues in the performance of their individual identity.

Activity in social media represents an important space of self-identity. As identified in Chapter 1, Butler (1990; 1993) argues that the self is a repetitive performance that builds on existing social norms and cues. According to Butler (1997: 99), 'a subject only remains a subject through a reiteration or rearticulating of itself as a subject'. Repetition is key for an individual's sense of self. Social media channels are sites that permit the continuous performativity of participants through what they share, like and comment upon. Social media is a continuous process and is constantly 'under construction' (Kennedy, 2006: 869). Building the profile is a ritual of contemporary selfhood (Boyd, 2007). Papacharissi (2002: 644) observes that personal homepages are 'a carefully controlled performance through which self presentation is achieved under optimal conditions'. Social media users navigate their way through various platforms, imagined audiences and artefacts (Lindgren, 2017). What this does is affect the user both through their senses (the sounds and images presented) and symbolically (through the meanings attributed to words and images). These meanings and feelings help present the individual or collective to a wider audience online.

In the stadium, the ultras coalesce to present a coherent whole, but that crowd is comprised of individuals. These find expression on social media – both through presenting the collective (through tifos, choreographies and chants) and of individualised expression (through images, comments and discussion). Goffman (1959) highlights that the individual presentation of self is comprised of social performances. These are an 'activity of an individual which occurs during a period marked by his continuous presence before a particular set of observers and which has some influence on the observers' (Goffman, 1959: 22). What differs for users of social media is the role of the audience. In the world Goffman was describing, it was an immediate face-to-face audience. On social media, however, there is an imagined audience (Marwick and Boyd, 2010). Users have to navigate between multiple audiences who could be friends, work colleagues, fellow fans or complete strangers. How users navigate this depends on the site; for example, Facebook is deemed more personal, whereas Twitter is more public (Marwick and Boyd, 2010). What is shared also depends on how it is targeted. When someone tweets another user directly (using an '@'), this is deemed more personal than when a hashtag is used to link to a broader (and more public) debate. Independent tweets are also carefully presented to an imagined audience of followers and how the individual wishes to present themselves. Users take their cues from the social media environment (Boyd, 2007). This draws on certain presumptions of the group the individual wishes to reflect.

Effectively, the construction of social media profiles becomes an exhibit, rather than a piece of theatre (Hogan, 2010). This was demonstrated by *Brigade Loire* from Nantes at their derby with Angers SCO in November 2018, when they displayed a huge picture frame that literally framed the ultras as if they were a work of art. Each image and video on YouTube, Instagram, Twitter or Facebook and other sites effectively becomes a growing exhibit of the group and the individuals within it. The image or video artefact is residual; it remains (Hogan, 2010; Marwick and Boyd, 2010). As Hogan (2010: 380) argues,

> Once a performance has been recorded, the nature of the performance has altered. It may still be a presentation of self, and undoubtedly it continues to signify an individual. However, it no longer necessarily bounds the specific audience who were present when the performance took place. Instead it can be taken out of a situation and replayed in a completely different context.

In relation to fandom, this residual post can be distributed across social media. Hills (2013: 136) argues that 'online postings, reviews or commentaries themselves become textual in the sense of being digitally reproduced and reproducible'. These images or videos are no longer simple representations of a fan group located in time and space, but texts that can be shared globally. As a consequence, they can be interpreted in a variety of ways, and integrated by ultras anywhere. While Jenkins (1992: 223) calls fans 'textual poachers', they are actually active producers of their own discourse and identity. Only those texts that merge with existing conceptions of self are incorporated.

In relation to the imagined audience, users have to self-monitor and reflect on what they post. Depending on how the users want to be seen, they emphasise or de-emphasise certain information (Leary and Kowalski, 1990). A fan who supports a team that finds itself in the media can choose to challenge or agree with the issue that is attracting attention, or alternatively, emphasise other aspects of the club or their fandom. These processes remain key aspects of the construction of self (Mead, 1934; Cooley, 1902; Goffman, 1959: Riesman, 1961). It is through reflexiveness that the individual turns experience back on themselves and adjusts their social behaviour (Mead, 1934). This phenomenon is not restricted to contemporary social life as Giddens (1991), Beck (1992) and Numerato (2018) suggest. Whether the ultra is in the stadium, a bar or online, the self is continuously presented through reflection and emotional cues. Emotions are key signifiers here of how an interaction takes place and how the individual performance has been received.

Language is a key aspect of this reflection. As 'nationally or globally dispersed fans have virtually simultaneous access to media texts and spatially transcendent online forums in which to socialise' (Guschwan, 2011: 1990), geographic and temporal boundaries have virtually dissolved. Consequently, English has become the dominant language online, particularly in forums with transnational fans (Gil-Lopez et al., 2017). This can be clearly demonstrated by the use of English in many of the ultras' tifos and banners. They are reflexively aware of their audience and recognise that their message may get circulated online. When the 'refugee crisis' affected Europe in 2015, fans and ultras, depending on the prevailing opinion of their group, presented banners saying 'Refugees Welcome' or 'Refugees Not Welcome', in English so as to communicate to a global audience. In this context Viktoria Plzeň ultras displaying an image of an axe-wielding man decapitating a visibly Muslim man, accompanied by the words 'Europe Wake Up', was clearly communicating to an audience outside the Czech Republic. But this performative act also presents those ultras as politically right-wing, masculine and defenders of Czech and European territory.

Reflection also takes time and is incorporated into future performances. The immediacy of social media can reduce this reflection, but often the audience interpretation will be clear. It is within the 'context collapse' of multiple audiences that problems occur (Marwick and Boyd, 2010). The difficulties in discerning front- and backstage are key here. Performances are perfected backstage before the action takes place out front (Goffman, 1959). Front- and backstage are relative spaces, not physically demarcated. A fan could be in a pub with friends and simultaneously be backstage with his friends, frontstage with the bar staff and performing a different frontstage on social media with work colleagues; yet the fan never leaves the barstool. What constitutes backstage is constantly negotiated. As Giulianotti (1995) observed in Sweden, a public toilet was seen as backstage by one inebriated Scotland fan, while another argued that when they are away from Scotland, they are always representing Scotland, so even out of the public gaze, they should not be acting like England fans.

Being out of the public gaze does not automatically make the performance backstage (Giulianotti, 1995). As Boyd (2010: 379) asserts, 'backstage is not private space'. This is particularly pertinent to social media as the interactions often take place at home, or in semi-private spaces like fan forums or Facebook. Even though the matchday choreography constitutes a frontstage performance, the preparations are not automatically backstage. Although the production of the choreography takes place before the match, backstage and in private, afterwards the performance remains. In some cases, the complete production, from the design and manufacture behind the scenes to the display in the stadium, becomes the full performance. For example, Schalke's *Ultras Gelsenkirchen* YouTube channel published a video on 20 December 2018 showcasing the preparation and display of their homage to the coal miners of the region. This well-produced video utilises professional software to present opening credits introducing the painting of the choreography before showing its unveiling in the Arena AufSchalke. Reinforcing the local history of the area around the city, the video incorporated indented videos of local (male) coal miners telling stories about their jobs. The backstage preparation became a new performance to embed the ultras and the club in the economic history of the city.

Marwick and Boyd (2010) identify how users vary their posts depending on the platform or who they think can see their posts. Consequently, the performance of individual ultras links to the collective performance of ultras groups. What is shared constitutes the cumulative performances of what it means to be an ultra. More importantly, these are a series of nested performances based on the audience. Each individual simultaneously will be front- and backstage to a variety of audiences, in the flesh and online.

Conclusion

The availability of information technologies such as the Internet, tablets and mobile devices has rapidly become an important part of social life generally and social media has become a major empowering tool for ultras as a way of making connections and building virtual communities specifically. Ultras, and fans in general, are active producers of their own identity and, in the stadium, the ultras coalesce to present a coherent whole, but that crowd is comprised of individuals. Social media helps present these identities. The collective is presented through tifos, choreographies and chants, while individual fans find expressions through their comments, discussion and shared images. It is within the relationships that the individual and collective are formed. Social media supports social networks and virtual communities where interests are shared, discussed and challenged.

Through social media, a much higher transparency in relation to the events on and off the field is created. Football fans get new content delivered directly from clubs and players, and receive – thanks to the increased transparency – a deeper insight into the inner mechanisms of a football club and the life of a professional footballer. Social media equally needs long-term planning and short-term flexibility. It allows the move from objective and fact-based traditional media messages to individual, subjective and crowd-sourced perceptions. The new and special proximity to selected clubs, teams or players also creates a new expectation among the fans. Apps and posts on social networks such as Facebook facilitate the kind of interaction that is needed, transforming these Web 2.0 communications tools into a potentially ideal means of appealing to an important number of faithful fans (Araújo *et al.*, 2014).

5

Ultras and the performance of gender

As the fans descended the steps of the Curva Nord at Lazio's Stadio Olimpico for their match against Napoli at the start of the 2018–19 season, they were confronted by pieces of paper placed on the seats of the front rows. This is not unusual for choreographies as coloured pieces of card or paper are often laid out in order to create the tifo. On closer inspection, these flyers were in fact not part of a display, but a decree to the fans:

> The Curva Nord represents for us a sacred space, an environment with an unwritten code to be respected. The first few rows, as always, have been experienced like the trenches. In the trenches, we do not allow women, wives and girlfriends, so we invite them to position themselves from the 10th row back. Those who choose the stadium as an alternative to a carefree and romantic day in [Rome's] Villa Borghese [gardens], should go to other sections. (Menezes, 2018)

The pronouncement, possibly from the leading group, *Irriducibili*, was clearly outlining how they envisioned themselves. The first ten rows represent the most important place for the ultras, where members prepare themselves for a war of attrition, and those who are not willing to engage should go for a stroll in the park instead. More pertinently, the message clearly stated that this space was for men, independent of wives and girlfriends. Through this exclusion they were inferring that all ultras are men.

The stands where ultras congregate are sometimes regarded as spaces of spontaneity; but in terms of gender, they are a 'permission zone' (Ben-Porat, 2009). The rituals of fandom reiterate who is a member and who is excluded. Despite allusions to the carnival and the transposing of conventions, existing hierarchies can remain within the liminal space of the ritual (Geertz, 1972). Gendered divisions can be reiterated and challenged within the ritual space of the stadium. Even though the Curva Nord is reserved for the home team's fans at Lazio matches, the ritual focus saw the front ten rows as a Durkheimian 'sacred space'. And this space, they argued, should be reserved for men. The flyer drew on heavily masculine language by using the metaphor of the trenches, inferring war, hardship and masculine solidarity. The implication was that these dangerous spaces are no place for women. Within the narrative, female fans were reduced to 'wives and girlfriends' who were only there to accompany male fans; clearly no woman could be a genuine fan of the club, let alone an ultra.

The fact that a flyer had to be distributed highlights how there are no permanent rules of fandom. Clearly, women attend Lazio matches, as many have for decades elsewhere (Cere, 2002; 2012; Williams, 2007; Caudwell, 2011; 2012; Pope, 2012; 2017; Dunn, 2014; 2017; Mintert and Pfister, 2014; 2015; Ratna and Samaya, 2018). The rules of fandom may be 'an unwritten code', as the Lazio ultras maintained in their written declaration, but this code is constantly negotiated. The flyers operated as clear assertion of their position and acted as symbolic violence against anyone choosing to challenge this verdict. Hierarchies within ultras groups are constantly negotiated and gender is a significant factor in this process. Ultras fandom privileges certain hypermasculine forms of behaviour such as physical strength, aggression and violence, and is symbolised through possession of territory. Those who do not conform to these behaviours are signified as emasculated or feminised.

As outlined in Chapter 1, performance is a central part of how ultras present and represent themselves. It was also highlighted how individuals continually present themselves to others. Significantly, gender is a key act of performance (Butler, 1990). Gender is cued through certain cultural signifiers, such as dress, bodily movement or language. Garfinkel's (1967) formative work on ethnomethodology highlighted that transgressing mundane everyday acts can have a deep impact on others. More broadly, he observed how transitioning between genders requires a significant amount of learning new bodily behaviours. One does not simply wear new clothes and become a new person; the individual has to learn a new set of behaviours, acts and mannerisms. Through analysis of such performances in the context of the ultras, for example the imagery, banners and choreographies, we can gain an insight into how they see gender and how they envision their members behaving. With rare exceptions, the imagery used is hypermasculine and draws on metaphors of war, physical strength and heroism. This chapter draws on the theory of 'hegemonic masculinity' (Connell, 1987) to illustrate how gender is a key part of the ultras identity and that this is constantly negotiated, as shown with the Lazio flyers, through a mixture of coercion and consent. As part of this negotiation, however, female ultras are beginning to assert themselves in the *curva* at some clubs.

There remains a prevailing 'gender blindness' in scholarship of football fandom (Free and Hughson, 2003). It is paradoxical that although sport is often seen as a male 'issue', and in the football field male fandom has played a dominant role for decades, the prevailing research on gendered aspects of fandom has been conducted by female scholars. There is a range of research evaluating the status of 'minority' female fans from a variety of regions, including Australia (Mewett and Toffoletti, 2011), Denmark (Pfister *et al.*, 2013), England (Caudwell, 2011; 2012; Dunn, 2014; Pope, 2017; Ratna, 2011; Ratna and Samaya, 2018), France (Ginhoux, 2018), Germany (Selmer, 2004; Sülzle, 2005), Italy (Cere, 2012) and Japan (Tanaka, 2004). Male scholars appear rarely in this context; examples include Chiweshe's (2014) exploration of phallocentric nature of the stadium in Zimbabwe or the study on the status of female fans in Poland by Antonowicz *et al.* (2018). With the exceptions of King's (1997) elaboration on masculinity, class and fandom, or Spaaij's (2008) study on violence, masculinity and hooliganism, masculinity is rarely analysed. The underlying inference is that fandom is inherently masculine, that there is only one way of being masculine and that femininity is articulated through masculinity. Yet men also have a gender and the collective performance of the ultras provides a clear insight into the performance of gender. This chapter represents a start at filling this lacuna.

Hegemonic masculinity and the performance of gender

In gender-oriented studies, the understanding of 'gender' as 'a way of referring to the social organisation of the relationship between the sexes' (Scott, 1986: 28) has been broadly adopted. Gender is distinct from sex, which is usually determined by biological differences in reproductive organs. Gender, in contrast, is socially constructed as different groups and cultures adopt different ways of signifying their gender. In many cultures, gender is signified through clothing and hairstyles. Traditional beliefs would have it that men often have short hair and wear trousers, while women wear dresses or skirts and present themselves through attention to their aesthetic qualities of physical beauty, make-up and grooming. As noted in Chapter 1, performance is a key aspect of gender, and Butler (1990) argued that an individual's gender is constantly performed. In her words, there is no 'doer behind the deed' (Butler, 1990:

142), so by using our bodies in various ways, we can present ourselves to the wider social world.

The football stadium is a significant male-dominated arena; the stands appear to be a refuge of masculinity (Marschik, 2003). For the hegemonic groups within the stadium it is a space with its own set of values, norms and rules where men celebrate dominance and power while women are considered as intruders (Crawford, 2004; Sülzle, 2005; 2011; Jones, 2008). As gender can be understood as 'doing' and displayed differently depending on cultural and social values, sport is one arena that not only permits a distinct performance of genders, but positively encourages it. Sport tends to be male-dominated and men occupy the privileged positions across governance, media, playing, managing and fandom (Messner, 1992). Consequently, 'like many other public environments, sports … have been associated with masculinity' (Wachs, 2003: 178). This is particularly true of football, which has traditionally been seen as a male domain and celebration of masculinity (Mintert and Pfister, 2014).

Although, historically, women have always been football supporters (Cere, 2002; Williams, 2007), the growth of violence in stadiums resulted in many fans, and female fans in particular, turning their back on match attendance. The dominant male presence in the stands has created an 'invented tradition' that only men can be football fans. Ben-Porat (2009: 883) remarked: 'The (male) Israeli spectator is likely to believe that football is a man's game and the presence of "the other sex" in the terraces is unnatural: What the hell is she doing in the stadium?' While this comment was made in reference to fans in Israel, the situation can be replicated in most, if not all, football stadiums across the world, as the opening paragraph to this chapter illustrates. This reaffirms that social basis of gender. Gender is not biological or 'natural'; if this were the case, social groups like ultras would not feel the need to reassert gendered differences. Yet these distinctions are constantly reaffirmed through regular performances, and the rituals of football create the space where this is enacted.

The statement by Lazio fans also emphasises the power dynamics implicit within gender relations. Connell (1987; 2002; 2012) under-scores the role of power with her illustration of 'hegemonic masculinity'. Connell draws on the work of Antonio Gramsci, who identified how power operated within wider culture to perpetuate the privileged posi-tions of social, economic and political elites. Applying this to gender, hegemonic masculinity privileges certain characteristics of the 'alpha male'. With constant performance, these behaviours become reified and self-reproducing as the men that master these acts are able to push themselves, both physically and emotionally, into dominant positions. Consequently, hegemonic masculinity as originally defined referred to an ideal: 'the currently most honoured way of being a man, it required all other men to position themselves in relation to it' (Connell and Messerschmidt, 2005: 832).

It is through the social articulation of emotion that hegemonic masculinity can dominate in fandom. Wider gendered social and cultural norms dictate how emotions are expressed and by whom (Lutz, 1988). These are associated with the power dynamics within wider society (Abu-Lughod and Lutz, 1990). Emphasising the Western underpinnings of hegemonic masculinity, suppression of emotion is considered to be a masculine virtue. Mastery and control of emotions, particularly those that display vulnerabilities like fear, anxiety or even love, emphasise certain hegemonic norms. Being 'emotional' is frequently viewed negatively and as 'feminine' in order to minimise non-masculine involvement (Lutz, 1986). Yet emotions like anger and joy are frequently displayed at football matches. The liminal space of the stadium permits certain transgressions, assuming they conform to other masculine norms. Crying after the team is relegated demonstrates loyalty and the importance of the team to one's identity, and demonstrates how the show of emotion at football transgresses wider gendered social norms. The display of anger and aggression to present the dominance of the group over rivals reinforces a masculine superiority over others. And hugging one's fellow ultras after a goal is scored on one level demonstrates undying love for the club, but really signifies the love of the social group.

Hegemonic masculinity therefore privileges a small number of men who exhibit certain behaviour traits, like confidence, or physical and emotional strength. When we privilege this type of masculinity, it excludes not only women but also other forms of masculinity. Returning to the statement by the Lazio fans, who determines that spending time with your girlfriend or wife makes you any less of a man? As King (1997b) observes with 'the lads', masculinity and class are socially constructed through specific acts and narratives. The group themselves determines how they present themselves and to whom, and this is constantly reiterated through regular matchday rituals. For some groups, violence and the taking of territory is what constitutes being a man (Newson, 2017); for others, it may be about sexuality, politics, locality or nationality (Hodges, 2018; Doidge, 2013, 2015a; Kossakowski and Besta, 2018). This process is a dialectic that is constantly performed and rearticulated through matchday rituals.

Analysis of the ultras highlights two forms of domination exhibited through hegemonic masculinity: internal and external (Demetriou,

2001). Internal hegemony refers to the relations between the different individuals within the group. This manifests itself in the hierarchies of capos and the leading members. As Gramsci (1971) highlighted, hegemony is practised through a dialectic of negotiation and enforcement between those with hegemonic power and those who are subservient. Within the ultras group, views and traditions are imposed or negotiated by those with the power to enforce their viewpoints. Consequently, certain views and practices are exhibited by the group, particularly around gender and 'being a man' where certain views of women and 'non-masculine' men predominate.

Hegemony can also be practised external to ultras groups. As argued elsewhere in this book, since the 1990s ultras have come to exert the greatest influence on fan culture in many countries. Because they are well organised, strongly committed and traditionally play the decisive role in the form of supporting the team, ultras have taken control of the spaces of fandom. They take ownership of the terraces and dominate the emotional space of the stadium with their chanting, choreographies and unity. In this way, the ultras demonstrate their values and viewpoints over the others in the stadium. It bears reiterating that football fans are not homogenous in their views or behaviours, so focusing on the behaviours of the dominant group only reinforces their privileged, hegemonic status.

Sport permits the recreation of hegemonic norms of masculinity through its association with strength, fitness and superiority over others. Consequently, it aligns with masculine traditions of 'being strong, successful, capable, reliable, in control' (Kimmell, 2003: 61). These qualities are supplemented by being loyal, not only to the football club, but also to one's own group. This is reflected in the framing of these groups as fraternal (a 'brotherhood') hierarchics dominated by capos and their directors. Despite these broad similarities, each group determines their own values and norms of behaviour, which reinforces the heterogeneous nature of ultras fandom. As will be analysed later, some qualities are more striking depending on the cultural context and identity of the group. In some cases, 'manhood' means also being homophobic, patriotic/nationalist, militant (in terms of formation of the group and some modes of behaviour, such as 'guerrilla' tactics for attacks on opponents) and entrenching traditional gender roles.

There is a paradox within these hegemonic forms of masculinity. This kind of masculinity is based on the legitimisation of men's supposed dominant position, and the ancillary subordination of women and marginalisation of alternative modes of maleness, which can include homosexuality. It favours 'homosociality' (Lipman-Blumen, 1976), which is the forming of social groups based on the same gender. Yet, frequently, there is a 'discursive gap between fans' inclusive attitudes and their practice of chanting homosexually themed language inside football stadia' (Magrath, 2017: 1). Homophobia is utilised to showcase the hegemonic, hypermasculine presentation of the group. In this denigration, they are inferring that gay men are not truly masculine and therefore subordinate in their gendered hierarchy. Homophobic chants aim to humiliate opponents by suggesting they are not tough, strong or masculine; the inference is that to be another type of masculine does not convey the same levels of strength or toughness, even though people of minority sexualities may have had to endure much more difficult experiences in society than those performing the homophobic chants.

Hegemonic masculinity constructs an intersectional hierarchy of masculinity. Certain races, ethnicities and nationalities are utilised to differentiate 'real masculinity' in opposition to 'others' (Kimmel, 2003; King, 2003). In the American context, this can be Italian, Jewish, Irish, indigenous or Asian (Kimmel, 2003). Back *et al.* (1998) identify the hierarchy of race and nation through chants of 'I'd rather be a Paki than a Scouse' to illustrate that while Pakistanis in Britain are seen as lower in the hierarchy than the chanters, people from Liverpool are seen as being lower again. Similar hierarchies are highlighted by Doidge (2015b) in his analysis of racism in Italy. Juventus ultras drew upon cultural images of blond Swedes to place not only the black Italian Mario Balotelli but also themselves as inferior. The paradox is that black masculinity was also seen as a threat and therefore something to be challenged (Carrington, 2010). Elsewhere in Europe, different cultural constructions are used to denigrate rival fans or assert racial superiority. In Eastern Europe using the term 'Jew' suggests that rival fans are weak or not true members of the nation. Likewise, African or Muslim men are portrayed as invaders, which necessitates local women needing protection (see Chapter 7).

Physical and emotional dominance of the group seeks to make other forms of masculinity and femininity subordinate (Messner, 1988; 1992; 1997). Power reinforces hegemonic masculinity by emphasising gender inequality and sexual stereotypes, and minimising the role of women. Wann *et al.* (2001) argue that 'spectator sports [are simply] supporting the gender order and masculine hegemony'. While many of the choreographies, group names and actions of male-dominated ultras reinforce hegemonic masculinity, the agency of female ultras should not be denied. Female ultras have also carved out a space in the stadium, just as other female fans have done. Many of the activities of ultras are not intrinsically masculine; they are just coded as masculine by the groups or wider society. Singing, clapping, choreographies and expressing unwavering loyalty and devotion to one's club is not inherently gendered. What the ultras style of fandom demonstrates, as with any other type of group mobilisation, is that people can become members by participating in the rituals of the group.

Performing masculinity

The ultras style of fandom provides an important space for the performance of a range of identities. The most prominent of these is performed within the stadium, particularly through choreographies. But identity is performed through everyday interactions. Social media, conversations in the pub and activities on the way to the ground all provide spaces for gendered performances. As highlighted in the previous section, hegemonic masculinity presents and reinforces a specific image of masculinity. Many ultras groups subscribe to the image of being strong and a 'real man'. Mostly, ultras' masculinity is based on presumed qualities of masculinity such as toughness, aggressiveness, strength, willingness to engage in violence (both physically and symbolically), assertiveness and excluding weak and 'non-hegemonic' males. These virtues suit the assumptions of the concept of hegemonic masculinity and should be regarded as a culturally idealised form (an 'ideal type' in the Weberian sense) and model to follow for many adherents of the ultras way of life. From a sociological point of view these qualities are distinctive from traditional societies and communities where there are clear divisions of gender roles (Hochstetler *et al.*, 2013). In the case of football fans, the modes of masculinity stem from a long tradition of dominance of predominantly white, working-class men who constituted the majority of the fan base in Europe. As a consequence, this group have determined the trajectory of behaving as and being an ultra since the inception of the movement.

In late capitalist societies, social life has become organised differently with the distinctions between traditional gender roles dissolving. Football becomes one space where men can 'prove' their masculinity, something they feel they cannot do in more progressive public domains. Rather than being uncivilised, masculine, working-class 'rumps', as argued by Dunning *et al.* (1988), masculinity and class are socially constructed (King, 1997b). Groups draw on their own traditions of masculinity to reassert their gendered hierarchies. This can come through dominating the leadership structures of ultras groups, as to date there have still been relatively few female capos. Similarly, men dominate supporters' associations (Dunn, 2014) and the business and management areas related to ticket redistribution and the selling of fan gadgets. The performance of hegemonic masculinity can be exhibited through violence or even with illegal activities, such as some ultras and *barra bravas* groups being linked to organised crime. In this way, these fans can still exert physical dominance over others.

The performance of masculinity occurs on many levels. Through the matchday performances, particularly the choreographies, it is possible to identify several key themes (Kossakowski *et al.*, forthcoming). This includes the image of the warrior, deliberate transgression of regulations, including illegality, and also reinforcing the homosocial fraternity of ultras fandom. The dominant masculine image of many ultras groups is that of the fighter with the well-muscled body. Critical feminist approaches have argued that intensive bodybuilding is an attempt to restore a feeling of self-control and self-worth for men (Gillett and White, 1992). Just as emotions are embodied responses that help the individual take control of their feelings (Katz, 1999), physical bodily activity can help one regain self-worth and control emotional responses, particularly in relation to trauma (van der Kolk, 2014). The fighter, and the related image of the clenched fist, link to the symbolic violence of the ultras (see Chapter 6) and also outline the values that ultras should pursue. Being ready for the physical confrontation is an important ideal, signifying that one is a 'real man' (Hochstetler *et al.*, 2013). This is exemplified by the image of the boxer. Ultras of Galatasaray used the figure of Hollywood boxing hero Rocky Balboa, standing in the boxing ring and wearing yellow gloves and red shorts (the colours of the club), before a derby against Fenerbahçe. Similarly, at a Champions League match against PSG in 2013 Olympiacos ultras displayed an image referencing Muhammed Ali's iconic victory over Sonny Liston accompanied by the message that 'Piraeus [the port where the club is based] means knockout'.

The warrior is a frequent image in choreographies. Many depict scenes with knights, soldiers or warriors with swords, axes and flags, often in club colours. As Chapter 6 highlights, this is symbolic of defending or invading territory. As Connell (2000) notes, for many men and boys, being 'a good warrior' and having the 'ability to defend himself against enemies' are important identity factors. Being an ultra reinforces this mentality; living with the continuous danger of facing physical confrontations from other ultras groups becomes the ultimate test of masculinity. This becomes symbolically represented through the actual performance of the group. It is for this reason that Dal Lago (1990) referred to the match as 'the representations of the battle'. The ultras' stands, filled with hundreds, even thousands of men, are the 'battlefield'. They are led by the capo who conducts the chants and the performative order of the match. The capo is the general directing the 'battle' by determining when to sing certain songs, when and where to display banners and tifos, and when to wave the flags.

The choreographies emphasise the warlike representations of certain groups. These choreographies festooned with knights, soldiers and warriors allude to an 'imagined' historical order and state, but are used anachronistically in the present. *The Union* of Spartak Moscow, for example, presented a huge image of an army of warriors from the Middle Ages to celebrate the group's fifteenth anniversary. These historical images are incorporated into contemporary portrayals to emphasise the masculine defenders of territory. These are invented traditions that suggest a link to time immemorial, but are new and contemporary. Even if it only lasts for the ninety-minute duration of the football match, the 'warrior' image makes contemporary men feel that there is still space for 'heroism' – in the name of the club or group, but in many ways in the name of a (dubious) masculinity. For these groups, there is a feeling that there are few spaces in contemporary society where these men can express an unreconstructed notion of masculinity with no nuances, no doubts and no feeling that they should reconcile gender roles. Braudy (2005: xii) asks: 'What has happened to heroism? But all also invoke a challenge that lies behind that: What has happened to men? Questions of heroism shade imperceptibly into questions of masculinity, which in turn often point to a deep and ongoing confusion over where we are going as a society.'

The nostalgia for heroism is noticeable in historical performances in Poland that glorify war heroes or people fighting with the authoritarian Communist system. Most of these choreographies are dedicated to heroes, with only a few of them to heroines. Heroism is linked to the tradition of chivalry that relates perfectly with the wider and more complex identity project in which males are the rulers and conquerors with exceptional combat skills and great commanding attitudes that predestine them to assume the supreme role in society. The liminality of the stadium indulges masculine performances. These men may feel that the real 'heroism' of war is unlikely (except during the Balkans wars of the 1990s, for example); instead, they choose to metaphorically fight symbolic others, such as Muslims, foreigners or rival ultras. Yet by playing with these symbols, they are reinforcing the social construction of masculinity. They are simply trying to enact a reified and mythical way of being a man. Being masculine does not necessarily mean that violence is inevitable, that space needs to be defended or that women have to be objectified.

These constructions of masculinity are both reifying and contradictory.

One part of ultras mentality is about being deliberately transgressive, particularly in relation to greater regulation and policing. It represents a mode of masculinity that cannot be controlled and is answerable to no authority. The use of pyrotechnics is one such 'game' that demonstrates the ultras' desire to be seen to challenge the rules. The irony of the creation of these rules is that they provide a barrier many ultras will want to subvert. As Giulianotti (1995) identified, official support of the carnivalesque can neutralise its power. Many choreographies, banners and chants suggest an engagement with the illegal world. For example, ultras from Polish club Motor Lublin displayed a giant choreography of a skull with a cowboy hat and masked face above a banner reading 'Bandit city, bandit club'. One of the chants of Motor's ultras contains the words: 'It is our habitat of lawlessness'. Similarly, the *Brigate Autonome Livornesi* displayed '*Fino all'ultimo bandito*' ('Until the last bandit'). This became immortalised in a song about the Livorno ultras by the Italian punks *Banda Bassotti* that highlights the crossover between wider subcultures associated with anti-establishment viewpoints.

These groups recognise the borders of social norms and seek to establish themselves as outsiders. There are two elements to this alleged deviancy. On one side are politicians, federations and the media, who use pejorative terms like 'animals', 'savages' or 'barbarians' to label these groups as deviants. On the other side is the reflexive and ironic dialogue with members and other groups that suggests that outsider status. Becker (1973) observed how members of groups labelled as deviant would determine their own boundaries and rules in order to differentiate themselves from others in order to reinforce that they were more authentic. King (1997a) observed similar traits with hooligans, who deliberately transgressed those boundaries in order to be seen as deviant. Being a renegade or bandit is a part of the self-defining performance of the ultras: 'With highly identified fans, a level of flirtation with the role of deviant is striking' (Winands *et al.*, 2017: 8). 'This role is attractive, but also provides another mode of differentiation from the ordinary and is thus connected with self-stylization as exceptional,' Winands *et al.* (2017: 8) assert, claiming that 'deviance is part of the group norms, and individual group members are ready to engage in deviant acts within the context of the group or scene'.

Drawing on Bakhtin's (1984) conception of the carnivalesque, everyday practices and hierarchies become subverted within the liminal space of the carnival. Yet this is not automatically a playful experience. Robson (2000) referred to the 'dark sense of the carnival' that permitted socially unacceptable behaviours within the carnivalesque terraces. Armstrong (1998) noted that hooliganism was a 'game' that required domination over rivals, whether they are rival fans, police or 'others'. However, this construction of others is gendered, racialised and sexualised. As outlined by Back *et al.* (1998), rival groups are stratified racially. The repeated construction of hegemonic masculinity also places women and gay men in lower positions in this gendered hierarchy.

These actions are not controlled or cathartic. Liminality is not a self-contained or neutral space (Turner, 1974; [1969] 1997). The catharsis argument has been suggested as a function of sport and spectacles for centuries. Juvenal suggested that political appeasement could be achieved through 'bread and circuses'. Zanker (1990) reasoned that the controlled release of frustration and anger towards political elites at public spectacles like the theatre and gladiatorial games was seen by the Emperor Augustus as a way of releasing tension and protecting those in power. Similarly, Elias and Dunning (1986) argued that sport was a mimetic exercise that permitted the controlled escalation and de-escalation of emotional energy; as modern society frowned on the public exhibition of emotion, sport became a space where this was tolerated. One reading of Bakhtin (1984) is that the carnivalesque permits the transgression of social norms, which return to normal after the carnival. Yet the liminal space is not dispassionate and ahistorical. The participants in the ritual are now acquainted through their participation and new ways of acting, and they form new relationships (Turner, 1974; [1969] 1997). Misogynistic views do not automatically dissipate upon fans' return from the stadium, as the figures documenting the rates of domestic abuse after high-profile matches attest to (Brooks-Hay and Lombard, 2018). This is not to suggest that football is causal, only that the subordinate view of females is continued away from the stadium.

The transgressive elements also cross into deeper illegal subcultures. In some countries, particularly in areas where fandom has a long tradition of violence like the Balkans, Poland, Russia or South America, there are connections between ultras (and hooligans) and criminal groups. Engaging in activities like drug trafficking, smuggling and robbery are part of the 'game'. These masculine groups seek to assert their independence from authority, particularly the police. Through the game of football, the police are resisted in protest at increasing regulation and matchday securitisation. Consequently, strictly enforced norms of behaviour are inculcated into members. Notably, there is a strict prohibition from cooperating with the police, as well as other actors such as the media, authorities and also academics. These homosocial groups form strong relationships of confidentiality and trust. The control within the ultras group becomes a matter of stability and safety that consolidates the borders of hegemonic masculinity.

The link between violence and masculinity connects to the dominance over rivals. This can be linked to the symbolic violence exhibited in choreographies (as Chapter 6 will discuss). Choreographies related to the derby between Inter and AC Milan showcase the symbolism ultras draw upon to infer their dominance. In 2012 Inter ultras displayed an impressive choreography of the *Madonnina*, the statue of the Madonna that sits atop Milan's cathedral, bedecked in Inter colours. Underneath bore the legend: *'Ti Te Dominet Milan'* ('You dominate Milan'), which comes from the unofficial anthem of the city, *Oh mia bela Madunina*. Metaphorically, it is a play on words, as the song refers to how the statue of the Virgin Mary 'dominates' over the city. In the context of the derby, combined with the use of Inter's colours, it gains an additional, ambiguous meaning. Likewise, ultras of AC Milan have presented many choreographies suggesting that they 'rule' the city. One of the performances included a slogan declaring *'Fin dall' antichita' tutta mia la citta'* ('from ancient times the city is mine').

Dominance is also demonstrated through the symbolic occupation of space. Matches against significant rivals will transform the wider city into another 'battlefield'. As Winands *et al.* (2017: 10–11) observe:

> It is not unusual, especially at highly charged matches such as local derbies, for there to be organized group marches from the railway station to the stadium. Here, the space that opposing fans claim as their own territory is deliberately violated. If the march comes off, then advances into enemy territory can be chalked up. On the other hand, such archaic actions – resembling invasions by enemy armies – are constantly subject to the risk of violent attack. The behaviour and attitudes of highly identified fans during these symbolic and territorial competitions are, in the final analysis, comparable to military confrontations.

The masculine 'warriors' and fighters are symbolically invading and defending their 'imagined homeland'. This is not necessarily cathartic and occasionally leads to violence, as outlined later in the book.

This leads to a second element of the ultras' masculine performance: fraternity. This homosociality (Lipman-Blumen, 1976) defines strong boundaries and norms within the group that entrenches a sense of unity and togetherness. This becomes symbolised in masculine notions of brotherhood and fraternity. These 'brothers in scarves' need to rely on their fellow ultras when in difficult situations, particularly in physical confrontations with rival ultras or the police. This cohesion is regularly performed through the shared activities of matchday rituals. As one ultra from the *Elephant Army* group in Malaysia declares,

> what unites them is their love for their club, their persistence to stay 90 minutes on their feet during the rain or cold, they are united by the warmth

from chanting at full voice, united while sleeping in a half-drunk state on a train that is taking them from an away game, united by the convoy through the center of the away team's city, united by one sandwich which is shared among four of them after many hours of hunger, united by one shared cigarette, united by one look, by one ideal, by a one and only mentality. (Wanmonster, 2011)

The language of unity is prevalent, particularly when describing time spent in the heart of their rivals' cities. Trust is important, such as when asleep, but also the solidarity of sharing the experience.

Unity and brotherhood are demonstrated through clothing. As Butler (1990) argues, the way people dress signifies their gendered identity. The ultras form of fandom is an excellent way of demonstrating the conflation of individual and group identity. Individual fans wear similar clothing to demonstrate their loyalty, as well as to obscure their individualism. Many groups will wear similar types of clothing so that the group provides one coherent image of unity and also so that individuals cannot be identified by the authorities. The illicit activities of the ultras have modified their choice of attire. Being the 'unknown perpetrator' is a part of ultras identity with members adopting various type of camouflage. The obscuring of individual identity is also presented through stylised images of the anonymous ultra (Doidge, 2015a), as described in Chapter 1. In a 2017 Europa League match against Nice, Vitesse Arnhem ultras unveiled a giant choreography depicting an ultra standing in front of the club's badge. The ultra was wearing a goggle jacket, which has a hood with an in-built pair of dark glasses that obscures the face. 'These "goggle jackets" completely remove any individuality from the ultra. The result is a character that resembles a ninja or militaristic individual who cannot be identified and prosecuted' (Doidge, 2015a: 170). A similar image is used on the logo of Pahang FC's *Elephant Army*: a skull wearing a gas mask, inferring their ability to withstand the police's tear gas. Emphasising this, the group declared:

> An Ultras [*sic*] has no name, only good friends know him. An Ultras has no face, most of the time a hood is covering his head, a scarf covering his mouth. An Ultras doesn't dress like others and doesn't follow trends and like the latest. (Wanmonster, 2011)

Underneath the ultra's hood and scarf, it is not possible to discern the gender of the wearer. The use of language and other performances, however, clearly infer that these ultras are male.

Brotherhood also extends to groups with shared colours or political viewpoints. These twinnings (Doidge, 2015a) structure relations with rival groups, drawing on the 'Bedouin syndrome', where 'the friend of a friend is a friend; the friend of an enemy is an enemy' (Dunning *et al.*, 1986). This contrasts with Evans-Pritchard's (1940) nested power relations observed within the Nuer people in Eastern Africa. The simplest fraternal relationship could lead to disagreement, but these brothers could unite when brought into conflict with rival tribes, and these tribes could then join forces to battle the British. This behaviour is not automatically replicated in ultras groups. While some may follow urban and nationalist lines (for example, rival club groups uniting at international tournaments), many of these groupings are contingent on a variety of factors that include previous encounters, political ideology, religion and geographical proximity.

More frequently, brotherhoods extend beyond national boundaries. The 'Triangle of Brotherhood' between Livorno, AEK Athens and Marseilles unites ultras groups with shared left-wing politics. Flags and banners of each group are waved at each other's matches to denote this friendship. Fraternities are also depicted in graffiti and choreographies of drinking together or handshakes, as demonstrated in graffiti of the 'Black-White Brothers' of *Gate 4* of PAOK of Thessoliniki and *Çarşı* of Beşiktaş. The material culture of fandom helps demonstrate and reinforce friendships. Mauss (1967) identified that the act of giving a gift builds relationships. Exchanging stickers or scarves helps symbolise the friendship between groups. These brotherhoods can be interpreted as broader imagined communities that draw on the 'invented traditions' of masculinity. To be a 'real man' is to be dismissive of authority, to drink together and to show solidarity with others.

The masculine foundation for these groups is frequently displayed through their names. The *Orthodox Brothers* fraternity between ultras who follow Belgrade's Crvena Zvezda and Olympiacos in Piraeus reinforces the fraternal norms of the groups. More conspicuous is the use of the moniker 'boys': examples include *Boulogne Boys* (PSG), *Ultras Boys* (Maccabi Haifa), *Boys Roma* and, even more simply, *Boys* at Inter. Many ultras groups draw on shared cultural symbols and performances that constantly reinvent tradition. The 'ideal type' of ultras brotherhood is full of honour, dignity, respect, unity, fraternity and sense of belonging to the collective that is associated with the football club. Yet these conventions can be adapted to be more inclusive. *Rude Boys and Girls* of Sampdoria added the inclusive suffix after meeting with German fans who suggested the change. The rituals and symbols of football are not inherently masculine, they are just gendered through the practice of their members.

The identity of groups is frequently articulated through a gendered, racialised and sexualised other. Hegemonic masculinity is continuously reinforced through repetitive practice. This is a dialectical process oscillating between masculine groups' notion of 'who we are' (which is tough, strong males who rule the city) and 'who we are not' (vulnerable, weak, defeated, non-masculine fans, including women and gay men). The first is accompanied by glorifying chants and choreographies. The latter is sometimes achieved through the symbolic degradation of opponents by attributing female/homosexual characteristics upon them. Many chants are misogynistic and bestow 'female' qualities such as 'whore' or 'bitch' on their rivals in order to humiliate them. The inference is that being female is humiliating. Sexualised images are also used to represent that 'real men' are the ones who dominate sexual relations. For example, in Austria a choreography was made that depicted the eagle symbol of Sturm Graz sexually exploiting a fan in the colours of their rivals, Rapid Vienna. Meanwhile in Poland, after fans of local rivals Arka Gdynia were prohibited from travelling to the derby, Lechia Gdańsk ultras placed sex dolls in Arka colours on the empty seats to demonstrate that they were sexual objects. This sexualised position has also been extended to rival players and managers. The *Red & Black Block* of Western Sydney Wanders displayed a choreography depicting a man resembling the Sydney FC coach performing oral sex. All of these performances create a clear distinction between hegemonic men as dominant figures and subordinated and feminised rivals who are dominated.

Female ultras and navigating masculinity

The unreconstructed practices and performances of hegemonic masculinity in the stands present a significant problem for female ultras. As the Lazio ultras declared in the introduction to this chapter, these masculine fan groups see the *curva* as a 'sacred space' for men. Consequently, the terraces are what Ben-Porat (2009) calls a 'permission zone'. There is nothing intrinsically masculine about much of the ultras' behaviour, such as their chants, choreographies and pyrotechnics. As King (1997b) identified, the groups themselves construct their own understandings of what it means to be masculine, just as the Lazio fans demonstrated with their declaration. Football provides the same sense of belonging and community, regardless of gender; there is nothing intrinsic about football fandom that privileges a particular gender. As Dunn (2014: 108) argues, 'female fans are no more a uniformly homogenous group than male fans because women perform their identity as football fans and assume different interpretations of their gender according to their audience'.

The hegemonic masculinity within the stadium means female fans are frequently confronted with hostility and trivialised sexism. Throughout football, women often remain marginalised, patronised and instrumentalised (Antonowicz *et al.*, 2018). At the start of the twenty-first century across Europe (in particular) there has been a rapidly increasing number of female fans in the stadium and among television audiences (Pope, 2017). Despite the image of the ultras as being hypermasculine, female members played an important role at the start of the movement in the 1970s (Cere, 2002; 2012). As the ultras emerged from the counter-cultural political scene in Italy, women were key actors. Cere (2002) argues that it is the focus on violence by the media and academics that has marginalised the role of female ultras. That said, each group emerges from its own particular milieu and draws on specific local traditions and cultures.

As stated earlier, there is nothing intrinsically masculine about football fandom. To be a fan is to engage in the rituals and practices of fandom. As with male fans, there are various modes of engagement among female supporters, from mere spectator to passionate ultra (Giulianotti, 2002; Crawford, 2004). Socialising with the community of fans is a major incentive in attending a football match every weekend (Mintert and Pfister, 2014, 2015; Pfister *et al.*, 2018). Women want to be known simply as fans, rather than female fans. For fans of all genders, being an ultra is a way of life that demands strong commitment and a high degree of identification with one's club (Cere, 2012). Unsurprisingly, female fans act and react at football matches in similar ways to their male counterparts (Sülzle, 2011). Male and female fans shout, swear, insult the referee, join in chants and cheer passionately for their team. 'Real' fans, men and women, wear similar clothing and are decorated with the same fan paraphernalia. As noted in the previous section, uniformity of clothing represents supposed masculine virtues of solidarity. The 'male gaze' has subordinated women to sexualised objects, but at football matches this can be challenged. Markers of feminine beauty, such as make-up and heels are removed or misplaced in the stadium (Pfister *et al.*, 2013; Mintert, 2015). As Jones (2008: 516) argues, 'women sometimes downplay their gender identities to reinforce their fan identities'.

To be accepted by the football community, one has to show dedication to the team and engage in the 'right' conduct, particularly in the stadium. Like their male counterparts, female fans are socialised into their fandom, which includes becoming familiar with the way to behave in the stadium: how to cheer and sing, how to dress and what to consume (Wann *et al.*, 2001; Cere, 2002; 2012; Kreisky and Spitaler, 2006; Llopis-Goig, 2007; Sülzle, 2007; 2011; Jones, 2008; Meuser, 2008; Mintert and Pfister, 2014; Pfister *et al.*, 2018). This is invariably learned from a male figure, such as a father or brother (Spaaij and Anderson, 2010; Dunn, 2014; Pfister *et al.*, 2018). Despite this early socialisation, competing social influences on female fans often provide female fans with different opportunities for presentation and identification. Male fans are often permitted the time and indulgence to attend matches, travel away and engage in their fandom over extended periods of time. Too often this luxury is not extended to female fans.

Although fandom is not gender specific but rather is simply about performance of the rituals, it remains dominated by masculinity. Female fans learn to not challenge men's way of doing fandom; they learn to keep silent in spite of affronts, and accept the sexism of male fans as well as the dominance of men in the stands (Dunn, 2014; Pope, 2017). Non-hegemonic genders are always in a precarious position as the hegemonic group determines acceptance. In the world of football, female fans do not want to lose their status and credibility as authentic supporters. In these processes, female fans become 'accomplices' of the majority of male fans and cooperate in the 'masculinisation' of football as a game and as a space of and for men (Chiweshe, 2014). In a personal interview (2016), a member of female fan group from Polish club GKS Katowice tried to legitimise the decision by male fans not to allow women to travel to away matches:

> Very often we are asked if we feel discriminated against by that. At the beginning, probably we considered it like this. But now we know that the first reason is our safety and the second – particular behaviour. During away matches we should support our club strongly. However, many women going away had more 'interesting' duties. Without going into details – their conduct had little in common with the real reason why they were travelling with their team.

Participation is not only contingent on performing the right actions but also on acceptance by the hegemonic bloc. Women are allowed only one particular style of supporting: that ascribed by male rules. And if women want to connect the matchday experience of supporting the team with other issues, they face firm resistance and critique.

Women are welcome in many in many fan groups but do not normally get access to ultras groups and the hooligan scene (Pilz and Wölki-Schumacher, 2010: 7). In Denmark, for example, Lyngby BK are supported by an ultras group called *Lyngby Syndikatet* and a hooligan group called *Blue Army*, neither of which accept women. The most important ultras groups in the country, *Urban Crew* (FC Copenhagen) and *Alpha* (Brøndby IF), likewise do not accommodate female fans (Joern, 2006). In some other groups, women are tolerated as they help to create the tifos, and they may even be able to smuggle fireworks into the stadium (Mintert, 2015: 106). For women, too, being an ultra is a form of life that demands strong commitment and a high degree of identification with their club (Cere, 2012). Even with acceptance there is still a gendered division of labour within the groups (Doidge, 2015a; Ginhoux, 2018). Female ultras often perform roles such as caring for injured (male) fighters or sewing together choreographies. With rare exceptions, however, capos and decision-making roles remain a male preserve.

Gender ratios and relations in the various fan groups reveal a clear pattern: the number of women decreases with the level of misogyny and violence. This is not helped by official strategies to try and use female fans to 'civilise' the behaviour of men at the stands (Pope, 2017). Female ultras form a minority that that has to cope with a measure of sexism but, as a rule, these women have developed strategies not only to survive in the group but also to enjoy football. One of these strategies is to establish women-only fan groups. This has been a prominent tactic in Italy, where female ultras have played an important role throughout the movement's history, and a national association of female football supporters has been established (Cere, 2002; 2012). For example, the women-only ultras group *All Girls* operates at a club, Parma, with a high proportion of female fans. Their name is also a counterpoint to the longstanding (male-dominated) ultras group *Boys 1977*. In Spain, women's *peñas* create a sense of community, acting 'as a counterbalance to the exclusion and derision previously experienced by these women' (Llopis-Goig, 2007). In Denmark, for members of the women-only fan group the *Female Vikings*, who follow Lyngby BK, it is most important to support their club in the best and most creative, acoustic and optical way but also to self-represent and socially experience the scene during the week. For them, it is the friendly bond between their fan club and the football club that symbolises their attitude to life (Mintert and Pfister, 2014; 2015).

The establishment of female fan groups is evidence for the increasing presence of women in the stands. Just as men are performing their (hegemonic) masculinity through participation in certain rituals at the stadium, female fan groups feel confident in displaying their femininity. Like the male groups, the naming conventions indicate their gender, for example *Forza Viola Girls* at Fiorentina, *Ladies Austria Wien 2005*, the aforementioned *Female Vikings* and their Danish counterparts *Pink Lions* of FC Copenhagen. The difficulty for female fan groups is how to negotiate the gendered boundaries of fandom. By establishing groups with names including 'girls', 'ladies' and 'pink', they are reinforcing those gender distinctions at the same time as they are resisting them. More militant groups also exist with more strident gender politics. The name of *Feministas Malmö* in Sweden clearly outlines the political direction of the group and aligns more clearly to the political origins of ultras fandom in Italy in the 1970s. In Germany a new strategy has emerged that refers to the anticipated sexism to which female fans are subjected. The movement *Titten Auswärts* (Tits Out) aims to take over and reinterpret the abuse and turn it into an ironic slogan for their group. Emphasising their femininity, members of the group wear their name across their chests on tight-fitting white T-shirts.

These female fan groups offer women new opportunities for leisure-time activities and reinforce an important space for the self-actualisation lacking in other parts of their lives. The establishment of women-only football fan groups indicates that for those devotees football has become a way of life in which a sense of community fosters the prospect of meeting like-minded women. That is as much a vital necessity for female fans 'doing gender' as a means of achieving a balance between staging femininity and displaying expertise in a male domain. By taking on both masculine and feminine behaviours they want to be seen first and foremost as supporters and prove their authenticity as fans (Mintert, 2015). As such, football opens up opportunities for supporters to imagine and experience qualities of life through fandom in their own way which are not directly linked to wider social norms and restraints from outside of football (Hognestad, 1997).

The foundation and activities of the female-only fan groups show how women can perform gender in the stands and how they play a significant role in the ultras movement. The proactive female fans' close connection with the official fan clubs, which were founded and dominated by men, made it possible to create and occupy a women's space. For these women it was crucial to participate actively, take responsibility, live out democracy, discuss and debate football on their own agenda. By longing for an affiliation with other female fans who share the same passion and understand the situation of women in a men's domain, the female active members found a space where values like emotionality and identification with their team can be addressed and lived out freely (Mintert, 2015).

Conclusion

Football fandom remains heavily gendered as the stadium remains a place where hegemonic masculinity is staged. Hegemonic masculinity reflects the continuous power and privileging of certain norms of behaviour (Connell, 1987). Physical and emotional dominance of the spaces of fandom (such as the stadium and social media) is performed by predominantly male fan groups who exhibit 'hypermasculine' behaviour. This hypermasculinity is demonstrated through the names of the groups, the chants and the banners. Many of these refer to the groups as warriors or armies who are metaphorically invading their rivals' symbolic spaces or defending their territory. Each of these represent a stylised version of hegemonic masculinity that seeks to exclude other forms of masculinity and femininity. It privileges certain masculine characteristics such as physical strength, emotional control and collective solidarity.

Despite the dominance of masculine fan groups, football increasingly attracts female fans. Amongst these will be female ultras and football enables these women to perform their gender in different ways. Even though many of the choreographies, group names and actions of male-dominated ultras reinforce hegemonic masculinity, the agency of female ultras should not be denied. Female ultras have also carved out a space in the stadium, just as other female fans have done. Some female ultras may take part in the male-dominated groups and broadly align to traditional gender roles, such as caring for those injured in fighting (Ginhoux, 2018). For others, the space of the stadium enables them to be liberated from the gendered norms and responsibilities of broader society, such as focusing on family. Female-only ultras groups, like *Forza Viola Girls* or *Female Vikings*, have been established to provide more freedom for female ultras to engage in their style of fandom. Despite this, large choreographies remain dominated by the masculine ultras groups.

6

Violence and the world of the ultras

It was the first time Hamburger SV had played their city rivals St Pauli in seven years. During the game, the Hamburg ultras unveiled a banner to taunt their neighbours: '*Eure werte sind fast so stabil wie eure Hools*' ('Your values are almost as strong as your hooligans'). This was not to celebrate the strength of their rivals' hooligans, nor their values; they were insinuating that St Pauli fans were weak, and their values likewise. St Pauli, as a club and fan scene, prides itself on being different from others due to their explicit anti-fascist and counter-cultural stances. These values have helped the club become one of the most supported outside Germany and their merchandise is one of the most successful for a German club outside the largest two, Bayern Munich and Borussia Dortmund. The implication from HSV fans was that St Pauli fans were supporting a club in the 2. Bundesliga (second division), with all the corporate values of any other club. They were using the symbol of violence and weakness to show their contempt for their rivals. This superiority had also been demonstrated with a huge choreography at the start of the match that showed HSV players lifting the European Cup, reminding their city rivals that they were the more successful club. Before the match, St Pauli fans sought to demonstrate their own superiority by marching through the streets of Hamburg on their way to the Volksparkstadion, all wearing white T-shirts to show their unity. Rather than refer to their team's success on the pitch, they were showing that their fans were superior through coordination and organisation. In both cases, symbolic dominance over the rival was the focus of both fan groups.

These images rarely entice the media, yet make up the majority of activities by ultras. While they draw on images of violence and domination, they are largely symbolic. Despite this, the media tends to focus on the rare episodes when physical violence takes place. They then apportion blame to the ultras and suggest that this is a moral failing of football fans in general and ultras in particular. As Cohen (1972) argued, moral panics are amplified by the media, which results in them attracting more participants but also more police, increasing the likelihood of conflicts occurring. Despite this, some in the media overwhelmingly focus on the violence and suggest that this is the primary modus operandi of ultras (see, for example, Hepburn, 2009). Often, these journalists will use on their own sensationalised media reports to reinforce their own arguments, thus amplifying the moral panic. Things have not moved on since Stuart Hall (1978: 36) declared that the way the English press portrayed hooliganism was 'brutal, short-hand and simplifying'. Similarly, Murphy *et al.* (1988) observed that the media go through phases of amplifying and de-amplifying issues of hooliganism. Poulton (2005: 42) observed that the argument had not moved on, and that 'the media regularly put all English football supporters in the frame for the hooligan element's misdemeanours'. These arguments are not restricted to hooliganism; they also apply to the ultras. In Italy the media play a role in constructing the ultras as 'folk devils' (Marchi, 2005; Doidge, 2015a). Cere (2002) also argues that the focus on violence has privileged masculine aspects of fandom and minimised the role and presence of female ultras.

This amplification becomes vitally important when considering the political mobilisation of ultras and other football fans (as will be shown in the following chapter). Alongside the economic transformation of football, there is a growing regulation of the ultras' activities. In the mediatised world of commercial football business, the ultras bring colour and spectacle, but their perceived excesses are curtailed in order to continue to present the sport as a family-friendly global product (Nuhrat, 2018b). Media companies have invested in football, in partnership with football clubs and governing bodies (King, 1998; 2003; Giulianotti, 1999; Doidge, 2015a). They thus have a vested financial interest in presenting a sanitised image of the game. Consequently, the media have a crucial role in presenting styles of fandom in a positive or negative light. On the one hand, they play a political role, presenting the ultras as dangerous in order to justify punitive regulations against their activities. Yet this can backfire: it should not be in the media's interest to paint ultras as constantly dangerous, as that could stop many other types of fans from attending the match. Doidge (2015a) has argued that in Italy, the punitive restrictions on *all* football fans aimed at curbing the perceived activities of a small number of ultras (particularly around violence) has actually had the opposite effect to the desired one. The regulations themselves have led to many fans remaining at home and watching matches on television, while the ultras are the only ones still going to the match, making them feel authenticated. As Contucci and Francesio (2013: 1) argue, 'they are trying to chase the violent people from the stadium. They have chased away everyone but the violent people.'

Considering the number of football matches that take place every weekend, and the many thousands of ultras that attend these games, violence is exceptional (Armstrong and Harris, 1991). Hooligan groups are mostly small (a dozen, several people) and do not constitute the whole picture of the fan community. Even if minor confrontations over queue jumping or spilt pints of beer were taken into consideration, violence at football matches is very rare. This is one of the reasons why the media focus on riots. Violence is so atypical that when it does occur, it becomes something worthy of attention. As Randall Collins (2008: 20) observes, violence in wider society is also rare:

> Violent interactions are difficult because they go against the grain of normal interaction rituals. The tendency to become entrained in each other's rhythms and emotions means that when the interaction is at cross-purposes – an antagonistic interaction – people experience a pervasive feeling of tension ... at higher levels of intensity ... [this tension] shades over into fear.

It is for this reason that Chapter 2 argued that emotions are an important factor in understanding fandom. Fear, anger, anxiety and tension can all contribute to violence, but it does not automatically equate to physical violence. The performances of bravado associated with masculinity are often individualised performances designed to take control of one's emotions in the context.

The main theoretical arguments of this book have centred on the performance and rituals of ultras fandom and the role emotion has within these groups. Violence is the clearest space where these aspects can be analysed. The work of Randall Collins in particular emphasises these aspects. Collins's (2008) analysis of the role of emotional energy in violent confrontations highlights that those who maintain the emotional dominance will succeed. In fact, without the correct emotional dynamics, then violence is unlikely to occur. Frequently, fear, anger and anxiety do not ensure that participants are in the correct emotional frame of mind. That said, there is a 'violent elite' (Collins, 2008) who constitute a small percentage that enjoy and thrive in violent situations. They have mastered emotional dominance and acquired strategies of draining the emotional resources of their rivals. For this reason, this chapter will reiterate the importance of emotions to matchday confrontations (and

the lack of them). It begins by distinguishing between violence associated with ultras and hooliganism, before outlining briefly the theories
of violence associated with football, particularly around hooliganism in
England. It will address the inter-group dynamics of the actual physical
confrontations that occasionally occur at football matches. Finally, it
will identify the symbolic violence of matchday choreographies and how
these both intensify the emotional energy at matches, as well as diffuse
tensions.

The difference between ultras and hooligans

Throughout this book, and particularly in Chapter 3, there have been
frequent comparisons between the English and Italian styles of fandom.
The frequency with which English fans travelled abroad in the 1980s
ensured that they took their aggressive, masculine approach to different places and confronted rival fans across Europe. It is this violent
approach, called hooliganism, that has then affected all discussion of
violence associated with football. Not all forms of spectator disorder are
hooliganism (Roversi, 1991; Mignon, 2002). As Hourcade (2002: 31)
outlines: 'Hooligans essentially seek incidents with rival hooligans or
with the police. They gather in informal gangs and often have a taste for
secrecy. On the contrary, ultras sometimes resort to violence, but they
do not focus on it. Their practice is of a larger type … the forms of these
groups are meaningful: ultras have their associations, while hooligans
merely have informal gangs'. It is important to differentiate between
violence resulting from match results or a pitch invasion, and arranged,
premeditated fights between well-organised fan groups (Hobbs and
Robbins, 1991). In this sense, hooliganism is 'the competitive violence
of socially organized fan groups in football, principally directed against
opposing fan groups' (Spaaij, 2006: 11). And as we have seen throughout this book, even though the ultras are well organised they are a very
different phenomenon to hooligans.

In the case of football-related violence, the crucial point is to distinguish certain fan practices. The ultras style can be considered quite
universal if it is understood as a unique, uncompromising style of supporting. Thus, being an ultra is a kind of lifestyle – irrespective of
the level of competition or nationality. Mostly, this *mentalita* involves
an aggressive attitude, in terms of supporting the team and insulting,
and fighting with, opposing fans. In most countries, ultras are also
responsible for the performative dimension. In some cases, there is a
clear distinction between ultras and hooligans. This is the case not only
in East-Central European countries, but also countries like Germany

or Sweden, where this distinction has developed since the formation of ultras groups in the respective countries in the 1990s. In Russia and Poland, groups of hooligans are devoted almost only to violent confrontation, and they consist of well-trained 'killing machines', fans with experience in boxing or mixed martial arts. Hooligans in these countries have undergone the process of professionalisation, and some of them compete in legal martial arts tournaments (Kossakowski, 2017c; Arnold and Veth, 2018). By contrast, in Britain it is difficult to find such a division, as for decades hooligans dominated most fan interactions and the development of an ultras style is rather modest.

This distinction should be considered while evaluating the phenomenon of violence. In the case of hooligans, especially in Europe, the tradition of arranged fights has become popular since the 1990s.[1] Ultras groups, who do not specialise in fights, are not engaged in this practice. However, ultras can also be involved in physical brawls – mostly during spontaneous situations like an attack by, or on, an opposing group while travelling to a match or near the stadium. In countries like Poland or Russia, however, it is true that 'only a small number of persons perform virtually all of the violence; this is a practical reality, known to those who are in violent situations, and it gives rise to a sense of stratification between a violent elite ... and the majority who back down from fights' (Collins, 2008: 231).

Arranged fights can be regarded as 'riot by appointment' (Johnston, 2000), but in more organised terms. Police surveillance, coupled with the illegal character of such encounters have caused hooligan groups in Europe to become specialised in 'guerrilla' strategies to mislead the police. For instance, Polish hooligans use expressions like 'rugby without a ball' (two hooligan teams attack each other in a manner bearing a vague resemblance to a rugby match) or 'mushroom picking' (many arranged fights take place in the woods) on Internet forums to confuse the police (Kossakowski, 2017b; 2017d). These kinds of violent encounters require trust between both sides and mostly take place according to pre-planned rules. The most common are an equal number of fighters on each side and a ban on the use of any tools or weapons. These rules are often locally and nationally contingent and can lead to confusion and anger when different groups follow different conventions, such as when St Etienne ultras encountered knives in Ukraine (Ginhoux, 2018). In some cases, there are also rules concerning the course of combat, such as stopping the fight when a rival lies on the ground or having both sides designate fighters of a similar age. Agreement between fighting groups is sometimes associated with a special 'honour code'. This is an unofficial norm, depending on the local context and arrangements between the competitors. This code is infused with notions of masculinity and what is considered 'noble'. There is no pride in attacking people who are not looking for a fight, families, children or women. Likewise, proceeding with a fight when a group significantly outnumbers their opponents is not considered honourable. However, different hooligan groups do not necessarily abide by these codes, as was the case in a confrontation between Russian hooligans and English fans during the Euro 2016 tournament in France. In these situations, as Collins (2008) identifies, the emotional energy of the dominant group can overpower and to ensure victory they then engage in 'forward panic', which sees the dominant individual(s) pre-empt a strike by capitalising on a perceived weakness of their opponent.

The dominance of hooliganism in academic studies

English hooliganism has dominated academic studies of football fandom. Indeed, the birth of football studies as an academic subject in the UK centred on hooliganism and violence. This, like the media coverage, has skewed the focus towards violence. Constant reminders are required that not all football fans are violent, and in particular that not all ultras are violent. It was not until the 1990s and new analyses of different type of fans that the field began to open up (Giulianotti, 1991; 1995; 2002; 2005; King, 1997a; 1998; 2003; Redhead, 1997; Sandvoss, 2003; Crawford, 2004). Scholarship on football has advanced significantly in the twenty-first century, with much of the focus examining the economic and commercial transformation of contemporary football and their impact on fandom (Cleland, 2010; 2011; Cleland *et al.*, 2018; Doidge, 2015a; Millward, 2011; 2012; and Poulton, 2014). There has been some residual focus on hooliganism that offers new insights into methodologies, media and literature analysis (Poulton, 2005; 2006; 2007; 2008; 2012a; 2012b; 2013; Redhead, 2007a; 2007b; 2007c). Most of the emphasis associated with violence at football has come from outside the UK (Spaaij, 2006; 2008; Tsoukala, 2009; Doidge, 2015a; Kossakowski, 2017b; Newson, 2017; Ginhoux, 2018), and has often been associated with the ultras.

A book on ultras is not the place for an in-depth overview of the literature on football hooliganism; this has been done much better and in greater depth elsewhere (Spaaij, 2006; Tsoukala, 2009). It is, however, useful to provide a quick overview in order to locate violence associated with ultras within the broader literature, to highlight the development of football fan studies and to reinforce the approach that centres on context, emotion and interaction. Early analyses took a Marxist approach that viewed fan violence as a consequence of working-class frustration about alienation from the commercialised game (Taylor, 1971a; 1971b). Although many ultras explicitly adopt the Against Modern Football stance, violence pre-dates this movement. Similarly, violence has become directed against the police (as we shall see later), but consumer alienation does not account for violence between groups with putatively similar anti-commercial outlooks.

Failure to control emotional impulses covers two different subsequent theories. Marsh *et al.* (1978) took a vastly different ethological approach and explained violence between fans as their inability to channel 'natural' inclinations to aggression in another way; fan violence involves 'catharsis', a ritual expression of these 'natural' instincts. They conclude that in many cases it is enough to perform an aggressive posturing or counter chanting to make the ritual of violence fulfilled. While Marsh *et al.* (1978) recognise the importance of ritual in the manifestation of violence, particularly the symbolic representations of superiority over rivals, this essentialist position fails to acknowledge how violence is learned, and that it cannot be simply reduced to animalistic drives. Not everyone engages in violence, and in some cases the performance of cho- reographies can intensify emotions towards rivals, rather than diffuse tensions, especially when external bodies (like the police) misunderstand the rituals and pre-empt violence with aggression of their own.

The 'Leicester School' draw on Eliasian theories of civilising social groups in relation to the suppression of emotions and accepted social behaviour (Dunning *et al.*, 1988; 1991; Murphy *et al.*, 1988; Williams *et al.*, 1989; Dunning, 1999). Rooted in a British class perspective, they argue that hooliganism is committed by those from the lower social strata – the 'rough' working class. They commit violence because they have not been incorporated into wider society's 'civilised' norms of conduct (Dunning *et al.*, 1988). These academics observe that violence is learned and denotes status within specific social groups. They also acknowledge the role of emotions, and highlight that violence can be pleasurable for some (Dunning, 1999). However, their focus on the pleasure of violence and its contrast with wider societal taboos under- plays the importance of other emotions like fear or anger. Also, the focus on class in Britain is not immediately transferable to other localities with different class structures or composition of ultras groups. Ultras across the globe are not necessarily all working class.

Later analyses of hooliganism have taken a more ethnographic approach that has provided key insights into context, interactions and the situational dynamics of confrontations (Armstrong and Harris, 1991; King, 1997a, 2001; Armstrong, 1998; Spaaij, 2006; 2008; Pearson,

2012; Doidge, 2015a; Ginhoux, 2018). One of the most significant developments in understanding hooliganism has come from social psychology, and applying social identity theory (Stott and Reicher, 1998; Stott *et al.*, 2001; Stott and Pearson 2007; Van Hiel *et al.*, 2007), and more latterly, fusion theory (Newson, 2017). The former work identifies the importance of intra-group and inter-group dynamics, particularly in relation to the role the police play in unifying a group of fans. If the police treat all fans as violent, then the group invariably unify as 'fans' against the 'police' (Stott and Reicher, 1998; Stott *et al.*, 2001; Stott and Pearson, 2007). In some cases, this newly unified group look to experienced hooligans to defend them (Stott and Reicher, 1998). This is not a process of deindividualisation; instead, people in the group reorient themselves towards shared group values and norms. 'Thus, it could be argued that group violence often reflects the operation of specific group norms, rather than being a sign of deregulation of conduct into thoughtless and aimless behaviour' (Van Hiel *et al.*, 2007: 173). In extreme cases, people in such situations are likely to experience a 'fusion identity', when the feeling of oneness with the group leads to pro-group actions (also willingness to fight for the group). It is clearly visible in football fan groups, particularly in hooligan ones, where the level of cohesion and solidarity is particularly high (Newson, 2017; Besta and Kossakowski, 2018; Kossakowski and Besta, 2018).

As outlined in the introduction to this chapter, the work of Randall Collins reiterated the importance of focusing on situations. Acts of violence are quite rare and typically short-lived. Consequently, most people try to avoid violent conflicts. 'In reality, most serious fights on the individual or small-group level are extremely short. If we cut out the preliminaries and the aftermath, with their insults, noise, and gesturing, and look only at the violence, it is often remarkably brief' (Collins, 2008: 14). Ethnographic accounts of violence associated with football support this – they generally last from several seconds to a few minutes (Armstrong, 1998). Discussions about the confrontation often last longer than the fight itself (King, 2001). By looking at the complete situation rather than the sporadic images on social media or television, the researcher gets a fuller understanding of the incident. It is for this reason that Collins (2008: 1) argues that any analysis of violence requires that the researcher should 'put the interaction in the centre of the analysis, not the individual, the social background, the culture, or even the motivation: that is to say, look for the characteristics of violent situations'.

By putting the interaction at the centre, we can begin to see the key foci for the behaviours. As outlined in chapters 1 and 2, social life is repetitive and this ensures that our behaviours are enacted habitually. Over time, these behaviours become ingrained and the individual can feel that they have some control in the situation. When placed in unfamiliar situations, individuals can feel anxious or fearful. One way of coping with those feelings is through acting a role. Anderson (1999) highlighted how in inner city America there was a 'code of the street', where trust in State authorities had eroded and men, specifically African American men, had to perform a type of masculinity of 'hardness' to suggest to others that they may be met with violence. This symbolic performance will be dealt with later in the chapter, but these behaviours are learned over time. This is not about an uncivilised 'rump', as Dunning *et al.* (1988) suggest hooligans are. Those who have engaged in violence regularly come to embody coolness in potentially violent situations (Contreras, 2018). Just as Wacquant (2004) observes how the boxer goes through a bodily apprenticeship before being allowed into the ring, the street fighter will have honed their skills over many interactions. It is for this reason that some ultras groups engage in 'mock fights' to initiate younger members into the group and to hone their skills for real confrontations. It takes time for ultras to 'learn to master the codes and the requirements of the "confrontational culture"' (Ginhoux, 2018: 843).

For Collins (2008), control of the emotional energy in the situation determines whether the conflict is diffused, or the relative success and failure of the assailants. Ultras culture is one that valorises 'the possession of this rare quality that is the ability to exert an emotional domination' (Bouton, 2011). Those who have mastered the 'confrontational culture' (Ginhoux, 2018) are those that gain a reputation for violence, maybe even of enjoying it (Spaaij, 2006). This 'violent elite' has learned the strategies, words and actions that allow them to dominate the situation and sap the emotional energy of the other side. In reality, this is about heightening fear, anxiety or panic in their rivals, which clouds their emotional judgement and leads to errors or weakness. One such strategy is 'forward panic' (Collins, 2008). Those enacting this strategy are the 'first line' (Ginhoux, 2018) who are the most skilful fighters and become the focal point of the confrontation. They are the ones who know when to attack and command the emotional space of the confrontation. They also attract the attention of police 'spotters' and rival groups who are observing them to see whether they are willing to engage.

The other crucial aspect of Collins's analysis relates to the role of the audience. Flashpoints often ignite violent conflicts. Preceding these flashpoints are ritualistic performances that ensure that participants save face and take control of their emotions. The audience can intensify and magnify the emotion within the situation. This can intensify the likelihood of violence, especially when police are involved: 'the more officers are called to the scene, the greater the chance of a forward panic or other kinds of police violence, quite apart from what the suspect does' (Collins, 2008: 464). The audience (and participants) can also reduce 'confrontational tension' (Collins, 2008). Without encouragement from bystanders, the emotional intensity does not increase, limiting the chances of a flashpoint. Similarly, the violent elite can also play a part. As experts in managing their emotions in these situations, they can read situations and diffuse tension (Contreras, 2018).

The police play a crucial role in predicting whether violence could ensue with ultras. When the police treat all fans as potential hooligans, this can temporarily unite all football fans (Stott and Reicher, 1998; Stott and Pearson, 2007). This treatment often begins far from the stadium. For example, in Italy the police division that is tasked with observing and controlling the ultras is the Digos, which also deals with terrorism and organised crime. As Ferreri (2008: 100–101) argues, the allocation of this remit symbolically shifted the public image of the ultras as 'they ceased to be simply hooligans from the stadium and were transformed into a subversive phenomenon, that needed repression with force'. The whole police operation at matches helps stoke the emotions of the crowd:

> The entire operation creates an overwhelming image of force and control and increases the tension and emotion of the situation ... the presentation of force at away games is potent. Not only does it criminalize all fans; it can present an altogether different image. Armoured police and carabinieri confront fans, while helicopters circle overhead. It feels like a war zone. This analogy reinforces the notion of a lack of legitimacy. It suggests that the authorities are an occupying force which has not won the 'hearts and minds' of the people they are supposed to be protecting. It also strengthens the suggestion that the police and fans are enemies. The police are acting not as intermediaries but as adversaries, and this provides ample opportunity for forward panic and potential violence. (Doidge, 2015a: 133–134)

This can then be exacerbated at the scene by perceived unfair policing practices (supporting local fans over away fans) or indiscriminate use of force. In fact, it can embolden the hooligans who become the defenders of the group, and they channel the fear and anxiety of those unused to violence into forward panic to liberate the group (Stott and Reicher, 1998). The potential for violence is increased because the police see the fans as potentially violent so strike first, which unites all the fans, or the violent elite sense their opportunity and engage in forward panic (Doidge, 2015a). It should be reiterated that, despite this, violence remains very rare.

The audience is also important for two other reasons. One is about substantiating the events to those who were not there and extending the emotional high of the victors. As Katz (1999) observed in relation to road rage, an audience after the event does not necessarily understand the situation, as their emotional engagement with it is vastly different. Audience members are needed 'to relive those violent encounters and elongate [the] emotional high [of the perpetrators]' (Contreras, 2018: 43). The other is to contribute to the collective memory of the group (King, 2001; Ginhoux, 2018). This contributes to their history and whether future confrontations will escalate or diffuse. These memories become reified in the history of groups, and hardened thanks to social media. The images become totemic symbols representing the group and reinforcing the feelings of love and solidarity produced.

The changing context of football violence

As Collins (2008) argues, it is important to focus on the whole situation, not just the usually short-lived violent conflict. Pulling back from the conflict itself, we can start to look at wider historical and social factors that can contribute to clashes between groups. With fan groups, there are longstanding rivalries and histories that add to the matchday ritual. Previous confrontational interactions can feed a narrative that effectively invents the tradition of rivalry between groups and can transcend temporalities. For example, the rivalry in the Soweto derby in Johannesburg between Kaizer Chiefs and Orlando Pirates stems from the former's perception of their own social and cultural superiority and the latter's perception that they are snobs. These antagonisms are taken into confrontations and fuel the emotions of the situation. Such conflicts are more pronounced in city derbies, but can exist over wider geographical areas, such as Fiorentina's hatred of Juventus, who are based 400 km from Florence in Turin, which stems from the 'theft' of the 1981 Italian championship (Foot, 2006).

Willingness to fight for the club is considered an essence of being a masculine fan in many countries. Violence can come from strong identification with the club (Hourcade, 2008; Newson, 2017) as a group seeks to assert their superiority and power. Fans from opposing clubs can treat rivalry as a way of gaining supremacy (regional, moral, physical), and physical violence can be a symbol of prestige or dignity (Armstrong and Harris, 1991). Through violent competition, fans from one club can gain a feeling of power and a reason for humiliating the defeated. Although most ultras fights are spontaneous, they still draw on specific practices, traditions and identities. Those who engage in violence have to learn to control the emotional space, and that comes with experience. In Argentina, '[f]istfights that come to blows are common in the contexts of socialization of the members of the hinchada. In everyday life, many conflicts are resolved in this way. Clashes are daily and common' (Moreira *et al.*, 2017: 67). Through practice, the group learn how to dominate their opponents, spot weaknesses and gain victory.

Even though face-to-face violence is rare, there have unfortunately been deaths associated with football. The first such in Italy occurred on 28 October 1979 when a firework fatally wounded a Lazio fan (Foot, 2006; Doidge, 2015a), although this did not stem from violence. The 1985 Heysel tragedy, in which thirty-nine Juventus fans were killed when Liverpool hooligans rushed at them and a wall collapsed crushing many underneath, was a landmark in European football. Meanwhile, a violent clash in 2012 between the Egyptian ultras of Al Masry and Al Ahly led to seventy-four people being killed and over five hundred injured. Often, these have the hallmarks of forward panic, where one group senses superiority and rushes forward to assert their advantage. More rarely, fatalities occur through face-to-face conflict. The mimetic aspect of ultras confrontations tends to ensure that weapons are not permitted, although (as noted earlier) Vincenzo Spagnolo, a Genoa fan, was stabbed to death by an AC Milan ultra in 1995, and the Napoli ultra Ciro Esposito was shot by a Romanista before the 2014 Italian Cup Final. In August 2018, after the derby between Persitara Jakarta Utara and ABC Wirayuda in Indonesia, a violent street clash in which knives were used resulted in the deaths of two fans. These situations only occur when certain fans endeavour to defeat their rivals at any cost, including through the use of dangerous weapons like guns (Archetti and Romero, 1994). Often these groups are quasi-criminal gangs who use their organisation to engage in other criminal activities such as drug trafficking. In Argentina the biggest fan groups have structures similar to organised crime gangs and many of their members are engaged in mafia-related activities. In the 1990s the organisation called *La 12*, established by Boca Juniors *barra bravas*, was recognised by a judge as a cover for illegal business (Grabia, 2011). Violence and death become ways of protecting their other activities.

As outlined in Chapter 3, many groups go through a period of fragmentation as younger members come along, often with different outlooks or influences. Football fans are not homogeneous, and even though the ultras make a great effort to present themselves as one coherent whole, there are constant power struggles as various groups try to assert their dominance over the terrace. Occasionally, these intra-group conflicts can turn violent as the dominant masculine groups resort to physical means in order to assert themselves. At PSG, members of the *Boulogne Boys* have long been associated with the far right and have engaged in racism at matches as well as following a more English hooligan style. In contrast, members of *Supras Auteuil* were known as an anti-fascist group at the club and adopted the ultras style. In 2010 'Yann L', a member of the *Boulogne Boys*, was assaulted by members of *Supras Auteuil* and subsequently died after a period in a coma. These conflicts have occurred in many political terraces. This is atypical in Eastern Europe as many of the groups eschew leftist politics. Despite this, there have been clashes between ideological factions among the ultras at Polonia Warsaw.

Despite the above descriptions of the more shocking incidents, it must be reiterated that deaths and physical violence are rare at football matches. Much of the violence is symbolic and this is reiterated through the tradition of stealing rivals' symbols, such as scarves, flags and other important icons. Snatching flags and scarves is not just about the physical loss, but the symbolic loss of honour. For instance, when the ultras of Grasshoppers Zurich took two flags belonging to the *Anthrax* group who follow FC Zurich, the latter group were disbanded. Fans of Śląsk Wrocław in Poland have been affected more dramatically. After they lost their flags in Seville before a Europa League match in 2013, the entire supporters' association that brought together all fans of Śląsk, including the ultras, was dissolved. These traditions are wrapped up in notions of masculine honour and bestow prestige on the individual claiming the spoils of conflict (Moreira *et al.*, 2017).

Supporting a football team is an emotional experience. For the ultras, this is more intense as they invest passionately in the rituals of the stadium and build up to games over days and weeks. As they participate in their own rituals, the events on the pitch are not the main driver of emotional fulfilment and, consequently, are not often likely to contribute to violence:

> Losing a game is generally emotionally deflating, and the crowd lacks the ebullience and the traditional rituals (such as tearing down goal posts), which can segue from a victory celebration into a destructive riot ... Defeat riots depend more on features extraneous to the game, since the emotional flow of the game itself will generally de-energize the defeated and energize the victors. (Collins, 2008: 312)

This is only partially true, as sometimes the extraneous factors are related to the team's relative standing in the league hierarchy. Relegation or missing out on a championship can arouse extreme emotions and even violence. In 2006 some fans of FC Basel attacked the players of FC Zurich after their team lost a decisive match for the Swiss league title. In 2012, meanwhile, the referee had to terminate a match between FC Köln and Bayern Munich in which the visitors were winning 4–1. Ultras of the host club set off so many flares that smoke completely engulfed the playing field. The ultras then invaded the pitch and clashed with the police as they expressed their anger about their team's impending relegation (Honigstein, 2012). Post-event instances of disorder are called 'expressive' as they stem from the high-level emotional state of triumph or suffering (Mann, 1989). For many fans, victory or defeat is something more, something connected to their sense of honour and identity. 'Militant fans', Archetti and Romero (1994: 38) argue, 'are *a priori* unable to convert disappointment brought on by the defeat of their team into praise for the opposing team and respect for its fans. Instead, physical force intended to injure, wound or destroy the adversary is the central element in acts of violence perpetrated by militant fans.' These fans seek to gain control of their emotions through externalising their anger towards the victors.

The police have become one of the most frequent targets for violence by ultras. Conflict occurs for two reasons. One arises in much the same way with other groups. Previous confrontations are woven into the narratives of the group and certain police forces become targets. Long histories of conflicts with police have helped create an anti-police narrative across Europe (Doidge, 2015a). The manifestations of this 'ACAB syndrome' (Stefanini, 2009; Doidge, 2015a) can be witnessed on T-shirts, banners, stickers and graffiti across the world. This 'All Cops Are Bastards' narrative feeds into violent situations by adding extra emotions into potential conflicts. Many ultras will see the police as enemies, based on ACAB syndrome or from past experience, and be more ready to engage in forward panic to pre-empt violence by the police (Doidge, 2015a). This is enhanced through sanctifying the victims of police violence, such as the banner declaring '*Giustizia per Paolo*' ('Justice for Paolo') that is dedicated to a Brescia ultra who became disabled after police physicality. Similarly, the message '*Speziale Libero*' ('Free Speziale') has been displayed across Italy, and also at Borussia Dortmund and Bayern Munich, calling for the release of Antonio Speziale, who was imprisoned following the death of a policeman in a riot after the Sicilian derby in 2007. Similarly, Eintracht Frankfurt ultras demonstrated their disdain for the police by stealing a police banner and displaying it upside down in 2019. These tropes unite rival ultras groups in common opposition to the authorities.

Interactions between police and fans can act as the ritual focus of fans' collective spirit and identity. As outlined earlier, when police are seen to be acting illegitimately this can temporarily unite all fans (Stott and

Reicher, 1998; Stott *et al.*, 2001; Stott and Pearson, 2007). In Mexico, for example, incidents of violence targeted at the police have become more common (Magazine and González, 2017). Police repression is justified through the media construction of the violent fan folk devil. As was detailed in the Chapter 3, the ultras' expertise at fighting the police has been very useful in specific political protests. At the Gezi Park protest in 2013, there was an unprecedented example of cooperation between ultras of three rival Istanbul clubs – Beşiktaş, Fenerbahçe and Galatasaray (Göksoy and Yilmaz, 2017). In Cairo, ultras of Al Ahly and Zamalek effectively became the armed wing of the Egyptian revolution in 2011 as part of the Arab Spring. Similarly, protests against police violence, as well as the country's political situation, united Ukrainian ultras who played an active part in the Euromaidan demonstrations in 2013 (Krugliak and Krugliak, 2017). Ultras are one of the few social groups who regularly encounter police and have developed strategies to evade, confront and challenge them. As with other forms of violence, through regular practice the individuals and groups become better able to handle the emotional cauldron of conflict.

Conflict with the police also occurs as they represent authority, law and State control. As clubs, leagues, football associations and governments seek to curb the excesses of the ultras, greater regulation has been imposed. Therefore, the police symbolise the repression of the ultras style of fandom. More importantly, they physically represent the enforcement of laws and regulations that the ultras see as illegitimate. For example, in 2011 members of the *Green Brigade* at Celtic launched a campaign called Fans Against Criminalisation, which mostly related to the Offensive Behaviour at Football and Threatening Communications (Scotland) Act 2012 that sought to criminalise certain aspects of fan behaviour. The police became the key focus in this campaign, as the organisers of Fans Against Criminalisation declared:

> We also entirely reject the notion that laws should be based on something as ridiculously ambiguous as offensiveness. This term is being used in this context as a catch-all to ensure that the police have almost limitless powers when it comes to using this act to criminalise and harass football fans. Equally pertinently, we object to being told when and where our rights to hold and express a political opinion can be applied, and this is an issue which should concern the public at large. (FAC, n.d.)

A campaign like this does not have to induce violent actions but rather serves as a platform for expressing discontent and civil disobedience. Such campaigns also provide a ritual focus for the activities of the groups and fuel their mobilisations.

Symbolic and performative violence

One of the central dynamics of football fandom is rivalries and attendant antagonistic conflict. Chapter 2 outlined the importance of rituals and emotion to denote who is part of the group and who is an outsider. In the joy of victory and despair of defeat, those emotions clearly delineate the two rival groups. Archetti (2001: 154) observes that, 'no identity can ever exist by itself and without an array of opposites, negatives and contradictions'. For many ultras, this relationship with fans of rival teams is characterised by very dramatic markers of distinction, despite the many similar practices, rituals and tropes they share. As Chapter 3 observed, supporters draw on various fan cultures, notably English and Italian, as well as localised histories and traditions to differentiate themselves. De Biasi and Lanfranchi (1997) call this the 'importance of difference'. Frequently, this is manifested in terms of the matchday performance of chants, gestures and choreographies.

It is within these matchday performances that a symbolic form of violence takes place. The anthropologist Allen Feldman (1991) identified in Northern Ireland that violence was not restricted to physical but also performative forms. Violence was enacted by individuals and groups through a variety of staged, symbolic acts to create a public and powerful political narrative which expressed political protest while also stoking fear in opponents and the wider public. In terms of the ultras, as we have seen throughout this book, their performance helps produce their own sense of self-identity while presenting the same to a wider audience. Part of this presentation of self is focused on domination and superiority of rivals. In many 'sanitised' societies,

> the non-violent expression of hot rivalry and opposition enlivens the football spectacle. On a broad level, the word rivalry brings with it thoughts and ideologies of conflict, domination, power and struggle ... which could be viewed in opposition to the functionalist ideals of what is often associated with modern sports. Therefore, it must be acknowledged that rivalries have both many negative and positive features. (Benkwitz and Molnar, 2012: 483)

The rituals of the stadium can both infuse and diffuse emotional tension. In some cases, the choreographies are a way for the collective to take control of their emotions and diffuse the anxiety and tension they feel. In other cases, the rituals can intensify the emotion. Football rivalries provide excitement and a high level of emotions for individuals and groups. In addition, many of the matchday rituals are about asserting the status of the group and engaging in performative violence, as this section will outline.

Performative violence is highly ritualistic. As outlined earlier, much of the violence associated with football comprises of chants, gestures and items being thrown. Actual physical violence is very rare. As Armstrong (1998) demonstrates, in some cases fighting groups only seek to put on a performance in front of the opposing side. They create a very loud atmosphere, full of offensive and threatening words, but in fact they await interruption by the police. This happens because a violent confrontation is only one part of the story, the other being the narrative connected with violence. Unlike hooligans, who seek to avoid the public gaze, ultras want to be conspicuous. This creates a symbolic representation of violence.

> First, during a football match every group fights to impose its symbolic strength in terms of the beauty and impressiveness of the choreography (flags, choruses and songs) and in terms of displaying courage (to steal in front of all other fans the enemy's flags, scarves, or even hats is considered by the youngest ultras the noblest of group activities). Second, every group, before or after the match, regards the end, the stadium and the open spaces surrounding the stadium (including underground stations, railway stations and so on) as its exclusive territory to be defended against the enemy's raids. (Dal Lago and De Biasi, 1994: 85–86)

In the case of the performative violence of the ultras, there are two key spaces: the stadium and public space approaching the stadium. Each of these ritual spaces becomes an arena where the symbols of the opposition are to be dominated, desecrated and defiled, while the symbolic power of the group is reified. These kinds of acts can lead to violent disorder as they are highly provocative, but mostly they serve as a substitute for real, physical fights. Thus, they are a very popular way of showing power in the context of fan rivalries.

The clearest example of performative violence is the extremely visible, and sometimes aesthetically impressive, choreographies. There are many violent tropes that are incorporated into these choreographies, from violent language, images of violence, strength and power to references to local history and the domination of one club over the other. Violent phrases are crucial for the formation of collective identity. Sometimes, they are just written on small banners held aloft by a few people, while others can cover the entire stand. The language presented by Legia Warsaw ultras that declared 'Ultras – We hate everyone' makes a clear statement of intent to others, particularly the authorities. The word 'hate' also appeared on a spectacular choreography by Hapoel Tel Aviv ultras who declared, 'We are driven by pure hate'. This was complemented by the figure of notorious movie cannibal Hannibal Lecter to symbolise the sociopathic tendencies of the group. *Elephant Army* of the Malaysian club Pahang exhibit a similarly uncompromising attitude: during one match they presented a large choreography depicting a black monster with red eyes and the motto 'We give you nightmare [*sic*]' written in English, reiterating that this was for a global audience.

Masculine imagery is frequently used to emphasise the strength and power of one group over its weaker (and feminised) opponents. This is more prevalent in countries where the ultras culture is interwoven with a hooligan one. Many choreographies present symbols of physical combat such as fists, muscles or the figure of a fighter ready to brawl. As mentioned in Chapter 5, Olympiacos ultras group *Gate 7* once unveiled a massive choreography depicting Muhammad Ali's famous victory over Sonny Liston, warning that they would 'knock out' their rivals. On the occasion of their former captain Steven Dufor returning to the stadium playing for their rivals Anderlecht, Standard Liege ultras presented a banner showing *Friday the 13th* villain Jason Voorhees holding the decapitated head of Dufor alongside the words (again in English) 'Red or Dead', referencing the colours of Standard. Undoubtedly, these symbolic pictures of readiness for violence and subsequent victory support the masculine character of ultras identity (Antonowicz *et al.*, 2018).

This masculine imagery is linked to notions of local patriotism around territory, particularly around which local rival has the rights to claim the city as theirs. As Ginhoux (2012) shows, ultras develop 'urban patriotism' and use many tools of communication, such as flags and banners, to present attachment to and love of the community and city. Doidge (2015a) identifies the Italian concept of *campanilismo*, which symbolises the love of one's city, and how this is depicted in ultras choreographies. At the 2011 Genoa derby, for example, the Genoa CFC ultras' choreography depicted a panorama of the city, with a griffin (the symbol of the club) firing a cannon at a sailor in Sampdoria's colours, accompanied by the motif 'The city does not want you … go from Genoa, Samp' (Doidge, 2015a). Elsewhere, in 2012 ultras from FK Sarajevo presented a banner reading '*Jedan Grad Jedan Klub*' ('One city one club') during the derby match against FK Zeljeznicar. During the Hamburg derby in March 2019, meanwhile, Hamburg ultras displayed a banner saying 'Our city and its club', while their St Pauli counterparts displayed a huge tifo stating 'Hamburg is brown and white'. In each case, the ultras propagated the vision that only one group can be entitled 'owners' of the city.

With the extreme focus on the locality, the city becomes a small 'mother country' (Podaliri and Balestri, 1998). This link to territory and masculinity also sees the incorporation of militaristic language. This is clearly depicted in the names of the groups, like the *Brigate Gialloblu* ('Yellow-blue Brigades') at Hellas Verona or *Elephant Army* at Pahang in Malaysia. In some cases, like the *Irriducibili* at Lazio, their name means 'steadfast' or 'indefatigable', inferring their resolute defence of the province. Lechia Gdańsk ultras are called the 'Lords of the North' to symbolise their territory. Links to the nation and monarchy are also incorporated. During the Madrid derby in 2008, *Ultras Sur* unveiled a choreography depicting a Nordic king seated upon a throne accompanied by two wolves and two ravens (Viersa, 2010). The Nordic theme was reinforced by runic symbols surrounding the image and the legend *'huestes a vencer'* ('Victory to the hosts') in a Gothic font. While this regal image portrays masculine control of a territory (a kingdom), the semiotics of a Nordic king in Iberia seem misplaced. The nuance is that the use of Nordic imagery denotes far-right and nationalist sympathies, themes which feature in many of the tifos of ultras in Eastern Europe. This Nordic imagery has also been adopted in Indonesia by one group, Persib Badung group *Viking Persib* who formed in 1993. Again, the masculine berserker style symbolises the never-say-die image that ultras want to present. This was reflected in a *Viking Persib* tifo against Persilja Jakarta in September 2018 when they depicted axe-wielding Vikings descending in longboats and attacking their rivals.

This nationalist defence of territory was clearly depicted during the summer of 2015 when Europe faced the largest mass migration of people since the Second World War. While some fans, particularly in Greece, Germany and the UK raised banners proclaiming 'Refugees Welcome', in Central and Eastern Europe banners and choreographies were clearly saying the opposite. As mentioned in Chapter 3, ultras at FK Jablonec in the Czech Republic raised a banner with a pig-faced Muslim being kicked back to Turkey by a blonde-haired white woman called Europa. In the same league, Viktoria Plzeň ultras raised a banner saying (in English) 'Europe wake up' alongside a graphic image of a blood-splattered, well-muscled, topless male wielding a large axe over a man wearing symbolic Muslim clothing and climbing out of a hole in the earth. These fans are clearly suggesting that refugees from Syria face a violent reception if they encroach on their territory.

Performative violence is not restricted to the imagery used in choreographies and banners at matches. The ultras repertoire uses chants and other verbal sounds, like musical instruments and pyrotechnics, to reinforce their symbolic domination. Many ultras use drums that raise the atmosphere, rhythm and level of emotion at a match. The sound of drums introduces the battle mood, evoking as it does images of historical warfare. Where once it provided the beat that soldiers marched to, it now generates the rhythm of the chants of hundreds or thousands of supporters. Sometimes, the banging of drums accompanies clapping or waving of the fists. All these gestures and sounds are used to sound and look impressively pugnacious. The following passage from a *Guardian* newspaper article illustrates how the journalist saw their contribution to the atmosphere at Borussia Dortmund:

> After a rousing rendition of You'll Never Walk Alone, long ago appropriated from Merseyside, the ultras facing the crowd at the bottom started banging their drums and the wall looked as insurmountable as ever. Banners were unveiled, complaining about the re-scheduling of the match: '6:45 kick-off: are you kidding? Fuck Uefa.' Supporters of French club Monaco, whose regular home game attendance is less than half of the capacity of Dortmund's southern terrace, looked briefly intimidated. (Oltermann, 2017)

Here, Borussia Dortmund ultras expressed their discontent at UEFA's decision to reschedule their match with AS Monaco the day after a terrorist attack had targeted the official team bus. The drums maintained the sombre emotions in the stadium, and the fans sought to intimidate those around, particularly the opposing players.

Militaristic chants have been incorporated into the repertoire of some ultras groups. Military music and songs are designed to build group cohesion and rhythm to ensure the battalion keeps to the same pace. It also functions as an emotional focus which brings the collective together, reinforces the dichotomy between 'we' and 'them', and valorises the locality or nation (Clark, 2006). At Beşiktaş, fans incorporated a military march into their chants:

> The rearticulation of marches into terrace songs seems to capture the embodied experiences of community, defence and strength. The national ethos of the marches is diminished, although the feeling of devotion towards the songs' objects, 'from cradle to the grave', prevails. The reasons for the popularity of marches can also be traced down to the history of football in Turkey, where the game has strong nationalistic connotations. (Kytö, 2011: 83)

Songs and chants serve as symbolic, discursive tools for arousing emotions related to war and desire (real or metaphoric) in order to kill enemies. The performative violence of chants can be seen in the song of Independiente ultras in Argentina who declare that 'we will kill one "bostero" [a derogatory terms for Boca Juniors' fans], a chicken [River Plate fan] and a "botón" [police officer]'(Moreira *et al.*, 2017: 65).

As noted earlier, the performative violence of the ultras is not restricted to the stadium. Ultras are about conspicuous display, so they visibly occupy public space, particularly on their way to the stadium. When groups of ultras march from their meeting point to the stadium, they create an impression of an incoming army. They walk in step with the accompaniment of loud chants, clenched fists, flags, banners and burning flares. They seek to intimidate observers as they present their symbolic power, feeling of unity and strength. As many hooligan memoirs published by 'retired' fighters demonstrate, turning up away from home, in numbers and with members walking together in formation was a way of performing the group's uniqueness in front of other fans, media or bystanders (Pennant, 2003).

The performative aspects of violence are not restricted to external audiences. As Chapter 3 argued, the narration of tifos and conflicts help construct the history of each group. King (2001) emphasises how hooligans care about the narrative side and their reputation as violent fighters. While the fight itself takes only a short moment, the story about it can develop at great length. For many fighters, symbolic narratives serve as a tool for building identity as well as respect. One of the most humiliating things that can happen in such a case is someone else presenting an account that portrays the storyteller as a weak fighter or coward. These discourses and narratives become a ritualistic focus of the group. They serve to reinforce the collective memory and collective identity, and to construct a historical mythology.

Social media also helps create the ritual focus for ultras groups. Images, in particular, become a powerful tool for presenting a group's values and identity. In ultras culture, visual and performative aspects of actions have played a crucial role since the movement's inception in the 1960s. Today, choreographies gain even more significance as all stadium spectacles can be broadcast in various media. Tifos are usually dedicated to supporting the ultras' own team, but the performative violence of the images seeks to assert the group's domination, while also denigrating their opponents. As Collins (2008) argues, the weakness of an opponent can strengthen the emotional energy of the group. These symbols heighten the emotional arousal of the collective and generate stronger feelings of belonging. It can also lead to frenzied excitement as the more powerful group devastates the opponent. This can be symbolically demonstrated in a large choreographies such as the one by Union Berlin ultras for their match against Dynamo Dresden in 2007 which depicted a large bear (the symbol of the city of Berlin), wearing Union's home jersey and a red and white scarf, savaging some lions (the symbol of Dynamo). The presentation was complemented by a slogan (in German) reading 'If a lion will invade our ground, it has to reckon with revenge'.

Local symbols conflate with those of the club to symbolise the superiority of the group, team and locality.

Conclusion

Despite the rarity of violence at football, the popular folk devil of the violent football fan persists. Consequently, new legislation, stricter policing and new stadium architecture continue to be introduced to try to prevent violent acts of any kind. The actions of external actors have had a direct impact on ultras culture. State authorities have introduced new legislative initiatives, such as harsher penalties for offences relating to behaviour at football matches (rules that do not apply to other sports). The police presence at matches has been increased, and some football authorities, such as UEFA, now require clubs to have all-seated stadiums if they are to participate in their competitions, which has made it more difficult for ultras to prepare choreographies. Additionally, the authorities in many countries have implemented extraordinary legal acts not only to prevent violent acts but also basically to create the legal and discursive space which frames some behaviours as illegal, violent or offensive. Although in many cases reliable rules are necessary, it is also possible to see how inadequate implementation of these rules, as well as a lack of dialogue in the drafting of these rules, will be seen as a significant intrusion into ultras culture, their freedom of speech or even infringing their human rights (Tsoukala, 2009; Giulianotti, 2011). Paradoxically, these actions have only emboldened ultras and reinforced their collective sense of identity. This ties in with the Against Modern Football movement, as will be discussed in the next chapter.

Yet football is a space for many different types of fan and many do not want to be involved in the physical or symbolic violence associated with the ultras. The challenge is how to create a space where all fans can enjoy the game while still respecting each other's differences, their right to express their identity and sense of belonging. The ultras could be more reflective and take a leading role as they pride themselves on contributing the atmosphere at matches. Sometimes this reflection has resulted from the 'moral shock' of a death, such as in Genoa in 1995 when Vincenzo Spagnolo was stabbed to death. Ultras from various groups across the country subsequently joined forces to established shared rules. Meanwhile, ultras have also joined forces in the face of police repression to resist the militarisation of the stadiums, particularly after Lazio supporter Gabrielle Sandri was killed by a police officer in 2007 (Doidge, 2015a). In Spain, two events at Espanyol – the deaths of a fan in a fight in 1991 and a 13-year old boy who was hit by a flare at a game against Cadiz in 1992 – also saw a period of reflection from the ultras and a change in behaviour. 'In the aftermath of these tragic events a significant change occurred in the violence provoked by the ultras, slowly developing towards a less physical and more ritual element within the ultra movement' (Spaaij and Viñas, 2005: 88). The memories of events like Heysel or Port Said should be one of the most important precautions that even though football is a deadly serious game for millions, rivalry need not be expressed through violence.

Fan cooperation is the way to embolden fans against the coordinated work of the State, governing bodies, media and police. In Mexico, fans from different clubs initiated the Movement of United Mexican Supporters in 2014, and the body adopted the motto 'No to violence in football stadiums' (Magazine and González, 2017: 102). Fans tried to commence a dialogue with many actors, from the police to the governing bodies. In Poland, meanwhile, cooperation between the football association, Ministry of Sport and Tourism, local councils and supporters' associations resulted in the launch of the Supporters United programme, operating in eighteen cities and dedicated to developing cultural and considerate ways of supporting football (Kossakowski, 2017d; Kossakowski and Bieszke, 2017). In Rio de Janeiro, supporters of six football clubs created the Federation of Rio de Janeiro Organised Football Supporter Clubs (FTORJ) in partnership with Ministry of Sports. FTORJ was founded in a hostile environment of rivalry saturated with 'a strong surge of conflicts and deaths among rival group members' (Hollanda and Teixeira, 2017: 90). Fans around the world need to work together to present their culture and interests and have a say in any legislation that affects them.

Authorities also need to understand fan culture and diffuse emotionally charged situations. The police in particular need to understand how to diffuse flashpoints and recognise that most confrontation is ritualistic and symbolic. Identifying the 'violent elite' in a conflict situation will minimise the likelihood of the rest of the fans identifying with that small group and exacerbating the situation. Authorities also need to recognise that working against the ultras, rather than with them, will only stoke up anger and resentment long before these passionate fans come to the stadium. These narratives help give the groups meaning and reinforce their unity. Many groups are fragmented, but having a ritual focus brings them together. This is the team, but it can also be narratives of fandom, particularly masculine traditions of territory, autonomy and honour. Challenging these, without dialogue, has simply entrenched the ultras mentality.

Note

1 Hooligan gangs from Germany, Denmark, France, Spain, the Czech Republic, Switzerland and the Balkans have been known to fight arranged 'battles', with many documented on fans' websites. Examples include a Danish case: http://cphpost.dk/news/danish-forest-fighting-hooligans-pining-for-legitimacy.html; an arranged fight between German and Danish hooligans: https://hooliganstv.com/arrange-fight-brondby-vs-dortmund-koln-18-06-2017/; an arranged fight in Spain: https://the18.com/soccer-news/real-madrid-hooligans-vs-malaga-ultras (all accessed 21 April 2019). These examples from different countries demonstrate that more and more hooligans are becoming engaged in a more 'professional' style of violence.

7

Ultras and politics

German football fans are at war with their football association (DFB) and national league (DFL). At least that is the image that *Ultras Dynamo* of Dynamo Dresden wanted to portray. On 14 May 2017 Dresden ultras sported military fatigues and marched to Karlsruher's Wildparkstadion to 'declare war' on the DFB. This was not a unique event. There were regular protests against the DFB and DFL throughout the 2017–18 season. Two in particular were directed at how the game was played, with ultras contesting the use of VAR and the introduction of Monday night football, a move which would impact on fans' ability to attend games. Further protests were held at the Champions League semi-final between Bayern Munich and Real Madrid in April 2017, as well as street protests away from matches. Munich fans were protesting Bavaria's proposed introduction of the *Polizeiaufgabengesetz* (PAG) to extend police powers to intercept phone calls and text messages, issue preventative banning orders and twenty-eight-day detention for those suspected of violence. Each of these powers target football fans only and represent a considerable infringement of human rights. At the end of the season, similar protests erupted as the region of North Rhine-Westphalia sought to introduce similar laws. Fans and ultras of Borussia Dortmund, Fortuna Düsseldorf and FC Köln joined forces in a protest on 7 July 2018 in Düsseldorf to challenge PAG. These protests continued into the 2018–19 season with ultras from Arminia Bielefeld displaying banners declaring '*Polizeigesetz NRW Stoppen*' ('Stop the NRW police law'); similar actions took place at Essen and Aachen. Social media helped promote these protests, particularly through the hashtag #NoPolGNRW.

These were not the only protests flourishing at the time. In August 2018, fans from across many different clubs all agreed to have a coordinated silence in all games. Chanting and clapping, the key elements of fan culture, were stopped for the weekend. At Borussia Dortmund, as in stadiums across the country, ultras unveiled a banner declaring '*DFB, DFL & CO Ihr werdet von uns hören oder auch nicht...*' ('DFB, DFL and co. You will hear from us or not...'). This protest was sparked after a delegation of fans from different clubs (including *Harlekins Berlin* of Hertha, *Block-U* of Magdeburg and Stuttgart's *Commando Cannstatt*) walked out of discussions with the DFB, who had expressed a desire to work with fans. Initial agreement over stopping collective punishments and streamlining regulations over the use of flags, drums and other equipment quickly evaporated. The fan representatives issued a statement:

> After two meetings between fan representatives and representatives of the DFB and DFL, the initial euphoria quickly dissipated. We increasingly got the impression that, as in previous decades, they were only using media-friendly words to avoid any actual action. We see no other option but to end all talks with immediate effect and continue our protests inside the stadiums with greater engagement than ever. We remain motivated to stand up for the basic values of football and against corruption and commercialization, and we know we can count on tens of thousands of supporters across the country. You will hear from us this season, too! (Ford, 2018)

The unifying factor to each of these protests was 'modern football', this commercial beast that the ultras felt was threatening the sport they loved, and more importantly, their ability to participate in the way they desired. Disruptions to games through VAR and moving fixtures for television were reinforced by the perception of the DFB's commercial focus. This was compounded by changes to policing laws that could seriously affect how fans, and ultras in particular, continued to operate. In Germany it also continued a recent history characterised by protests against greater police repression. In 2012 many ultras groups conducted a protest declaring '12:12 without voices – no atmosphere', a slogan referring to the Secure Stadium Experience Act, a law designed to increase cooperation between police and clubs; the numbers in the slogan were connected to the date on which the law was to be implemented – 12 December 2012 (Brandt *et al.*, 2017) .

German fan protests were not restricted to complaints against the football and law enforcement authorities; they also took a leading role in challenging the rise of the far right in the country. In April 2017 at a Regionalliga Nordost (fourth-tier) match between SV Babelsberg and Energie Cottbus, a section of the away fans performed Nazi salutes and directed anti-Semitic chants at the home fans, whose ultras are noted for their left-wing stance. They also launched pyrotechnics at the home fans and some attempted to storm the home end of the stadium. The Babelsberg fans responded with chants of '*Nazischweine raus!*' ('Nazi pigs out'). The NOFV (the local football association), however, fined the home team for their fans' use of that phrase, and for their failure to control the pyrotechnics and crowd incursions. Cottbus were fined for their supporters' behaviour, but not specifically for the Nazi salutes and chants. Babelsberg refused to pay the fine on moral grounds, arguing that the NOFV were turning a blind eye to right-wing extremism. They were threatened with exclusion from the league if they refused to pay. The Potsdam club were supported by others such as Werder Bremen, Borussia Dortmund and FC Köln, and many fans displayed solidarity through the hashtag #nazisrausausdenstadien (Nazis out of the stadiums) and displayed '*Nazis Raus*' banners at matches. Eventually, Babelsberg came to a settlement, with both the club and NOFV agreeing to use half of the fine to fight racism.

In one season in Germany we can see the many political performances of the ultras. There are sustained protests against the introduction of new regulations, laws and processes that affect the game, which are brought in without engaging in dialogue with fans. The Against Modern Football movement has become the catch-all for such protests against changes to the game (King, 2003; Numerato, 2013; Doidge, 2015a; Hill *et al.*, 2016, Cleland *et al.*, 2018; Perasović and Mustapić, 2018). This can include the manner of and approach to policing, new laws of surveillance, the introduction of membership cards or regulations to purchase tickets, greater commercialisation by clubs, increased televised games, changes to club ownership or name changes. These transformations are not restricted to Germany. There is a range of research on fan activism in single-nation or single-group case studies, including, but not restricted to, England (King, 1997b; Nash, 2000; Brown, 2008; Cleland, 2010; Burdsey, 2011; Millward, 2011; 2012; Caudwell, 2012; Cleland and Dixon, 2014; Millward and Poulton, 2014), Italy (Testa and Armstrong, 2010; Contucci and Francesio, 2013; Doidge, 2013; 2015a), Croatia (Hodges, 2014; 2018; Hodges and Brentin, 2018; Perasović and Mustapić, 2018), Turkey (Erhart, 2011; 2014; Nuhrat, 2013; 2018a; 2018b; McManus, 2014), Germany (Merkel, 2012; Brandt and Hertel, 2015), Poland (Antonowicz *et al.*, 2016; Kossakowski *et al.*, 2018), France (Lestrelin *et al.*, 2006; 2013; Ginhoux, 2018), Brazil (Hollanda and Teixeira, 2017), Mexico (Magazine, 2007; Magazine and González, 2017) and Denmark (Mintert and Pfister, 2014; 2015). Although King (2003) took a European approach, it focused predominantly on Western Europe. Cleland *et al.* (2018) focused chiefly on England, but also recognised the importance of pan-European cooperation. Numerato (2018), similarly, acknowledged the transnational character of fan activism through an analysis of the struggles over policing, governance and the ownership of symbols in England, Italy and the Czech Republic.

Alongside the fan activism around football politics and changes to the game, ideological politics also feature in the activities of ultras. As Chapter 3 highlighted, the ultras emerged in a politically turbulent period of Italian history, and the paraphernalia of protests in the streets and piazzas was taken into the stadium. We have now come full circle and the same props are used to make political messages (Doidge, 2015a), including some use outside the stadium, as in Algeria (Mezahi, 2019). While most political messages are attributable to the football politics of Against Modern Football, some groups do display ideological politics. This can range from the left-wing or anti-fascist slogans of St Pauli, Babelsberg, Livorno, AEK Athens, Cadiz, Celtic or Marseilles, to the right-wing and nationalist slogans drawn upon particularly in post-communist Eastern Europe. But these groups are not homogenous. Not all fans of the same club share the same ideological politics. As outlined in the previous chapter, intra-group violence can occur between fans of rival ideologies, such as at PSG when members of *Supras Auteuil* fought the *Boulogne Boys*. Ideological politics is still important for some fans, and in some cases, this can get woven into the Against Modern Football narrative. For more left-wing fans, the commercial changes to the game are a reason to resist, as well as the changes to police power. For right-wing fans, attempts to clamp down on offensive banners and racist chanting are drawn under the same resistance. The result is that fans and ultras from all hues proceed to actively resist any changes being brought into football.

The ultras perform politics in various ways, and all through their existing fan culture. They also mobilise around issues pertinent to their fandom as the German examples at the start of this chapter demonstrated. Political expressions become part of the ultras' performance. This is not unique to the ultras, but is a tried and tested formula of contemporary politics. As Alexander (2017: 91) states: 'Voters do not decide whom to vote for by weighing their objective costs and benefits. They are not calculating machines, but emotional and moral human beings. Searching for the meaning of things, they want to make sense of political life, working out grand narratives about where we've been, where we are now, where we're going in the future.' Politics has become a performance and politicians sell themselves to their electorate (McGinniss, 1969; Habermas, 1989: Doidge, 2015a; Alexander, 2017). They have skilled speechwriters, strategists, media managers, spin doctors, pollsters and access to the media so that they can present their narrative clearly. Contemporary politics is about creating a powerful narrative and presenting this to the audience. The ultras also have a clear narrative that is Against Modern Football. However, it is not clear who their audience is. The narrative is definitely performed to each other, and there are occasionally performances against the police and those in authority.

Football fans, and ultras in particular, represent a significant political movement. This chapter seeks to expand this argument and contends that football fans engaged in forms of social protest are part of a wider global social movement. This chapter builds on existing understandings of fan activism in discreet local and national contexts. It reinforces this with literature from studies of social movements as well as reiterating the ideological dimension of some fan groups, particularly around nationalism and a broader link to racism. This is not to say that all ultras are right-wing; many are resolutely anti-fascist and others will claim to be politically neutral. It is also not saying that all ultras are racist. Like other fans, some exhibit various forms of racism, and only some of this is ideologically driven (Back et al., 2001). Much of the success in challenging racism has come from fan movements, as well as players. Just as not all ultras engage in violence, there are some who display behaviours that attract negative media attention. As has been argued throughout the book, football provides a regular space where groups can present themselves. Through an analysis of the Against Modern Football movement, followed by a discussion of nationalism in ultras identities, this chapter demonstrates that not only do they constitute a sizeable political force, their political performances are simply part of the broader narrative the groups are presenting. One should not automatically assume that being in a social movement means that the members want to change things. Being part of something can bring a sense of belonging and identity that can unite members. As with football fandom in general, this can be an end in itself.

The formation of ultras as a social movement

Football fans are increasingly well-connected and socially active, thereby forming a global social movement. Although scholars such as Harvey et al. (2013) have highlighted the importance of social movements to sport, this did not include football, nor presented fans' activities as a social movement in itself. More people globally engage in football-related activity than any other social activity. Its popularity brings many disparate groups of people together; yet these groups are not homogenous. They comprise a wide range of people from a variety of backgrounds and with different motivations for supporting their club (see Bromberger, 1993; Back *et al.*, 2001; Caudwell, 2011; Dunn, 2014). Sometimes, historical enemies with a high level of hatred between them can establish a common platform of activism and protest. In the case of the FTORJ, supporters of hostile local fan clubs in Rio de Janeiro gathered to fight against the police force, the modernisation of Brazilian stadiums and football, as well as murders among fans (Hollanda and Teixeira, 2017).

Despite this, certain trends can be observed. Cleland (2010) has noted that some fan groups are moving from 'passive' and apolitical to 'active'. They are engaged in a variety of activities to campaign and lobby on behalf of their perceived rights as fans. Others have also challenged the different forms of discrimination still present in the stadium and in the game as a whole. Particularly in the UK, many of the independent supporters' associations that emerged in the 1990s were key drivers for diversity awareness in football. In 2019, the Football Supporters' Federation and Supporters' Direct, two fan organisations in England and Wales, agreed on a merger. The result was a new organisation, the Football Supporters' Association (FSA, 2019), which with a combined membership of over 500,000 fans represents a greater membership than any of the political parties in England and Wales. National supporters' associations operate in other nations too, such as the Association Nationale des Supporters in France, the Danish Fans Federation and Federación de Accionistas y Socios del Fútbol Español (FASFE). All of these are also part of FSE, which has members from forty-eight European countries. Local, national and regional collaboration is a key part of lobbying for change.

The politicisation of fans around a form of leisure consumption constitutes an important social movement in the twenty-first century. Crossley (2002: 7) suggests that 'there are doubtless many reasons' why social movements should be central to sociology. This becomes more pertinent at a time of deindustrialisation and migration, when financial crises are impacting a significant section of the European population, particularly the young. Social movements used to derive from the collective solidarity of working in the same industry, or living in the same area. Decentralisation of production has resulted in the breakdown of these traditional solidarities, in what Castells (1996: 265) calls the 'individualisation of labour'. While Calhoun (2006) observes that these processes limit protection to workers and privatise risk. The resulting shift to a post-Fordist service sector economy in many areas of Europe has facilitated the formation of new social movements (Touraine, 1981: Melucci, 1996). More importantly, the emergence of a technologically driven, globalised world has created new spaces for fans to explore and shares ideas. For Touraine (1981), the ability to identify with others in the group, and outsiders, is a key factor to new social movements. For many fans, their fandom is a primary form of identity. This provides motivation and focus for their political action. Meanwhile, Melucci (1996) argued that one of the requisites of collective action was to have a group of people coming together regularly with a shared purpose. The basic act of a football fan is to ritualistically attend the stadium in order to watch a match. Those fans that identify the strongest with the fan group are more likely to engage in fan activities (Besta and Kossakowski, 2018). While collective action is not a prime requisite of football fandom, it can be an outcome.

Protest has become a significant part of the repertoire of ultras fandom. According to Tarrow (1998: 4): 'Movements mount challenges through disruptive direct action against elites, authorities, other groups or cultural codes.' Testa and Armstrong (2010: 69) suggest that ultras are 'an emerging social movement'. Extending this, Millward and Poulton (2014: 3) note that the protests by Manchester United fans against the club's owners had hundreds of thousands of participants, arguing that this made them 'among the best supported forms of social movement in the world'. Yet this was just one protest at one club. At varying times and frequencies, fans at different clubs can be engaged in forms of protest. Such actions can be taken to challenge club management or specific players, fight against discrimination or raise money to save the club. Yet protests do not have to be regular; groups can go through 'latent' periods (Melucci, 1996). In order to understand fandom as a social movement, it is important to recognise that some political issues do not affect *all* fans at the same time. Some issues are due to specific factors within the club or locality. Jasper (1997) suggests that movements occur from a 'moral shock' that helps mobilise activists who work to build on this outrage and anger to focus attention. Issues that affect the football clubs can generate this moral shock and represent a call to arms for fans.

Four basic properties of social movements have been identified: collective challenge, common purpose, solidarity and collective identity, and sustainability. Football fans have been collectively challenging various groups since the 1970s. As Tarrow (1998: 5) argues, 'collective challenges are often marked by interrupting, obstructing, or rendering uncertain the activities of others. But ... they can be symbolised by slogans, forms of dress or music, or by renaming familiar objects with new or different symbols.' Taylor (1971) suggested that hooliganism was a form of resistance to commercialism in English football. Although Taylor has been heavily critiqued (see Dunning *et al.*, 1986; Giulianotti, 1994), he does highlight how fans began to mobilise collectively against other groups in the 1970s. Similarly, as already noted, the ultras in Italy brought the political banners from the piazzas into the stadiums and have often sought to challenge different groups, including politicians, rival ultras and, latterly, the police (Dal Lago and De Biasi, 1994; Roversi and Balestri, 2000; Doidge, 2015a). Over time these different fan groups began to adapt their clothing. Hooligans adopted the casual style of dress, while politically affiliated ultras adopted specific fashions that reflected their political leanings (Doidge, 2013). These various groups sustain significant solidarity. More than forty years since they first emerged, the ultras in particular have cemented themselves as a major football movement in Europe. The central feature of the ultras style of fandom is its unwavering support for the local club. The rituals of the game and supporters help generate significant collective solidarity.

As Durkheim (1964) has demonstrated in relation to religion, regular congregation, such as the gathering of fans and ultras in the stadium, generates a 'collective effervescence' that promotes solidarity and group cohesion. This solidarity is embodied in the symbol of the club – a sacred totem connecting 'devotees' in the common ritual. This emotional sense of belonging that football fandom produces can be a powerful motivating factor when 'moral shocks' occur. According to Goodwin, Jasper and Polletta (2001: 7): 'The motivation to engage in protest – a process overflowing with emotions – has been largely ignored in recent research because it has so often been taken for granted under the structuralist assumption of objectively given interests.' While politico-economic factors provide an environment in which protest and mobilisation can occur, emotions and a collective sense of belonging are vital when considering the motivations of fans. The collective solidarity of ultras and fans unifies members and encourages mobilisation. 'Personal ties of love and friendship among members were an important cultural ideal. A willingness to shape personal relationships around the cause was, in large measure, what made possible the intense commitment of members' (Taylor, 1989: 769). Sociability, and being around like-minded people, helps produce the social relations that facilitate the politicisation of fans.

Although they support the team, and engage in debates about the sport, from the early days it is not clear that the ultras, hooligans or football fans in general have had a common political purpose. Tilly (2004) observed that protests were, historically, local in character and directed at local patrician owners. Throughout the twentieth century, meanwhile, social protests became predominantly national in character. In football this change began to occur in the 1990s as economic transformations accelerated. Various masculine fan groups, particularly ultras, began to coalesce under the Against Modern Football banner

(Numerato, 2015). In Germany fans also aligned to this banner, but successfully fought for and retained ownership of their clubs (Merkel, 2012). English fans began forming independent supporters' associations and supporters' trusts (King, 1997b; 2003; Giulianotti, 1999; Nash, 2000). This phenomenon has spread further afield, resulting in the formation of national associations across Northern Europe (Cleland *et al.* 2018), the Balkans and Eastern Europe (Brentin and Tregoures, 2016; Hodges and Brentin, 2018; Perasović and Mustapić, 2018).

More significantly, disparate fan groups started to collaborate and share ideas. It was during the 1990s that football fandom began to emerge as a political movement. In England the seeds were sown earlier with the formation of the Football Supporters' Association in 1985 in the aftermath of the Heysel tragedy. This became the umbrella organisation for various independent supporters' associations that were formed to challenge changes to football in the 1990s. In 2002 it merged with the National Federation of Supporters' Clubs to form the Football Supporters' Federation, before another merger, detailed above, saw it readopt the FSA name. Other organisations including Kick It Out, Supporters' Direct and Level Playing Field also formed from specific fan movements associated with English football. Similar situations occurred across Europe. For example, Bündnis aktiver Fußballfans (BAFF, the Association of Active Football Fans), established in 1993 in Germany as a nationwide federation of fan groups from a variety of different clubs, principally deals with issues around commercialism, discrimination and stadium issues. This highlights the importance of the 1990s to fan activism, and also shows how fans have put aside differences to establish unified political movements.

Against Modern Football

One of the themes of the book, as illustrated in the opening paragraphs to this chapter, has been opposition to 'modern football'. As noted, football has undergone a profound economic transformation since the 1990s. The formation of the Premier League in England and pan-European Champions League in particular, as well as a reorganisation of FIFA and the men's World Cup, have commercially organised the sport around marketing products, television exposure and corporate partnerships (King, 1998; 2003; Sugden and Tomlinson, 1999; Giulianotti, 1999; Giulianotti and Robertson, 2009; Millward, 2011; Doidge, 2015a). These commercial developments have been adopted in various ways across clubs and competitions across Europe and the rest of the world as clubs seek to increase revenue, expand markets and promote their brand globally. The fact that clubs are using the business terminology of brands, markets and profit is anathema to many football fans, and ultras in particular, and this symbolises the shift from local pride, on-field success and enjoyable football to commercial exploitation.

In parallel, police powers have been strengthened to try to regulate the perceived excesses of football fans. As noted in the previous chapter, ultras are seen as a convenient folk devil against which the media and state can justify more draconian measures. King (1998) argues that one of the drivers for the commercial transformation of the Premier League was Lord Justice Taylor's (1990) report that was commissioned after the Hillsborough tragedy. Although Hillsborough was not linked to hooliganism, some of the problems affecting antiquated British stadiums were measures introduced to combat hooligans, such as high perimeter fences and excessive numbers of police who were focused on violence and ill-prepared for health and safety issues. The Taylor Report recommended treating fans like customers and the introduction of all-seater stadiums. These recommendations came at the same time as new directors were seeking to profit from football with the formation of the Premier League and significant television deals.

This pattern has been adopted across Europe as governing bodies and state authorities seek to control potential violence, with the police being the primary enforcers (Tsoukala, 2009; Doidge, 2015a; Antonowicz and Grodecki, 2018). As outlined in the introduction to this chapter, regions of Germany have attempted to introduce PAG, a measure that will permit the police to intercept phone calls and text messages, confiscate mail without warrant and pre-emptively detain suspects before they have even committed a crime. In Italy, the anti-terror police, the Digos, have the remit to investigate ultras, which symbolically denotes them to be as dangerous as terrorists and the Mafia (Doidge, 2015a). More worryingly, these laws were passed as decrees, meaning they did not go through the usual legislative process (Testa, 2013). As with the PAG in Germany, this gives the police the power to act without obtaining prior judicial approval, effectively making them law enforcement, judge and jury. The Italian police also have the power to issue Daspos, or football banning orders, an instrument that has been open to abuse, as the example of two Pisa fans who were given bans for being in possession of toilet rolls, or 'inflammable materials' as the police described them, demonstrates (Doidge, 2015a). The result is 'ACAB syndrome' among fans (and ultras in particular) and a perception that the police are against them, which then influences how they react when they are in confrontation (Stefanini, 2009; Doidge, 2015a).

Alongside the changes to stadium architecture and the increased power and visibility of the police, different governing bodies have tried to introduce regulations to restrict access to games for those they perceive to be troublemakers. After a police officer was killed in riots after the Sicilian derby between Catania and Palermo in 2007, the Pisanu Laws were introduced in Italy (Doidge, 2015a). These required the installation of fences and additional security gates around stadiums. They also introduced regulations that stipulated that each individual ticket had to have the fan's name printed on it, with the names cross-checked against a database to see if they were on a banned list. This also meant that each fan had to show a form of identification at the turnstiles to prove they were the designated ticket holder.

The Pisanu Laws also introduced the *tessera del tifoso*, or fans' membership card, which was tied to a corporate bank and a national database. The authorities tried to enforce all football fans to have one, for instance by restricting ticket sales for some matches, and for away fans at all matches, to *tessera* holders only. Italian fans united to successfully resist the enforced use of the *tessera* (it is now voluntary). However, their counterparts were less successful in Turkey where the authorities introduced a similar scheme called the *Passolig*. Like the *tessera* this was putatively to stop violence, but was also linked to a national bank with links to the Erdoğan regime, as well as databases at the Ministry of the Interior and Ministry of Finance (Nuhrat, 2018a). The fact that these cards are linked to discounts on merchandise illustrates a commercial dimension to their introduction. These cards are also illustrative of the way that ultras are seen as being subversive and how State authorities wish to use various means to monitor them. Foucault (1991) argued that the possibility of constant surveillance forced prisoners to change their behaviour and produced 'docile bodies'. Prisoners never knew when they were being observed, so adapted their behaviour *in case* they were being watched. The threat of constant surveillance by the State is an attempt to produce docile ultras. The *Passolig* is linked to State databases, and both this system and the *tessera* are linked to police databases. One wrong move and fans could be banned from attending matches.

State repression has gone to another level in certain countries. As mentioned in Chapter 6, fans of Mexican clubs have established the Movement of United Mexican Supporters and 'their principal objective was to begin a campaign against abuse, stigmatization and criminalization of Mexican supporter groups' (Magazine and González, 2017: 102). After their role in the Arab Spring unrest, ultras have been banned from Egyptian football stadiums since 2015 after conflicts at Port Said and a deadly stampede in the Air Defence Stadium in Cairo (Ibraheem,

2015). Although the regime permits other fans to come to the stadium, ultras are still specifically prohibited (Schietti, 2017).

Clubs are also attempting to prohibit ultras. As a result of vandalism, club officials at Real Madrid removed *Ultras Sur* from the stadium in 2013, establishing a new group *Grada Joven*, which, thanks to its close cooperation with the club, was to be the civilised and predictable alternative. *Ultras Sur* tried to continue to attend matches, but in 2015 the club introduced additional restrictive rules for the distribution of tickets for away games.

Political expression is one area of increased regulation of ultras. The ultras have had their roots in ideological politics since their emergence in 1960s Italy. Yet authorities are challenging many forms of political expression. Governing bodies and clubs are starting to seek prior approval of banners before entering the stadium. As with history, this has to take into account the power relations of the protagonists. As Guschwan (2014: 896) observes,

> In practice, any political expression that upholds the *status quo* is not considered political. Corporate logos *do* political work in promoting consumerist capitalist values, while politician expressions that deviate from accepted norms attract negative attention, bland patriotism is accepted as apolitical, dissent is not. Radical dissent is violently opposed. Signs can be banned, and chants and songs can be punished, but unless fans themselves are eliminated, the possibility for political expression will be part of any gathering, except, perhaps, in the most repressive regimes.

Commercial sponsors are political expressions of capitalist relations, and national flags are expressions of nationalism. Authorities never legislate against the waving of national flags, even though these may symbolise fascism to their members or rivals (Doidge, 2015a). In Belarus the authoritarian regime of Alexander Lukashenko also sees the ultras as subversive and has clamped down on any activities seen as contrary to the regime (Bylina, 2013). Banners in English are banned as the police cannot understand them, and any political expressions have to be performed outside the country, as BATE Borisov ultras did at Panevėžys in Lithuania when they chanted 'May he die!' in reference to Lukashenko. In Portugal laws were introduced in 2007 to force the registration of any group that wanted to present a choreography with its own name in the stadium. Some groups perceived this form of regulation as a betrayal of the ultras' ideals. As a result, some groups specifically became *No Name Boys* so that they did not meet the requirements of registration. These groups would present their choreographies without their names or logos so they could continue to operate as before and subvert the regulations. In so doing they continued to perform their anti-authority ideals.

The use of pyrotechnics has become one of the biggest battles in the early years of the twenty-first century. Pyrotechnics became popular in Southern Europe as the ultras style developed. They have since been adopted by ultras across the globe. On the one hand, they provide a visual spectacle, particularly during night matches. Football clubs and governing bodies, particularly for important fixtures, often use pyrotechnic displays to welcome the players onto the pitch or to celebrate victories. The authorities claim that the ultras' use of pyrotechnics is dangerous, and while exceptionally rare, there have been deaths attributed to the use of flares. The first such death at a football match in Italy occurred when a nautical flare killed a Lazio fan in 1979 (Foot, 2006). A similar incident occurred in 2013 in South America when a 14-year-old Bolivian boy was killed after a firework launched by Corinthians fans pierced his eye (Marshall, 2013). Despite the small number of deaths or injuries, many states and governing bodies (especially UEFA) have banned any use of pyrotechnics by fans, including those performed by trained users. In some cases, notably Norway and German, there has been dialogue and agreement about the use of flares being legal under some circumstances. But in general, the prohibition has resulted in another opportunity for ultras to perform their anti-authority credentials. Smuggling pyrotechnics into the stadium becomes a game. In some cases, it becomes a deliberate provocation and reaction to the authorities. In 2013 UEFA closed Legia Warsaw's Zyleta ('razor blade') stand for their next European match after Legia fans chanted racist abuse. At their next home match in the Ekstraklasa (Polish football league), these same fans deliberately provoked the European governing body by unfurling a banner running the length of the Zyleta stand that declared (in English) 'Ultra extreme fanatical atmosphere' and then proceeded to use hundreds of flares. The abbreviation of their message was of course 'UEFA' and thus was clearly targeted at the perceived illegitimacy of the European governing body. Pyrotechnics have become a symbol of protest against both governments and football authorities. Additionally, as it is illegal in most countries, for an ultra to light flares and not be charged is a matter of 'victory' over the legislative and commercial order. Deliberate transgression of boundaries becomes pleasurable for fans (King, 1997a).

The perceived regulation of all ultras activity has seen the conflation of *any* sanction as illegitimate. All attempts to regulate ultras have been swept under the umbrella of Against Modern Football and therefore seen as an attempt to change ultras behaviours from their perceived traditions. The use of sanctions, rather than dialogue, also entrenches the ultras' position. Even when the authorities are legitimately challenging damaging behaviours like racism, the lack of legitimacy of the governing bodies sees some ultras resisting all forms of sanction because they are seen as symptomatic of 'modern football'. The example of the display by Legia Warsaw fans above demonstrates that the closure of the stand after incidents of racism collectively mobilised the fans to resist in other ways. When the Italian authorities attempted to stop the 'territorial discrimination' meted out between fans based on their region, ultras of different clubs joined forces (Doidge, 2015a). What was worse is that the Italian football federation (FIGC) attempted to clamp down on racism at the same time as this territorial discrimination. This occurred after AC Milan were sanctioned with a stadium ban after their ultras showed a banner stating '*Napoli colera*', inferring that Naples was unhygienic and living in the nineteenth century. But this punishment only unified the rival ultras groups, including Napoli fans who displayed a banner saying '*Napoli colera: e adesso chiudeteci la curva!*' ('Naples cholera: now close our stand!'). The fans actively tried to close their own stands to challenge the rules.

While there are some similarities across the globe that unite the Against Modern Football movement, including anti-commercialism and anti-police sentiments and challenging regulations over pyrotechnics and membership cards, there are also many local factors at play. As ultras in Belarus, Egypt and Turkey demonstrate, there are broader factors around authoritarian regimes. In Italy, territorial discrimination was a motivator for resistance, while at Legia Warsaw it was anti-racism. In Croatia the Against Modern Football movement not only challenges police repression and the commercialisation of the game, it is also a movement against corruption in both football and politics (Perasović and Mustapić, 2018). HNS, the Croatian football federation, has been blighted by corruption for several years. In 2010 twenty-two players were convicted of match-fixing, followed by fifteen more the following year. That same year Zeljko Sirić, the former vice-president of HNS, and the president of the referees commission, Stjepan Djedović, were arrested and subsequently convicted of accepting a bribe for 'fair refereeing'. Four years later, two HNS executive vice-presidents, Zdravko Mamić and Damir Vrbanović, were arrested on suspicion of embezzlement of €15 million from GNK Dinamo. Mamić was also vice-president of GNK Dinamo and became the symbol of corruption and criminality in Croatia (Perasović and Mustapić 2018). It is in this context that we can see other forms of ultras protest. Before the qualifying match between Croatia and Italy in June 2015, ultras broke into the stadium and used weedkiller to mark a swastika measuring 14 m on the pitch. Although Croatian fans have been noted for nationalist and extreme right-wing sympathies, they demonstrated the reflexivity that Numerato (2015) observes by choosing the one symbol they knew would get their football federation into trouble. The swastika attracted global condemnation for the HNS and its chief executive, Damir Vrbanović, and they both received fines from UEFA and the local courts (Milekic, 2018).

The paradox of the ultras is that the clubs are attracted to the atmosphere they bring to stadiums. In a televised commercial spectacle, this is highly engaging for other fans and television audiences. As Chapter 3 observed, this visual spectacle is one of the reasons the phenomenon has spread globally. The ultras grew at a time when football was experiencing a commercial hiatus, what King (2003) calls 'Eurosclerosis'. Attendances were falling, the quality on the pitch was not endearing and violence was a constant problem across Europe. Thanks to good relations with club authorities, the ultras gained access to the stadium for choreographies, received free tickets or preferential ticket prices and other benefits (Spaaij and Viñas, 2005; Doidge, 2015a). Clubs enjoyed the atmosphere created by the ultras, which affected the players of the home team, referees and the opposing team. The ultras also gave their support to club presidents during elections to the board and this helped guarantee a lot of privileges (Doidge, 2015a). For example, Nuhrat (2018b: 873) highlights how club officials at Beşiktaş welcome the passionate support from Çarşı, but that this comes at a price: 'Wishing to be in total control of football as a spectacle, administrators praise or rather tolerate fervour and passion so long as they have the final say in relation to how they can be packaged – in a way that can generate profit for the club.' The ultras style of support is highly marketable and contemporary football clubs seek to commercialise the passion the ultras represent.

This commercialism brings the ultras into further conflict with clubs and authorities. The performances of the ultras derived from political protests of the 1960s. Consequently, they draw on the full range of tactics of political protests. As Perasović and Mustapić (2018: 969) identify:

> Against Modern Football is the common denominator of a worldwide, heterogeneous social movement comprised of various actors and the methods of conflict: simple, symbolic actions like slogans written on flags, banners or walls; boycotts, petitions, demonstrations, direct actions and the foundation of new football clubs by supporters.

Football fans across Europe, including ultras, have engaged in various protests to assert their symbolic rights over their sport. Some have established their own clubs, like Hapoel Katamon Jerusalem (Ha-Ilan, 2018) or FC United of Manchester (Brown, 2008; Millward and Poulton, 2014). Others have established localised organisations to protest specifics of their clubs, such as club ownership at Liverpool and Manchester United (Millward, 2011; 2012), corruption in Croatian football (Perasović and Mustapić, 2018) or, in the case of a group of Leeds United fans, racism and fascism (Thomas, 2010). There is a slow movement towards the formation of national and international organisations to campaign and lobby on behalf of fans, such as FSE, BAFF in Germany, the FSA in England, Taraftar Haklari Derneğli (Fan Rights Association) in Turkey and FASFE in Spain. These seek to represent all fans and want to open a dialogue with State authorities, governing bodies and the police.

Working in partnership with authorities contravenes the perceived autonomy of the ultras. Consequently, they seek to remain outsiders so they can continue to be transgressive. As Giulianotti (1995) observed, official support of the carnival undermines the qualities of the carnivalesque. What the Against Modern Football movement demonstrates is how the 'moral shock' (Jasper, 1997) and emotional response (Goodwin *et al.*, 2001) to changes to the game to which the ultras devote their lives helps mobilise their responses.

The rituals of the ultras rely on a symbolic focus. Tradition dictates that this is on the symbols of the club and the ultras group themselves. The profane symbols of rivals are also mobilised against. With Against Modern Football, new foci are emerging, in particular the police and football authorities, which unite ultras in different ways. Choreographies will regularly include various tropes, such as 'ACAB' or 'UEFA Mafia'. The opening of Chapter 1, for instance, described the choreography of Legia Warsaw fans challenging the decision to exclude their team from the Champions League. Fans of Swedish side Malmö chanted 'UEFA Mafia' during their Champions League match against Juventus after the referee sent off one of their team's players (Wilman, 2014). Perceived injustices are focused at the governing bodies, rather than the opposing players or referees.

Although ultras pick up on these patterns through social media and face-to-face contact, they are also starting to actively coordinate activity. The traditions of football that seek to differentiate on the basis of 'us' and 'them' have been a continued obstacle for coordinated resistance to 'modern football'. Having UEFA, national federations or the police as a focal point helps emphasise their role in 'modern football' and creates the ritual focus for ultras that transcends club rivalries. As the opening paragraphs of this chapter demonstrate, German fans have coordinated their responses to police laws and the failure of the DFB to honestly engage in dialogue. As also noted earlier, ultras across Italy, and into Germany, displayed 'Speziale Libero' banners and T-shirts in protest at the incarceration of an ultra following the death of a police officer in Sicily (Doidge, 2015a). In Istanbul and Cairo, ultras from rival groups united to actively protest against government measures. Those that unite are more likely to present a unified front and challenge national and international bodies. Where there has been some measure of success, mainly in Northern Europe in countries including the UK, Germany, Sweden and France, this is because there has been some unified mobilisation. In countries like Italy and Spain, ultras culture continues to face strong pressure from legal restrictions. These are also the countries that have seen the most recent attempts at working together.

Ultras need to recognise who the audience for their protests is. Alexander (2017: 38) identifies the paradox:

> Social movements do not succeed because they are materially powerful; they become materially powerful because they succeed. To explain this seeming paradox … social movements should be understood as social performances. To seize power in the state, one must first seize the collective imagination, projecting drama on the stage of social life that depict the triumph of justice, so powerfully fusing with distant audiences that dangerous insurrection becomes legitimate.

Social movements are successful as a social drama that recognises their audience and present themselves accordingly. The ultras are clear in their presentation. They have no problem presenting themselves to themselves. The issue they have is engaging those who do not identify as ultras. As argued in the previous chapter, the ultras have become a folk devil and a convenient symbol of deviance for governments, governing bodies and the media. In this way they can justify evermore draconian legislation to pacify and eliminate the ultras.

The ultras are not a coherent movement with clear leadership. They encapsulate what Castells (2012) calls 'rhizomatic' properties. They are grassroots, networked and sporadic. But what weakens them is their lack of coherence. The ultras mentality is about being against 'modern football' in all its guises. As demonstrated by the Legia Warsaw ultras saying 'we hate everyone', they are deliberately contrary and confrontational. Being an ultra is to challenge authority and be autonomous. This results in every perceived manifestation of 'modern football' being challenged. Because of this, any attempt to regulate violence or racism is met with instant rebellion. In some cases, racism is increased to deliberately challenge the rules (Doidge, 2015a). Yet it is not clear that the ultras actually want to change rules or make football inclusive. Most of the literature on social movements tends to focus on outcomes as though that is what participation is all about. Yet participation can be an end in itself; taking part is the pleasure and being deliberately obstructive is the outcome. Although this chapter has touched on ideological and social politics, politics themselves may not be the outcome, just the vehicle to confront and challenge.

The authorities invariably do not speak to the fans, let alone the ultras, and this results in weak or ineffectual legislation. This is easy to resist and challenge through protest and intellectual argument. But when the ultras are perceived (and this perception is partly produced by the ultras themselves) as merely being deliberately obstructive, the authorities impose their rules anyway. In the end, all fans lose out. The ultras' lack of coherence means a lack of clear outcomes. It is not clear what the ultras want other than a situation where the authorities are not regulating them. But this anarchistic, contrary persona invites regulation. Only the most ardent ultra sees violence and racism as an acceptable byproduct of their activities. This approach can continue for so long, but it is not sustainable. The forces of consumerism and the State will endure unless the ultras follow their peers in Egypt or take an explicitly more anti-neoliberalism role. Nationalism reinforces State control and the quest for on-field success ensures a concentration of ownership in a small number of global entrepreneurs. The love–hate relationship will continue but with the power of the ultras diluted through a growing focus on global television audiences and marketing partnerships.

Nationalism

'*Dijeli zemlju na tri zadrta politika Zavadi, pa kradi, nacionalna taktika*' ('It divides the land into three – it is rotten politics. To divide and to steal – it's the nationalist tactic'). This is a fragment of 'Kontra sistema', a popular song performed by ultras of Bosnian club Celik Zenica. This ultras group is extraordinary in the context of the Balkan region as in its frames there is space for Bosnian Muslims, Catholic Croatians, Orthodox Serbians and even Albanians and Gypsies. It is an explosive mixture when you consider the Balkan war, the case of Kosovo, and inter-religion and ethnic animosities in that region. It is hard to explain the phenomenon of Zenica. The Balkan conflict seemed to bypass this city and, as a result, a multicultural unity among the population has been preserved. Ultras of Celik, united by a love of the club and not divided by national or ethnic differences, represent a unique bunch of friends.

This example is the exception, not the rule. In many cases, the structure of ultras groups is ideologically unified. Sometimes, in the environs of elite clubs with large fan bases there are cases of divided ultras groups in terms of political engagement (examples include FC Seville, l'OM and PSG, where both left- and right-wing groups operate). Many politically minded ultras groups are strongly attached to nationalist, right-wing attitudes, particularly in Russia, Poland and the Balkans. There are also those with groups supporting left-wing, progressive perspectives such as at St Pauli and Babelsburg (Germany), AEK Athens (Greece), Livorno (Italy) and Rayo Vallecano (Spain). Many more will declare political neutrality (particularly groups from the US, UK, South America and some in European contexts). It is difficult to assess which tendency prevails; however, qualitative observation suggests nationalism is a significant underpinning philosophy for many groups, even those claiming to be apolitical.

Nationalist tendencies between ultras groups can be classed as a type of 'invented tradition'. Hobsbawm (1983: 4) argued that these are 'essentially a process of formalisation and ritualisation, characterised by reference to the past, if only by imposing repetition'. However, inventing tradition does not mean only to recall the past; it implies a visionary and performative creation of the 'old' in a 'new' way – mostly by making past ceremonies and values suitable for contemporary group ideology. This practice is also a way of struggling with political-cultural changes: 'It is contrast between the constant change and innovation of the modern world and the attempt to structure at last some parts of social life within it as unchanging and invariant' (Hobsbawm, 1983: 2). Some ultras groups observe remembrance of the past but they also imagine a utopian fatherland with staunch culture and norms.

Inventing tradition underpins the performative presentation of 'imagined community' (Anderson, 1991). It is the performative mechanism where many ultras choreographies draw on symbols that seek to present an imagined 'promise land'. These choreographies present a distinctive, visible image with a loud voice envisaging 'old, good times' in new, invented/imagined ways. Slogans like 'Great Russia' or 'White-red Poland' are simple and persuasive. In a Durkheimian way, these symbols of nation become sacred for these groups and act as a point of reference for the community. These groups also relate to Durkheim's (1997) 'mechanical solidarity' as many are not democratic, but resemble traditional tribes or societies where individuals were important only as a part of the collective consciousness. The masculine conception of these groups refers to fraternities, brotherhoods and the Fatherland. In each case, nationalism is seen as 'natural' and above criticism. Even those groups who identify as left wing still conform (in most cases) to masculine forms of conduct, which includes group solidarity and violence if required.

The Balkans provides a key insight into nationalism, ethnic identity and ultras. With memories of the disintegration of Yugoslavia and the establishment of new states still vivid, many groups, ethnic or religious, have regained the right to express their identity, and their large number means that conflict is inevitable. Football serves here as a platform for the expression of such emotions and resentments. The history of Dinamo Zagreb is part of such identity work. After the overthrow of communism, the club changed its name three times: firstly, the name 'HSK-Građanski' – referring to pre-communist era – returned; next it was 'Croatia', tied to the project of building new nation; finally, from 2000, the name 'Dinamo' has been resurrected.

> These changes in Dinamo's name were deeply disputed, reflecting diverging opinions about which parts of history – and consequently which version of Croatian national identity – the team was to be associated with. In essence, what unfolded around Dinamo and the name dispute was a struggle over history and identities, especially national identity. (Sindbæk, 2013: 1)

Ultras groups have taken key positions within these debates as nations, clubs and groups construct their own invented traditions and collective memories over their respective imagined communities.

These contestations, debates and conflicts are actively performed in and around football through the use of nationalist symbols. Many Croatian fans, ultras and players have performatively expressed the *Ustaše* salute of *Za Dom Spremni* (Ready for the homeland), that is connected to the official salute of the Independent State of Croatia, a fascist quisling-state in existence during the Second World War (Brentin, 2016). After the Croatian national team returned from the 2018 World Cup in Russia having lost to France in the final, the singer Marko Perković Thompson (known for his right-wing views) performed the song '*Herceg Bosnia*' in Zagreb in front of half a million citizens. This song referred to the nationalist project emphasising Croatian dominance in Bosnia and Herzegovina (Pisker, 2018). Nazi insignia have also been incorporated into choreographies with political rivals. In 2006 Croatia fans stood in the form of a human swastika symbol during a friendly match against Italy in Livorno. This was deliberately provocative to a city with noted communist sympathies (Doidge, 2013; Brentin, 2016), but was dismissed by one of the members of Croatian football association as a 'funny joke' (Brentin, 2016: 6). As mentioned earlier in this chapter, Croatian fans also faced international condemnation after marking a large swastika on the pitch with weedkiller in a protest against the Croatian FA. The latter examples recognise an understanding that nationalist symbols are provocative, while also reflecting the wider political culture in the country (Hodges, 2018).

Elsewhere, ultras groups recall the old order in performative ways. Chants and banners with the message '*Kosovo je Srbija*' ('Kosovo is Serbia') presented by Serbian ultras are a good example. The ultras of Belgrade giants Crvena Zvezda are active in this area, and presented a banner declaring 'UEFA supports terrorism' when Kosovo was incorporated into the structure of the European association. They proclaim their own tradition to treat Kosovo as a part of Serbia despite the fact that it is acknowledged as independent region (legally since 2008, although the Serbian government treats Kosovo as part of Serbia as there are important places for Serbian identity in the region, such as the monasteries in Gračanica and Visoki Dečan). Gaining independence has become an excellent opportunity to express ethnic Albanian identity openly by many ultras group in Kosovo. The flag of Albania is often waved during matches and the Albanian eagle is the symbol of an ultras group called *Kugezinjet e Jakoves* who support KF Vellaznimi. During the 2017 Gjilan derby (KF Gjilan vs Drita Gjilan), the ultras of the home team presented a huge choreography referring to Serbian war criminals with the words: 'Our heroes die in war, yours die in the Hague'. Nationalist memories are performed in the football stadium and these recreate the divisions that led to war.

The Balkans is not the only region where the nationalist attitude of ultras is vigorously performed. Generally speaking, Central and Eastern Europe is a region with a substantial level of such activity. In Poland there is no group with an inclination to leftist ideology. All ultras groups support patriotic, conservative values based on the commemoration of war heroes, people fighting against both Nazi forces during the Second World War and the Communist regime afterwards. The lack of a progressive group in Poland is a result – among others – of associating left-wing movements with communism (even if contemporary leftist organisations have nothing to do with communism). The shared conservative values are also connected to the part played by the Roman Catholic Church in Polish history (Kossakowski *et al.*, 2018). The specificity of political and ideological engagement between fans has to answer questions regarding local history and context.

Engaging with local circumstances is also required when analysing the situation in Russia. It is not enough to state that Russian ultras (and hooligans as well) just share right-wing values. As Arnold and Veth (2018: 2) observe, in the case of Russian fans, 'the far right attained such a level of prominence because they entered the *bolel'shchiki* (supporters' groups) subculture when its development was nascent, underinstitutionalized, and unable to defend itself'. On the other hand, Glathe (2016: 1523) shows that the readiness of Russian fans to engage in right-wing activity stems from wider group pursuits associated with masculinity and violence. Being organised into 'legions' and 'firms', with regular fight training, a passion for violence and 'a collective self-image with military undertones' highlights the gendered aspects. Once again, male, cohesive and highly hierarchical solidarities seem to be more likely in nation-building discourses.

Local circumstances, identities and history are not restricted to Eastern and Central Europe. Similar performances exist with the *La Familia* ultras group at Beitar Jerusalem, who are well known for their ultranationalist ideals. The word 'Beitar' is connected to the right-wing formation of revisionists promoting an image of Jews as strong and courageous people. '*La Familia* is known for its noxious brand of far-right, Islamophobic politics. While *La Familia* represents a minority of Beitar's fan base, it has come to define the club to outside observers as a bastion of xenophobia and racism in Israel. ... [W]hen the team signed two Chechen Muslim players, fans, led by *La Familia*, revolted. They displayed a massive yellow banner that declared "Beitar will be pure forever"' (Tharoor, 2014). This highlights the hegemonic position that many ultras groups have within their fan bases and present a specific identity to others. In Beitar's case, the only form of resistance to this ideological hegemony has been the formation of a new club – Agudad Sport Nordia Jerusalem.

Many ultras groups refer not only to national identity but also to 'local patriotism' (Ginhoux, 2018). Localism has had a growing influence in Western Europe, thanks to a reconfiguration of the global economy and the growth of the EU (King, 2003). In Italy this adherence to localism has been ingrained since the early days of the ultras. In particular, there was shift from ideological politics to localism in the 1980s. 'Their logic of the *curva* as a liberated space is replaced by that of the *curva* as a small "mother country", which produced a clannishness, a cult of toughness and paramilitary organisation. This link to the small "mother country", which is very close to extreme right-wing values, facilitated racist and xenophobic behavioural patterns inside the stadia' (Podaliri and Balestri, 1998: 93–94). This is not true of all groups, as many are apolitical or hold left-wing views (Doidge, 2015a) as previously noted, but the rituals associated with the matchday experience, as well as the emotions generated, help create these localised ultras groups as small imagined communities (King, 2000).

The case of football fandom highlights how groups form on a local level. The football club becomes a focal point for groups' solidarity and is deeply associated with the historical and cultural background of the city. Most football clubs are a part of the heritage of a place, its districts, as well as class segments (Giulianotti, 1999). Studies in Norway have revealed that 'contemporary football provides a space in which the meanings of partisan fanhood are more focused on local than on national conditions and realities, whether "the local" means the physically immediate surroundings or the location of a club located elsewhere or in a different country' (Hognestad, 2003). This is emphasised and reinforced through the regularity of local rivalries, particularly those with different political views as in the case of the Nicosia derby in Cyprus between Omonia and APOEL. Ultras of the former display left-wing symbols connected to socialism and Che Guevarra, while the latter raise nationalist symbols, even with the swastika (Kassimeris and Xinari, 2018). These patterns are reproduced across Europe in particular and make collaboration between groups extremely difficult.

Conclusion

Forms of political action are constrained by national factors. Frequently, the media present all fans, and ultras in particular, as one homogenous bloc of violent or parochial thugs. This limits fans' access to governance. The ultras in Italy, for example, have had a limited say in the running of their clubs. Leading ultras have been incorporated into the patrimonial networks of club presidents, but this has marginalised the wider group membership (Doidge, 2015a). When combined with the political traditions of the ultras, this has led to a situation of confrontation between the authorities and ultras. This limits dialogue and inhibits progress. Both sides become locked into a cycle of conflict that fails to resolve itself. In contrast, German clubs engage in a continual process of dialogue with fans. Through fan projects, the employment of supporters' liaison officers and communication with fan federations like BAFF, the authorities and fans engage in constructive dialogue that gives the fans a voice, while limiting areas of conflict. A good example of this is in relation to the use of pyrotechnics. The use of flares and fireworks has been a longstanding tradition among ultras as they provide a visual and spectacular choreography. In some countries, notably Italy and Poland, the use of pyrotechnics has been banned. This has led to acts of rebellion from fans, and flares have become the symbol of spontaneity, freedom and uncompromising spirit. They are smuggled into stadiums and detonated out of sight of the surveillance cameras. In Germany the

DFB has discussed the situation with ultras groups and agreed upon a compromise that allows certain individuals to use pyrotechnics provided they have had the relevant health and safety training.

Dialogue and compromise provide a key outcome for the movement. This is true at a European level. Fan organisations like FSE are committed to maintaining a dialogue with various footballing bodies. In particular, blanket bans and stadium closures become key foci of the discussions. The problem with sanctions that punish all fans is that they can have the effect of creating a bigger problem. As Stott and Reiter (1998) argue, if all fans are treated as potential hooligans, then those innocent fans who are badly treated will identify with their fellow supporters rather than the forces of law and order. This can be extended to stadium closures for racism, where innocent fans are penalised for the actions of others. Rather than focus their ire on those who committed the acts that caused the closure, they identify with them and this reinforces the wider solidarity. In Italy in 2013, the FIGC introduced full and partial stadium closures for 'territorial discrimination' (Doidge, 2015a). This racialised form of abuse was directed at fans from the south of Italy. During the crackdown, one of the stands at AC Milan's San Siro stadium was closed after a banner was displayed that denigrated Napoli fans as cholera sufferers. The following week, fans of Inter and Juventus, Milan's biggest rivals, joined forces to perform similar chants so that their stadiums should be closed too. More significantly, Napoli fans themselves unveiled a similar banner which explicitly dared the authorities to close their stand. They were engaging in the same forms of ritualised abuse to challenge the authorities. In Rome, two stands were closed for similar behaviour. At the match in question, fans in the remaining stands engaged in the same abuse, which resulted in three stands being closed at the next match. Fans frequently identify and have solidarity with fellow supporters in opposition to the authorities. Dialogue is more likely to produce a positive outcome than confrontation.

The ultras: a conclusion

It was due to be one of the greatest moments of Eintracht Frankfurt's history. They had drawn with Shaktar Donetsk in their Europa League game in Ukraine and were looking forward to returning to the Commerzbank-Arena to complete a famous victory. Two hours before kick-off the police stormed into the *curva* to confiscate a large banner, which led to altercations with fans, with some sustaining serious injuries. The reason for the police involvement was that they claimed that the banner contained a 'foul and offensive' message concerning Peter Beuth, the local interior minister for the state of Hessen (Ford and Tamsut, 2019). In a statement, the Frankfurt group *Nordwestkurve e.V.* admitted that the banner was 'neither friendly nor particularly sophisticated', but reiterated that the police reaction was disproportionate and reflected a growing repression of the ultras' activities. Beuth had been vocal in condemning the use of pyrotechnics in Germany and police were issued a warrant to search the Frankfurt stadium for pyrotechnics before the match. They did not find any, but confiscated a banner instead. All of these heightened reactions came after a season of ultras protests against new police laws being imposed in Germany.

The result of this act of police repression was a show of solidarity from across a range of German ultras groups. Freiberg ultras raised a banner saying 'Ultras against Peter Beuth'. Borussia Dortmund's ultras displayed their solidarity with a banner reading 'Beuth, Reul, your law and order politics fog your mind!' Many more groups, including those from Babelsberg, Bayern Munich, Bochum, Braunschweig and Dynamo Dresden, all displayed banners in support of the Eintracht Frankfurt fans. It was clear that many groups felt empathy with the situation, recognising that while it may have been Eintracht Frankfurt today, tomorrow it could be any of them. It is this emotional engagement with protests that will make or break the ultras in the future. Recognising that they are all ultras and share a common activity will be crucial in overcoming the various regulations and legislative acts that are attempting to restrict ultras activities across the globe. In contrast, if the emotional attachment to one's own club overrides any attempt to collaborate with rivals, then it is harder to challenge the repression.

It is hard to generalise in a diverse movement that reflects and reacts to a variety of local, national and regional traditions, cultures, regulations and expectations. The German ultras are particularly active and political; many other groups are not as collaborative. Each group engages in different activities and for different intrinsic purposes. Some are socially engaged, while others are openly racist and nationalistic. Many are apolitical in an ideological sense, but will engage with football politics that affect their activities. What unites all ultras is an emotional, passionate support for their local club. This fandom extends well beyond the ninety minutes of a football match and comes through social media posts, planning choreographies and conversations in the pub. The ultras have a fairly common form of expression through the performance of choreographies, chants and sustained support throughout the game. Through the rituals of the performance, members build an emotional attachment to their club that valorises the colours and symbols of that team, while denigrating those of their opponents.

Since their emergence in Italy in 1968, ultras have become the most dominant style of football fandom in the world. In the decades since, the ultras style has spread from Southern Europe across North Africa to Northern and Eastern Europe, South East Asia and North America. This book has argued that ultras are an important site of enquiry into understanding contemporary society. They are a passionate, politically engaged collective that base their identity around a form of consumption (football) that links to modern notions of identity like masculinity and nationalism. This collective identity is generated and reinforced through the collective rituals associated with matchday attendance. The match provides a focal point for the group. These regular, repetitive congregations are not a passive act, but active engagement which continues throughout the week as chants, banners and tifos are planned. The football season provides many of these focal points and this has a cumulative effect for the group. Key matches, notably local derbies, require more attention. Choreographies will be planned months in advance, which helps intensify the individual group members' attachment to the ultras group throughout this preparation.

These regular, repetitive acts generate a range of emotions. From the pleasure of sociability and being around people like yourself (Simmel,

1950) to the joy and ecstasy of celebrating a goal or a hard-fought victory, fans will experience emotions that contrast with their daily lives. As Durkheim (1964) argued, the contrast with mundane everyday life helps intensify the identification with the group. This is magnified through the collective effervescence generated from the chants, choreographies and pyrotechnics. This collective ritual entrains the individuals into the wider collective such that the group moves, sings and applauds as one. This produces a feeling of flow (Csikszentmihalyi, 1992; 2008) that lifts the individuals out of themselves and provides feelings of achievement, happiness and pleasure. These emotions only intensify the feeling of belonging as they are experienced as part of the collective. This emotional connection helps the individual identify ontologically with the group (Katz, 1999). Yet the individual is key to producing these emotions. They invest in the ritual, they relax their inhibitions to engage in the activities and they contribute to the overall success of the performance. The performance only succeeds as a series of collective individual acts working in unison. In this way, ultras demonstrate the importance of shared cooperative actions to individuals' feelings of belonging (Sennett, 2012).

The global ultras phenomenon

Ultras culture, despite its Italian roots, is a global phenomenon. This is tied to the overall globalisation of football since the nineteenth century (Goldblatt, 2007; Giulianotti and Robertson, 2009). The ultras have not just emerged independently around the world, but are specifically tied to the global interest in the sport. Although ultras activities have passed into other types of sports fandom, like basketball, football is their primary driver. The colonial and imperial expansion of the British in the nineteenth century helped disseminate the sport well beyond Europe. As sport became tied to various national projects, international tournaments helped entrench football as a marker of national identity (Sugden and Tomlinson, 1998; Martin, 2004). In parallel, football has become a source of local attachment since its origins (Mason, 1980; 1988; Holt, 1989; Russell, 1997). Football clubs invariably took the name of the locale in which they were located (Giulianotti, 1999). In many places, particularly Western Europe, this has become more pronounced since the 1980s as fans identify with their home city, often in opposition to or the absence of the national team (King, 2000; Gabler 2010; Doidge, 2015a).

Engagement and support for the game of football helped develop a more active interest in the sport. People started to love the game, and some of them took a more active engagement in their support. Since at least the 1920s, fans have been organising supporters' clubs to watch the match together, or organise transport and end-of-season parties (Taylor, 1992; Doidge, 2015a). From the 1950s in Europe, various types of fan groups emerged, from *peñas* in Spain, groups like Inter's *I Moschettieri* (The Musketeers) in Italy and *Torcida* from Hajduk Split in Croatia (Guerra *et al.*, 2010; Llopis-Goig, 2015; Perasović and Mustapić, 2018). It is from supporters' groups such as these that the ultras emerged in the late 1960s in Italy. They grew out of a particularly fertile and febrile period of Italian political history that saw the re-emergence of fascism, an increase in political terrorism and growing discontent on the streets. The political paraphernalia from the protests was taken into the stadiums and early ultras groups had explicitly ideological affiliations.

Thanks to growing contact with English hooligans at the 1982 World Cup, 1984 European Championships and European club matches, violence became more central to the next generation of ultras in the 1980s. These European matches also helped spread the visual, passionate style of the ultras outside of Italy. The commercial, televised expansion of the Champions League and national leagues like Serie A and the Premier League in particular helped broadcast the ultras style around the world. From Portland, Oregon, to Jakarta, football fans have seen new ways of supporting their team. This has been enhanced as clubs utilise the spectacular images of ultras to sell their club globally, at the same time as authorities criminalise the ultras' activities and the clubs themselves try to curb some of the activities they do not like (Nuhrat, 2018a).

Thanks to social media, the ultras have a more global impact. Fans around the world that are looking for inspiration for their style of fandom can easily find numerous images, videos and websites. No longer does interest or inspiration come from witnessing the choreography in person inside the stadium; the images have a permanence that extends well beyond the ninety minutes of the match. Ultras around the world draw on these visual and performative inspirations and integrate them into their own styles. Local images, traditions and histories are incorporated into the choreographies, chants and banners as each group seeks to assert its own individuality and difference from their rivals. In this way, they engage in similar performances in order to differentiate themselves from others. This can come from enacting a particular performance, like Lech Poznan ultras turning their back on the match and jumping up and down, to designing greater and more impressive choreographies in the stadium. In each case, the group are constructing their own sense of localised identity through these performances.

These local circumstances influence the different political and ideological attitudes of groups. As we have shown in this book, nationalist performances in Eastern Europe derive from particular histories and memories of communism and war. Across the Balkans, ethno-nationalism has shaped wider political identities. These have found expression within the stadium, both as a form of identity under the unified Yugoslavia, and collective memories after the civil war (Hodges and Brentin, 2018). In Italy specific local histories have shaped other ideological engagement, such as that in Livorno with its particular historical link to communism in the country (Doidge, 2013; 2015a). Despite these local political traditions, this does not automatically translate to all ultras groups, and specific groups will develop their own political outlook. Even though the performance at the match is one of unity for the team, diverse political outlooks can in fact exist within the same fan base, such as the case of the *Boulogne Boys* and *Supras Auteuil* that existed contemporarily at PSG. At any one time, a political or apolitical group can gain hegemony within the *curva*, but this can always be contested.

Consequently, it is hard to state there is one ultras culture. In this case, the term 'culture' is used in the manner of Geertz (1973: 452), who stated that 'the culture of a people is an ensemble of texts, themselves ensembles, which the anthropologist strains to read over the shoulders of those to whom they properly belong.' Academically, it is problematic to homogenise large groups of people under one 'culture' and this effectively leads to essentialism (Ortner, 2006). Arguing that there is an 'ultras culture' essentialises their actions and denies the groups any agency in changing things. Alternatively, we essentialise ultras within a particular national culture, for example Italian ultras compared to Greek ultras. Throughout this book we have shown that there are many differences within groups, even opposing political ideologies. While there are many similarities in terms of style and form, such as clothing, naming conventions of groups, choreographies and use of pyrotechnics, each group will have their own group dynamics that will influence how they operate as they adopt local and national acts into their repertoire. We can read and interpret these 'texts', but have to be careful not to homogenise and essentialise.

Recognising culture as a process, it is possible to see how the various groups operate within the confines of global, commercialised football. As the game has become more commercialised at the elite male level, ultras have mobilised to resist these changes. Under the banner of Against Modern Football, many fans, including ultras, draw upon an image of 'modern football' with which they can resist (Doidge, 2015a; Numerato, 2015; 2018; Hill *et al.*, 2016; Perasović and Mustapić, 2018). Against Modern Football becomes an invented tradition that is constructed by the groups themselves in order to link to an imagined golden age of fandom from the past (King, 1997b). Other groups, meanwhile, adopt the image of an urban guerrilla into their style. This can include wearing clothing of the casuals style, in particular wearing apparel that obscures the face. Jackets with hoods and goggles, combined with scarves in club colours covering the face, all help to de-individualise the individual ultra and highlight how they are one collective. Despite their resistance to the commercialisation of football, the style of clothing is still a consumption and many styles have become brands as individuals seek to identify themselves as an ultra.

The absorption of the individual into the collective is achieved within the prescribed hierarchies of the groups. They can be seen as one of the last bastions of what Durkheim (1997) called mechanical solidarity. This reflects strong group cohesion through the enduring influence of 'elders' within the group. Most ultras groups do not operate as a democratic order, but as a hierarchy with the capo as a leader. While all members have a voice and are free to express their opinions, this does not necessarily mean that those views are taken into account. Activities and strategies are controlled by the *direttivi* that organise the groups' activities. Bonds between members are based on trust, reliability and the sacrifice of individual interest for the sake of group. To be an ultra is to be subsumed within the broader collective.

These structures, which resemble those of militant groups, are also a consequence of the gendered aspects of ultras fandom. As demonstrated in Chapter 5, the majority of the members of ultras groups are male. In this sense, there are gendered expectations of solidarity, protection of territory and of rules of engagement, particularly with a readiness to be violent (sometimes physically but always symbolically in order to offend rivals). Female fans are still in the minority and some will have their own groups. The political origins of the ultras ensured a high proportion of female members in the phenomenon's formative years in Italy (Cere, 2002). Female participation, however, has fluctuated with the growing focus on violence. In these situations, there remains a gendered division of labour with female ultras invariably undertaking caring responsibilities (Ginhoux, 2018). As with other aspects of the ultras, these dynamics vary greatly depending on the group and location. For example, there are many more female ultras at Werder Bremen than there are at Lech Poznan.

The collective performances of the ultras help generate spectacular atmospheres in the stands. As Emile Durkheim and Randall Collins have shown, high levels of emotional energy emerge during group rituals, which makes the group experience even stronger. This helps to reinforce the solidarity of the group as well as contrasting with the mundane routine of everyday life. This emotional response ensures continued practice and engagement with the groups. As Katz (1999) argues, emotions are an embodied response and help the individual to take control of the situation. Even if the team is losing, the performance of the ultras still produces the collective effervescence that unites the group. Key symbols become venerated by the group within the emotional cauldron of the stadium. These symbols, political ideas and practices are presented to a broader audience thanks to the extraordinary manner of communication in the ultras' performance. The spectacle is created with huge flags, choreographies, flares, collective singing, clapping and jumping, which all produce powerful images. These are then presented around the world through social media or through the commercial activities of football clubs, leagues and television. In this way, these images are consumed, interpreted and incorporated continually across the globe.

The future

The ultras represent one of the largest and most visible social collectives in the world today. There are few activities where many thousands of people across the globe engage in a shared set of practices on a weekly basis. It is for this reason that the ultras phenomenon has grown in popularity and power since the late 1960s. Regular congregation strengthens the emotional connection individuals have to the group, as relationships and friendships build while the excitement of the match provides opportunities to express emotions publicly, which is not usually socially acceptable elsewhere. As clubs, leagues and media companies continue to expand their markets, it is unlikely that there will be a reduction in the number of matches being played. This will mean that there will continue to be numerous opportunities for ultras to meet, perform and create their spectacles. There will be continuing passion and performance in stadiums across the world, all of which will intensify and magnify the image of the ultras. It is for this reason that the ultras are not going away.

Since their inception, ultras have regularly been seen as a folk devil; this has led to increased repression of certain types of activities (Marchi, 2005; Doidge, 2015a). Becker (1973) identified that deviant behaviour was not intrinsically deviant, but was just labelled as such by others. Many activities of the ultras have been undertaken in a similar way for decades. The dramatic commercialisation of the game has led to football clubs attempting to change the behaviours and demographics of the fans in the stadium. Consequently, certain activities are now deemed deviant. This has led to the hypocritical position where clubs and media companies use the passionate image of the ultras to sell their brand, while at the same time criminalising the activities that create that image (Nuhrat, 2018a). These feelings of repression and persecution are symbolised under the banner Against Modern Football and reflect a general point of resistance for ultras. The continued criminalisation and debate around the use pyrotechnics highlights that increased regulation will not fade away. There are certainly health and safety issues related to the use of flares, as the death of Lazio fan Vincenzo Paparelli in 1979 attests. Yet the footballing and State authorities rarely engage with the views of fans. This results in the hypocritical situation where football clubs will use pyrotechnics when welcoming the players onto the pitch, but not allow the regulated use of similar devices by fans. The use of flares and fireworks then becomes a pleasurable, transgressive act that provides status to those who manage to do so without sanction. It is also likely to lead to more injuries as fans take greater risks in order to ignite pyrotechnic devices without being caught.

Anger at the growing regulation of ultras is particularly focused on key symbolic targets: the football authorities and the police. Throughout this book there have been numerous examples of ultras protesting about sanctions or actions by UEFA, football leagues or football associations. From Legia Warsaw displaying an image of a pig dining on money within the UEFA logo, to German fans protesting against the Bundesliga, the football authorities have become the targets of the ultras' wrath as the symbolic gatekeepers of 'modern football'. This is despite the fact that football club owners and directors have been the main drivers of the commercial changes within the sport (King, 1998; 2003; Doidge, 2015a). Ultras have been known to protest against their club; the relationship between owners and supporters is often fractured as those in the boardroom are not seen to be as committed as the fans (Portelli, 1993; Klugman, 2008). Clubs will only attract the ire of the ultras if they have not succeeded in ways that the fans think they should have, for instance if it is perceived that the owners have not invested adequately in the team, or are actively trying to undermine the privileges of the ultras (Doidge, 2015a). As UEFA and leagues assert more power, they will continue to be the focus of protests from fans. This provides the clubs a certain amount of distance from the protests (even though they are constituent members of the leagues). How the clubs manage future regulation of the ultras will determine whether the clubs also become symbolic of 'modern football' as UEFA and the leagues have.

As noted, the police have become a key area of conflict and this will continue as regulation is increased. This is manifested in an anti-police mentality symbolised with the acronym ACAB (Stefanini, 2009; Doidge, 2015a). The difference between the police and football authorities is that the ultras come face-to-face with the police on a regular basis. How the police act has a dramatic impact on the outcomes of any potential conflict, as well as how fans perceive the enactment of legislation and regulation (Stott and Pearson, 2007). They symbolise the regulation of modern football. Yet the regular interactions between fans and police mean that they learn each other's actions and strategies. As demonstrated in Cairo, the ultras of Zamalek and Al Ahly became skilled in engaging the Egyptian police (El-Zatmah, 2012). This meant that they effectively became the armed wing of the Egyptian revolution in 2011 as part of the Arab Spring. Yet the inverse is also the case as the authorities can use policing at football matches as training opportunities for wider strategies for policing the general populace. How the police treat ultras becomes an advanced warning system for State repression.

It should not be forgotten that not all the acts of the ultras are pleasant or legal. There are many reasons why their activities understandably lead to confrontation with the police and authorities: violence, racism, misogyny and criminal activity mean that many of activities necessitate police involvement. The challenge for the police is not to treat all ultras as potentially criminal or violent (Stott and Pearson, 2007). Some of the ultras' activities are financed through organised crime, particularly drug dealing. There has been a long running police investigation into ticket touting by Juventus ultras with links to the Calabrian organised crime network 'Ndrangheta (Jones, 2016). The main conduit between Juventus and the *Drughi* was a fan called Ciccio Bucci. For twenty years he was able to access tickets from the club and then sold them for the ultras. This was lucrative and attracted the attention of the 'Ndrangheta. In 2016 Bucci was found dead at a well-known suicide spot near Turin; however, there are suggestions that this was not a suicide (Conticello, 2018). Not all ultras are innocent victims of draconian laws and policing.

Repression and regulation of ultras (and fans in general) will continue. The commercial expansion of global men's football is unrelenting. Capitalism ensures that consumers are either incorporated or excluded. Ultras will either be regulated out of the stadium through increasing legislation, banning orders and extra policing, or certain activities will be incorporated into the commercial package. Fans are an important part of the game; football without fans is nothing, as many fan groups argue. Clubs recognise the important fact that fans enhance their 'brand' and use images of their supporters to sell the club (Nuhrat, 2018a). The ultras add colour and spectacle to the stadium, when it is done on their terms. But as Giulianotti (1995) argued, official backing of the carnivalesque aspects of the festival nullifies the spectacle. Ultras have to remain autonomous in order to provide the power, energy and emotional connection to the club. Stripping away that emotion and turning people into customers would not only lead to sanitised stadiums, but require clubs to find evermore innovative ways of bringing new customers through the doors – which basically means having the best players on the pitch. Unlike the theatre or opera, sport is ultimately a results-driven business and someone has to lose. For many, fans and ultras alike, they want to see commitment on the pitch and feel part of a collective. This emotional attachment is what sustains their regular participation.

Challenging regulation and repression is vital to maintaining the emotional core of football fandom. Yet the path to successful resistance is often contrary to the ultras mentality. Part of the performance of ultras fandom is to be confrontational and to resist 'modern football'. But it is also about being different from your rivals and differentiating yourselves from others. Successful resistance will only come through a united approach, which will require cooperation between rival factions and groups. The tactic of divide and conquer makes it easier for clubs, authorities and politicians to force through changes. In reality, few owners will wish to confront their own fan base, but a fragmented *curva* is easier to deal with. There is evidence that ultras have collaborated in the face of increased repression. Italian fans successfully fought the mandatory imposition of the *tessera del tifoso* membership cards. The Poznan Pact and Genoa agreement between rival ultras groups also showed certain rules of engagement could be agreed upon. And the ultras from Cairo demonstrated that they can have an impact on revolution. Clearly, much of this rests on the power of those in authority and local issues will always take precedence.

Resisting everything, however, demonstrates little self-reflexivity and wins little sympathy. Despite Numerato's (2015; 2018) assertion, there is little evidence that many groups exhibit reflexivity of their actions. Continuing racist abuse or engaging in dangerous and violent acts while blindly resisting everything is not a strategy that will produce victory. There is no moral case for racism, an act that systematically undermines individuals based on one aspect of their physical appearance. Similarly, there is little support for the indiscriminate use of violence, particularly when there are innocent victims. This has to be about picking the right battles. For example, while the use of pyrotechnics is controversial, it is not universally despised; it unites most ultras groups where ideological politics does not. While there are obvious dangers to using such devices in crowded spaces, there have been advances in smokeless flares. Danish fans, for example, have been in dialogue with Brøndby IF about developing safe pyrotechnics (FSE, 2017). Although discussions with legislators are more problematic, winning the support of clubs is an important step. In the UK, the debate about standing at football ignited in 2018 when West Bromwich Albion and Shrewsbury Town applied to introduce standing areas in their stadiums. After the then sports minister Tracey Crouch declared that it was only a 'vocal minority' who wanted to stand, over 100,000 fans petitioned the government and forced a review of the legislation. Elsewhere, Ajax Amsterdam installed a standing section in 2016 and this was expanded two years later after its initial success. Clear, coordinated campaigns are more likely to work when the power imbalance is weighted in favour of clubs and authorities.

Ultimately, it depends on what the various groups actually want. As has been argued throughout, there is not one unified ultras culture or approach; there is a heterogeneity of opinions and approaches within the ultras. It is not clear that the ultras actually want to overturn the current system. According to a lot of observers, their resistance is performative and demonstrates their transgressive outlook. For many, there is a pleasure in deviance (Katz, 1988; King, 1997a). Therefore, no matter what the authorities do, the ultras will continue to resist. In fact, the authorities may actually be contributing to the maintenance of this transgressive mentality through continued repression. As Doidge (2015a) argues in relation to Italy, increased regulation affects all football fans, which can actually dissuade many non-ultras from attending matches. The result is that the ultras are the only ones left regularly attending, which gives them a greater sense of entitlement to be the 'authentic fans' and reinforces their behaviour. Continued repression only adds fuel to the ultras' narrative of persecution. The result is that both sides are locked into what Albert Camus called a 'fatal embrace' where both sides are incapable of uniting and are willing to fight until the end.

References

Abercrombie, N. and Longhurst, B. (1998). *Audiences: A Sociological Theory of Performance and Imagination*. London: SAGE.

Abu-Lughod, L. (1986). *Veiled Sentiments: Honor and Poetry in a Bedouin Society*. Berkeley: University of California Press.

Abu-Lughod, L. and Lutz, C. (1990). *Language and the Politics of Emotions*. Cambridge: Cambridge University Press.

Ahmed, S. (2004). *The Cultural Politics of Emotion*. London: Routledge.

Alexander, J. (2006). 'Cultural pragmatics: social performance between ritual and strategy', in: J.C. Alexander, B. Giesen, J.L. Mast (eds), *Social Performance: Symbolic Action, Cultural Pragmatics, and Ritual*, pp. 29–90. Cambridge: Cambridge University Press.

Alexander, J. (2017). *The Drama of Social Life*. Cambridge: Polity.

Amado, C. (2008). 'The ugly side of the beautiful game – hooliganism in French football', unpublished MA thesis. Provo: Brigham Young University.

Anderson, B. (1983). *Imagined Communities*. London: Verso.

Anderson, E. (1999). *Code of the Street: Decency, Violence and the Moral Life of the Inner City*. New York: Norton.

Antonowicz, D. and Grodecki, M. (2018). 'Missing the goal: policy evolution towards football-related violence in Poland (1989–2012)', *International Review for the Sociology of Sport*, 53(4): 490–511.

Antonowicz, D., Szlendak, T. and Kossakowski, R. (2016). 'Flaming flares and football fanatics and political rebellion', in: M. Schwartz, H. Winkel (eds), *Eastern European Youth Cultures in a Global Context*, pp. 131–144. London: Palgrave.

Antonowicz, D., Jakubowska, H. and Kossakowski, R. (2018). 'Marginalised, patronised and instrumentalised: Polish female fans in the ultras' narratives', *International Review for the Sociology of Sport*, published online 25 June, https://doi.org/10.1177/1012690218782828.

Araújo, N., Carlos, P. de and Fraiz, J.A. (2014). 'Top European football clubs and social networks: a true 2.0 relationship?', *Sport, Business and Management*, 4(3): 250–264.

Archetti, E. (2001). 'The spectacle of a heroic life: the case of Diego Maradona', in: D.L. Andrews and S.J. Jackson (eds), *Sport Stars: The Cultural Politics of Sporting Celebrity*, pp. 151–163. New York: Routledge.

Archetti, E. and Romero, A.G. (1994). 'Death and violence in Argentinian football', in: R. Giulianotti, N. Bonney and M. Hepworth (eds), *Football, Violence and Social Identity*, pp. 37–72. London and New York: Routledge.

Armstrong, G. (1998). *Football Hooligans: Knowing the Score*. Oxford: Berg.

Armstrong, G. and Harris, R. (1991). 'Football hooligans: theory and evidence', *Sociological Review*, 39(3): 427–458.

Arnold, R. and Veth, K.M. (2018). 'Racism and Russian football supporters' culture', *Problems of Post-Communism*, 65(2): 88–100.

Ashmore, P. (2017). 'Of other atmospheres: football spectatorships beyond the terrace chant', *Soccer and Society*, 18(1): 30–46.

Back. L., Crabbe, T. and Solomos, J. (1998). *Lions, Black Skins and Reggae Gyals: Race, Nation and Identity in Football*. London: Goldsmiths College, University of London.

Back, L., Crabbe, T. and Solomos, J. (1999). 'Beyond the racist/hooligan couplet: race, social theory and football culture', *British Journal of Sociology*, 50(3): 419–442.

Back, L., Crabbe, T. and Solomos, J. (2001). *The Changing Face of Football: Racism, Identity and Multiculture in the English Game*. Oxford: Berg.

Bairner, A. (2012). 'For a sociology of sport', *Sociology of Sport*, 29(1): 102–117.

Bakhtin, M. (1984). *Rabelais and His World*. Bloomington: Indiana University Press.

Barbalet, J. (1998). *Emotions, Social Theory, and Social Structure*. Cambridge: Cambridge University Press.

Barbalet, J., ed. (2002). *Emotions and Sociology*. Oxford: Blackwell.

Barthel-Bouchier, D. (2001). 'Authenticity and identity: theme-parking the Amanas', *International Sociology*, 16(2): 221–239.

Battani, A. (2012). 'Reshaping the national bounds through fandom: the ultr-Aslan of Galatasaray', *Soccer and Society*, 13(5–6): 701–719.

BBC (2017). 'Celtic v Linfield: Police make 12 arrest over banners', BBC News, 1 August. Available online at: www.bbc.co.uk/news/uk-scotland-40788465 [Accessed 28 February 2019].

Beck, U. (1992). *Risk Society*. London: SAGE.

Becker, H. (1973). *Outsiders: Studies in the Sociology of Deviance*. New York: The Free Press.

Benkwitz, A. and Molnar, G. (2012). 'Interpreting and exploring football fan rivalries: an overview', *Soccer and Society*, 13(4): 479–494.

Ben-Porat, A. (2009). 'Not just for men: Israeli women who fancy football', *Soccer and Society*, 10(6): 883–896.

Besta, T. and Kossakowski, R. (2018). 'Perception of in-group and out-group members as two predictors of collective action tendencies among football supporters', *Revista de Psicología del Deporte/Journal of Sport Psychology*, 27(2): 15–22.

Borisov, T. (2015). 'The fall of the Bulgarian giants', *Balkanist*, 14 February. Available online at: https://balkanist.net/the-fall-of-the-bulgarian-giants/ [Accessed 1 December 2018].

Bourdieu, P. (1986). 'The forms of capital', in: J. Richardson (ed.), *Handbook of Theory and Research for the Sociology of Education*, pp. 241–258. Westport: Greenwood.

Bouton, E. (2011). 'Corps sublimés: le prix de la virilité et de la gestion du pouvoir pour des jeunes de la culture des rues' [Sublimated bodies: the price of the virility and the management of the power for young people of the culture of streets], *International Review on Sport and Violence* 3: 95–108.

Boyd, D. (2007). 'Why youth (heart) social network sites: the role of networked publics in teenage social life', in: D. Buckingham (ed.), *MacArthur Foundation Series on Digital Learning – Youth, Identity, and Digital Media Volume*, pp. 1–26. Cambridge, MA: MIT Press.

Boyd, D.M. and Ellison, N.B. (2007). 'Social network sites: definition, history, and scholarship', *Journal of Computer-Mediated Communication*, 13(1): 210–230.

Brandt, C. and Hertel, F. (2015). 'German ultras as political players? An analysis of the protest against the "Secure Stadium Experience"', *Miscellanea Anthropologica et Sociologica*, 16(4): 64–82.

Brandt, C., Hertel, F. and Huddleston, S., eds (2017). *Football Fans, Rivalry and Cooperation*. London: Routledge.

Braudy, L. (2005). *From Chivalry to Terrorism: War and the Changing Nature of Masculinity*. New York: Vintage Books.

Brentin, D. (2016). 'Ready for the homeland? Ritual, remembrance, and political extremism in Croatian football', *Nationalities Papers*, 44(6): 1–17.

Brentin, D. and Tregoures, L. (2016). 'Entering through the sport's door? Kosovo's sport diplomatic endeavours towards international recognition', *Diplomacy and Statecraft*, 27(2): 360–378.

Bromberger, C. (1993). 'Fireworks and the ass', in: S. Redhead (ed.), *The Passion and the Fashion: Football Fandom in the New Europe*, pp. 89–103. Aldershot: Avebury.

Brooks-Hay, O. and Lombard, N. (2018). '"Home game": domestic abuse and football; the role of research in policy and practice', *Journal of Gender-Biased Violence*, 2(1): 93–108.

Brown, A. (1998). 'United we stand: some problems with fan democracy', in: A. Brown (ed.), *Fanatics! Power, Identity and Fandom in Football*, pp. 50–68. London: Routledge.

Brown, A. (2008). '"Our club, our rules": fan communities at FC United of Manchester', *Soccer and Society*, 9(3), 346–358.

Burdsey, D. (2007). *British Asians and Football: Culture, Identity, Exclusion*. London and New York: Routledge.

Burdsey, D. (2011). *Race, Ethnicity and Football: Persisting Debates and Emergent Issues*. London: Routledge.

Butler, J. (1990). *Gender Trouble*. London: Routledge.

Butler, J. (1993). *Bodies That Matter: On the Discursive Limits of 'Sex'*. London: Routledge.

Butler, J. (1997). *The Psychic Life of Power: Theories in Subjection*. Stanford: Stanford University Press.

Bylina, V. (2013). 'Belarus ultras and the regime', *Belarus Digest*, 29 January. Available online at: www.belarusdigest.com/story/belarusian-ultras-and-regime-12915 [Accessed 4 March 2019].

Calhoun, C. (2006). 'The privatization of risk', *Public Culture*, 18(2): 257–263.

Carlson, M. (1996). *Performance: A Critical Introduction*. Abingdon: Routledge.

Carnogurská, T. (2012). 'Fotbaloví fanoušci jako součást občanské společnosti', unpublished MA thesis. Prague: Univerzita Karlova.

Carrington, B. (2010). *Race, Sport and Politics: The Sporting Black Diaspora*. London: SAGE.

Carter, T.F. (2008). *The Quality of Home Runs: The Passion, Politics and Language of Cuban Baseball*. London: Duke University Press.

Carter, T.F. (2018). *On Running and Being Human: An Anthropological Perspective*. London: Palgrave.

Castells, M. (1996). *The Rise of the Network Society*. Oxford: Blackwell.

Castells, M. (2012). *Networks of Outrage and Hope: Social Movements in the Internet Age*. Cambridge: Polity.

Caudwell, J. (2011). 'Gender, feminism and football studies', *Soccer and Society*, 12(3): 330–344.

Caudwell, J. (2012). *Women's Football in the UK: Continuing with Gender Analyses*. London: Routledge.

Cere, R. (2002). '"Witches of our age": women ultras, Italian football and the media', *Sport in Society*, 5(3): 166–188.

Cere, R. (2012). '"Forever ultras": female football support in Italy', in: K. Toffoletti and P. Mewett (eds), *Sport and Its Female Fans*, pp. 46–60. Abingdon: Routledge.

Chambliss, D. (1989). 'The mundanity of excellence: an ethnographic report on stratification and Olympic swimmers', *Sociological Theory*, 7(1): 70–86.

Chiriac, M. (2012). 'Club bankruptcy highlights plight of Romanian football', *Balkan Insight*, 5 December. Available online at: https://balkaninsight.com/2012/12/05/romanian-football-club-asks-for-insolvency/ [Accessed 1 December 2018].

Chiweshe, M. (2014). 'One of the boys: female fans' responses to the masculine and phallocentric nature of football stadiums in Zimbabwe', *Critical African Studies*, 6(2–3): 211–222.

Church, B. (2019). 'Europa League: Zenit St Petersburg's fiery welcome', CNN, 29 January. Available online at: https://edition.cnn.com/2019/02/22/football/zenit-saint-petersburg-europa-league-welcome/index.html [Accessed 23 February 2019].

Clark, T. (2006). '"I'm Scunthorpe 'til I die": constructing and (re)negoti- ating identity through the terrace chant', *Soccer and Society*, 7(4): 494–507.

Cleland, J. (2010). 'From passive to active: the changing relationship between supporters and football clubs', *Soccer and Society*, 11(5), 537–552.

Cleland, J. (2011). 'The media and football supporters: a changing relation- ship', *Media, Culture and Society*, 33(2): 299–315.

Cleland, J. and Dixon, K. (2014). '"Black and whiters": the relative powerless- ness of "active" supporter organization mobility at English Premier League football clubs', *Soccer and Society*, published online 25 February, https://doi. org/10.1080/14660970.2014.891988.

Cleland, J., Doidge, M., Millward, P. and Widdop, P. (2018). *Collective Action and Football Fandom: A Relational Sociological Approach*. Basingstoke: Palgrave Macmillan.

Clough, P.T. and Halley, J., eds (2007). *The Affective Turn*. Durham, NC: Duke University Press.

Cohen, S. (1972). *Folk Devils and Moral Panics*. London and New York: Routledge.

Coleman, J.S. (1988). 'Social capital in the creation of human capital', *American Journal of Sociology* 94: 95–120.

Collard, A. (1989). 'Investigating "social memory" in a Greek context', in: E. Tonkin, M. McDonald and M.K. Chapman (eds), *History and Ethnicity*, pp. 89–103. Abingdon: Routledge.

Collins R. (1975). *Conflict Sociology: Towards an Explanatory Science*. New York: Academic Press

Collins, R. (1981). 'On the microfoundations of macrosociology', *American Journal of Sociology*, 86(5): 984–1014.

Collins R. (1990). 'Stratification, emotional energy, and the transient emotions', in: T. Kemper (ed.), *Research Agendas in the Sociology of Emotions*, pp. 27–57. Albany: State University of New York Press.

Collins, R. (2004). *Interaction Ritual Chains*. Princeton: Princeton University Press.

Collins, R. (2008). *Violence: A Micro-Sociological Theory*. Princeton: Princeton University Press.

Connell, R.W. (1987). *Gender and Power: Society, the Person and Sexual Politics*. New York: Polity.

Connell, R.W. (2000). *The Men and the Boys*. Sydney: Allen & Unwin Australia.

Connell, R.W. (2002). *Gender. Short Introductions*. Cambridge: Polity.

Connell, R.W. (2012) 'Gender, health and theory: conceptualizing the issue, in local and world perspective', *Social Science and Medicine*, 74(11): 1675– 1683.

Connell, R.W. and Messerschmidt, J.W. (2005). 'Hegemonic masculinity: rethinking the concept', *Gender and Society*, 19(6): 829–859.

Conticello, F. (2018). 'Curva Juve e 'ndrangheta: Bagarini ancora attivi, *La Gazzetta dello Sport*, 23 October. Available online at: www.gazzetta.it/

Calcio/Serie-A/Juventus/23–10–2018/curva-juve-ndrangheta-bagarini-ancor a-attivi-300899729157.shtml [Accessed 28 February 2019].

Contreras, R. (2018). 'Que duro! Street violence in the South Bronx', in: E.B. Weininger, A. Larueau and O. Lizardo (eds), *Ritual, Emotion, Violence; Studies in the Micro-Sociology of Randall Collins*, pp. 27–45. London and New York: Routledge.

Contucci, L. and Francesio, G. (2013). *A Porte Chiusi: Gli Ultimi Giorni del Calcio Italiano*. Bologna: Sperling & Kupfer.

Cooley, C.H. (1902). *Human Nature and the Social Order*. New York: Charles Skribner's Sons

Crawford, G. (2004). *Consuming Sport: Fans, Sport and Culture*. London: Routledge.

Crossley, M. (2002). *Making Sense of Social Movements*. Buckingham: Open University Press.

Csikszentmihalyi, M. (1979). 'The concept of flow', in: B. Sutton-Smith (ed.), *Play and Learning*, pp. 335–358. New York: Wiley.

Csikszentmihalyi, M. (1992). *Flow: The Psychology of Happiness*. London: Rider.

Csikszentmihalyi, M. (2008). *Flow: The Psychology of Optimal Experience*. London: Harper Perennial.

Csikszentmihalyi, M. and Csikszentmihalyi, S., eds (1988). *Optimal Experience: Psychological Studies of Flow in Consciousness*. Cambridge: Cambridge University Press.

Dal Lago, A. (1990). *Descrizione Di Una Battaglia: I Rituali Del Calcio*. Bologna: Il Mulino.

Dal Lago, A. and De Biasi, R. (1994). 'Italian football fans: culture and organisation', in: R. Giulianotti, N. Bonney and M. Hepworth (eds), *Football, Violence, and Social Identity*, pp. 73–89. London and New York: Routledge.

Damasio, A.R. (1994). *Descartes' Error: Emotion, Reason and the Human Brain*. London: Papermac.

Damasio, A.R. (1999). *The Feeling of What Happens: Body and Emotion in the Making of Consciousness*. New York: Harcourt Brace and Company.

De Biasi, R. and Lanfranchi, P. (1997). 'The importance of difference: football identities in Italy', in: G. Armstrong and R. Giulianotti (eds), *Entering the Field: New Perspectives on World Football*, pp. 87–104. Oxford: Berg.

Deleuze, G. (1988). *Spinoza: practical philosophy*. San Francisco: City Light Books.

Deleuze, G. and Guattari, F. (2013). *A Thousand Plateaus*. London: Bloomsbury.

Della Porta, D. and Diani, M. (2006). *Social Movements: An Introduction*. Oxford: Blackwell.

Della Porta, D. and Tarrow, S. (2005). *Transnational Protest and Global Activism*. Oxford: Rowman and Littlefield.

Demetriou, D.Z. (2001). 'Connell's concept of hegemonic masculinity: a critique', *Theory and Society*, 30(3): 337–361.

Denzin, N. (2007). *On Understanding Emotion*. New Brunswick and London: Transaction.

Dixon, T. (2003). *From Passions to Emotions: The Creation of a Secular Psychological Category*. Cambridge: Cambridge University Press.

Djordjević, I. (2012). 'Twenty years later: the war did (not) begin at Maksimir: an anthropological analysis of the media narratives about a never ended football game', *Glasnik Etnografskog Instituta SANU*, 60(2): 201–216.

Djordjević, I. and Pekić, R. (2018). 'Is there space for the left? Football fans and political positioning in Serbia', *Soccer and Society*, 19(3): 355–372.

Doidge, M. (2013). '"The birthplace of Italian Communism": political identity and action amongst Livorno fans', *Soccer and Society*, 14(2): 246–261.

Doidge, M. (2014). *Anti-racism in European Football: Report to UEFA*. Brighton: University of Brighton.

Doidge, M. (2015a). *Football Italia: Italian Football in an Age of Globalization*. London: Bloomsbury Academic.

Doidge, M. (2015b). '"If you jump up and down, Balotelli dies": racism and player abuse in Italian football', *International Review for the Sociology of Sport*, 50(3): 249–264.

Doidge, M. (2017). 'The Italian ultras: from local divisions to national co-operation', in: B. Garcia (ed.), *Whose Game Is It? Supporter Activism and Regulation in European Football*, pp. 45–64. Basingstoke: Palgrave.

Doidge, M. and Lieser, M. (2013). 'The globalisation of ultras culture: an international comparison of Japanese and Italian fan-groups', in: *Global Research Project on Fan Communities and Fandom Conference*, Harris Manchester College, University of Oxford, 22–23 March 2013.

Doidge, M. and Lieser, M. (2018). 'The importance of research on the ultras: introduction', *Sport in Society*, 21(6): 833–840.

Doidge, M. and Sandri, E. (2018a). *Active Integration*. Brighton: University of Brighton.

Doidge, M. and Sandri, E. (2018b). '"Friends that last a lifetime": the importance of emotions amongst volunteers working with refugees in Calais', *British Journal of Sociology*, published online 13 May, https://doi.org/10.1111/1468-4446.12484.

Duke, V. (1991). 'The sociology of football: a research agenda for the 1990s', *Sociological Review*, 29(3): 627–645.

Duke, V. and Crolley, L. (1996). 'Football spectator behaviour in Argentina: a case of separate evolution', *Sociological Review*, 44(2): 272–293.

Dunn, C. (2014). *Female Football Fans: Community, Identity and Sexism*. London: Palgrave.

Dunn, C. (2017). 'The impact of the supporters' trust movement on women's feelings and practices of their football fandom', *Soccer and Society*, 18(4): 462–475.

Dunning, E. (1999). *Sport Matters: Sociological Studies of Sport, Violence and Civilization*. London: Routledge.

Dunning, E., Murphy, P. and Williams, J. (1986). 'Spectator violence at football matches: towards a sociological explanation', *British Journal of Sociology*, 37(2): 221–244.

Dunning, E., Murphy, P. and Williams, J. (1988). *The Roots of Football Hooliganism*. London: Routledge.

Dunning, E., Murphy, P. and Williams, J. (1991). 'Anthropological versus sociological approaches to the study of soccer hooliganism: some critical notes', *Sociological Review*, 39(3): 459–479.

Durkheim, E. (1952). *Suicide: A Study in Sociology*. London: Routledge & Kegan Paul.

Durkheim, E. (1964). *The Elementary Forms of the Religious Life*. Oxford: Oxford University Press.

Durkheim, E. (1997). *The Division of Labor in Society*. New York: The Free Press.

Ekman, P. (1972). 'Universals and cultural differences in facial expressions of emotions', in: J. Cole (ed.), *Nebraska Symposium on Motivation*. Lincoln, NB: University of Nebraska Press.

Ekman, P. (2003). *Emotions Revealed: Understanding Thoughts and Feelings*. London: Weidenfeld and Nicolson.

Ekman, P. and Davidson, R.J., eds (1994), *The Nature of Emotion. Fundamental Questions*. Oxford: Oxford University Press.

Elias, N. (1978). *What Is Sociology?*. New York: Columbia University Press.

Elias, N. (2000). *The Civilizing Process*. Oxford: Wiley-Blackwell.

Elias, N. (2001). *The Society of Individuals*. London: Continuum.

Elias, N., and Dunning, E. (1986). *Quest for Excitement: Sport and Leisure in the Civilizing Process*. Oxford: Blackwell.

Elster, J. (1999). *Strong Feelings: Emotion, Addiction and Human Behaviour*. Cambridge, MA: MIT Press.

Elster, J. (2008). *Alchemies of the Mind: Rationality and Emotions*. Cambridge: Cambridge University Press.

El-Zatmah, S. (2012). 'From terso into ultras: the 2011 Egyptian revolution and the radicalization of the soccer's ultra-fans', *Soccer and Society*, 13(5–6): 801–813.

Erhart, I. (2011). 'Ladies of Besiktas: a dismantling of male hegemony at Inonu Stadium', *International Review for the Sociology of Sport*, 48(1): 83–98.

Erhart, I. (2014). 'United in protest: from "living and dying with our colours" to "let all the colours of the world unite"', *International Journal of the History of Sport*, published online 18 June, https://doi.org/10.1080/095233 67.2014.929116.

Evans-Pritchard, E. (1940). *The Nuer: A Description of the Modes of Livelihood and Political Institutions of a Nilotic People*. Oxford: Clarendon Press.

FAC (n.d). 'More about FAC', Fans Against Criminalisation website. Available online at: http://fansagainstcriminalisation.com/more-about-fac/ [Accessed 22 April 2019].

Farred, G. (2002). 'Long distance love: growing up a Liverpool Football Club fan', *Journal of Sport and Social Issues*, 26(1): 6–24.

Feldman, A. (1991). *Formations of Violence: The Narrative of the Body and Political Terror in Northern Ireland*. Chicago: University of Chicago Press.

Ferreri, A. (2008). *Ultras, I Ribelli del Calcio: Quarant' Anni di Antagonismo e Passione*. Milan: Bepress.

Foot, J. (2006). *Calcio: A History of Italian Football*. New York: Harper Perennial.

Ford, M. (2018). 'German fan groups quit DFB talks, promise further protests', Deutsche Welle online, 21 August. Available online at: www.dw.com/en/german-fan-groups-quit-dfb-talks-promise-further-protests/a-45161140 [Accessed 2 March 2019].

Ford, M. and Tamsut, F. (2019). 'Eintracht Frankfurt's Europa League success marred by "disproportionate" policing', Deutsche Welle online, 23 February. Available online at: www.dw.com/en/eintracht-frankfurts-europa-league-success-marred-by-disproportionate-policing/a-47642946 [Accessed 28 February 2019].

Foster, W. and Hyatt, C. (2007). 'I despise them! I detest them! Franchise relocation and the expanded model of organisational identification', *Journal of Sport Management*, 21(2): 194–212.

Foucault, M. (1991). *Discipline and Punish: The Birth of the Prison*. Harmondsworth: Penguin.

Free, M. and Hughson, J. (2003). 'Settling accounts with hooligans: gender blindness in football supporter subculture research', *Men and Masculinities*, 6(2): 136–155.

Freud, S. ([1921] 2001). *Group Psychology and the Analysis of the Ego*. Vol. 18 of *The Standard Edition of the Complete Works of Sigmund Freud*. London: Vintage.

Frosdick, S. and Marsh, P. (2005). *Football Hooliganism*. Cullompton: Willan Publishing.

FSA (2019). 'Affiliates and associates', Football Supporters' Association website. Available online at: www.fsf.org.uk/about-us/affiliates-and-associates/ [Accessed 2 August 2019].

FSE (2017). 'Brøndby IF: club and Danish Football Fanclubs (DFF) develop safe flares', Football Supporters Europe website. Available online at: www.fanseurope.org/en/news/news-3/1535-brondby-if-club-and-danish-football-fanclubs-dff-develop-safe-flares-en.html [Accessed 28 February 2019].

Fuchs, C. (2012). 'Some reflections on Manuel Castells' book *Networks of Outrage and Hope: Social Movements in the Internet Age*', *tripleC*, 10(2): 775–797.

Fuller, A. and Junaedi, F. (2018). 'Ultras in Indonesia: conflict, diversification, activism', *Sport in Society*, 21(6): 919–931.

Gabler, J. (2010). *Die Ultras: Fussballfans und Fussballkulturen in Deutschland*. Cologne: PapyRossa.

Gabler, J. (2013). 'Of structured emotions and emotionally charged structures: spotlight on recent developments in the ultra scene', in: M. Gabriel, N. Selmer and H. Thaler (eds), *Fan Work 2.0: Future Challenges for the Pedagogical Work with Football Fans*. Obertshausen: Fan Project Coordinating Centre at German Sport Youth.

García, B. and Welford, J. (2015). 'Supporters and football governance, from customers to stakeholders: a literature review and agenda for research', *Sport Management Review*, 18(4): 517–528.

Garfinkel, H. (1967). *Studies in Ethnomethodology*. Cambridge: Polity.

Geertz, C. (1972). 'Deep play: notes on a Balinese cock fight', *Daedalus*, 101(1): 1–37.

Geertz, C. (1973). 'Thick description: toward an interpretive theory of culture', in: C. Geertz, *The Interpretation of Cultures*, pp. 3–30. New York: Basic Books.

Geertz, C. (1983). *Local Knowledge: Further Essays in Interpretive Anthropology*. New York: Basic Books.

Gerke, M. (2018). '"Supporters, not consumers." Grassroots supporters' culture and sports entertainment in the US', *Sport in Society*, 21(6): 932–945.

Gibbons, T. and Dixon, K. (2010). '"Surf's up!": a call to take English soccer fan interactions on the Internet more seriously', *Soccer and Society*, 11(5): 599–613.

Giddens, A. (1990). *The Consequences of Modernity*. Stanford: Stanford University Press.

Giddens, A. (1991). *Modernity and Self-identity*. Stanford: Stanford University Press.

Giddens, A. (1992). *The Transformation of Intimacy*. New York: Wiley.

Gillett, J. and White, P.G. (1992). 'Male bodybuilding and the reassertion of hegemonic masculinity: a critical feminist perspective', *Play and Culture*, 5(4), 358–369.

Gil-Lopez, T., Ahmed, S. and Taylor, L. (2017). 'Understanding fandom in the multilingual Internet: a study of "El Clasico" fans' commenting behavior on YouTube', *International Journal of Sport Communication*, 10: 17–33.

Ginhoux, B. (2012). 'L'interdiction de stade: Analyse de la mise à l'épreuve de la carrière des supporters de football ultras', *Sociétés et jeunesses en difficulté*, 13 Printemps.

Ginhoux, B. (2018). 'Openers, witnesses, followers, and "good guys": a socio-logical study of the different roles of female and male ultra fans in confronta-tional situations', *Sport in Society*, 21(6): 841–853.

Giulianotti, R. (1991). 'Scotland's tartan army in Italy: the case for the carnivalesque', *Sociological Review*, 39(3): 503–527.

Giulianotti, R. (1994). 'Social identity and public order: political and aca-demic discourses on football violence', in: R. Giulianotti, N. Bonney and M. Hepworth (eds), *Football, Violence and Social Identity*, pp. 9–36. London: Routledge.

Giulianotti, R. (1995). 'Football and the politics of carnival: an ethnographic study of Scottish fans in Sweden', *International Review for the Sociology of Sport*, 30(2): 191–220.

Giulianotti, R. (1999). *Football: A Sociology of the Global Game*. Cambridge: Polity.

Giulianotti, R. (2002). 'Supporters, followers, fans and flaneurs: a taxonomy of spectator identities in football', *Journal of Sport and Social Issues*, 26(1): 25–46.

Giulianotti, R. (2005). 'The sociability of sport: Scotland football supporters as interpreted through the sociology of Georg Simmel', *International Review for the Sociology of Sport*, 40(3): 289–306.

Giulianotti, R. (2011). Sport mega-events, urban football carnivals and securitised commodification: the case of the English Premier League', *Urban Studies*, 48(15): 3293–3310.

Giulianotti, R. and Robertson, R. (2009). *Globalization and Football*. London: SAGE.

Glathe, J. (2016). 'Football fan subculture in Russia: aggressive support, readiness to fight, and far right links', *Europe-Asia Studies*, 68(9): 1506–1525.

Goffman, E. (1959). *The Presentation of Self in Everyday Life*. London: Penguin Random House.

Goffman, E. (1961). *Encounters: Two Studies in the Sociology of Interaction*. Indianapolis: Bobbs-Merrill.

Goffman, E. (1967). *Interaction Rituals: Essays on Face-to-Face Behavior*. London: AldlineTransaction.

Goffman, E. (1971). *Relations in Public: Microstudies of the Public Order*. New York: Basic Books.

Göksoy, E.C. and Yilmaz, O. (2017). 'Istanbul united: a short-lived experience of agonistic pluralism', in: C. Brandt, F. Hertel and S. Huddleston (eds), *Football Fans, Rivalry and Cooperation*, pp. 158–169. London: Routledge.

Goldblatt, D. (2007). *The Ball is Round*. London: Penguin.

Goodwin, J. and Jasper, J.M., eds (2004). *Rethinking Social Movements: Structure, Meaning and Emotion*. Lanham: Rowman and Littlefield.

Goodwin, J., Jasper, J.M. and Polletta, F., eds (2001). *Passionate Politics: Emotions and Social Movements*. Chicago: University of Chicago Press.

Gordon, S.L. (1989). 'Institutional and impulsive orientations in selectively appropriating emotions to self', in: D.D. Franks and E.D. McCarthy (eds), *The Sociology of Emotions: Original Essays and Research Papers*, pp. 115–135. Greenwich, CT: JAI.

Gould, D. (2004). 'Passionate political process: bringing emotions back into the study of social movements', in: J. Goodwin, J.M. Jasper (eds), *Rethinking Social Movements: Structure, Meaning and Emotions*, pp. 155–176. Lanham: Rowman and Littlefield.

Gould, D. (2010). *Moving Politics: Emotion and ACT UP's Fight Against AIDS*. Chicago and London: University of Chicago Press.

Grabia, G. (2011). *La Doce: La Verdadera Historia de la Barra Brava de Boca*. Buenos Aires: Sudamericana.

Gramsci, A. (1971). *Selections from the Prison Notebooks of Antonio Gramsci*. New York: International Publishers.

Greco, M. and Stenner, P. (2008). *Emotions: A Social Science Reader*. London: Routledge.

Gregg, M. and Seigworth, G. (2010). *The Affect Theory Reader*. Durham, NJ: Duke University Press.

Guerra, N., Imperi, V. and Vardanega, C. (2010). *I Poeti della Curva*. Roma: Aracne.

Guschwan, M. (2011). 'Fans, Romans, countrymen: soccer fandom and civic identity in contemporary Rome', *International Journal of Communication*, 5(1): 1990–2013.

Guschwan, M. (2013). 'La tessera della rivolta: Italy's failed fan identification card', *Soccer and Society*, 14(2), 215–229.

Guschwan, M. (2014). 'Stadium as public sphere', *Sport in Society*, 17(7), 884–900.

Guţu, D. (2017). '"Casuals" culture. Bricolage and consumerism in football supporters' culture. Case study – Dinamo Bucharest Ultras', *Soccer and Society*, 18(7): 914–936.

Habermas, J. (1989). *The Structural Transformation of the Public Sphere: An Inquiry into a Category of Bourgeois Society*. Cambridge, MA: MIT Press.

Haenfler, R. (2014). *Subcultures: The Basics*. New York: Routledge.

Ha-Ilan, N. (2018). 'The (Re)Constitution of football fandom: Hapoel Katamon Jerusalem and its supporters', *Sport in Society*, 21(6): 902–918.

Hall, S. (1978). 'The treatment of football hooliganism in the press', in R. Ingham (ed.), *Football Hooliganism: The Wider Context*, pp. 15–36. London: Inter-Action Imprint.

Hardt, M. and Negri, A. (2005). *Multitude: War and Democracy in the Age of Empire*. London: Penguin Books.

Harvey, J., Horne, J., Safai, P., Darnell, S. and Courchesne-O'Neill, S. (2013). *Sport and Social Movements: From the Local to the Global*. London: Bloomsbury.

Haynes, R. (1995). *The Football Imagination: The Rise of Football Fanzine Culture*. Aldershot: Arena.

Heidegger, M. (1962). *Being and Time*. Trans. by J. Macquarrie and E. Robinson. New York: Harper & Row.

Hemakom, A., Powezka, K., Goverdovsky, V., Jaffer, U. and Mandic, D.P. (2017). 'Quantifying team cooperation through intrinsic multi-scale measures: respiratory and cardiac synchronization in choir singers and surgical teams', *Royal Society Open Science*, 4(12): 1–23.

Henderson, H. and D'Cruz, B. (2004). 'The role of virtual communities in the English Premier Football League', in: L.M. Camarinha-Matos (ed.), *Virtual Enterprises and Collaborative Networks. PRO-VE 2004. IFIP International Federation for Information Processing*, vol. 149. Boston: Springer.

Hepburn, R. (2009). '"Red Ultras" banner at Aberdeen spoilt classic Celtic clash', *Sunday Mirror* 25 January. Available online at: www.mirror.co.uk/sport/football/red-ultras-banner-at-aberdeen-spoilt-657394 [Accessed 5 March 2019].

Hesse, U. (2013). *Tor! The Story of German Football*. London: WSC Books.

Hill, T., Canniford, R. and Millward, P. (2016). 'Against modern football: mobilizing protest in rhizomatic movements', *Sociology*, 52(4): 688–708.

Hills, M. (2002). *Fan Cultures*. New York: Routledge.

Hills, M. (2013). 'Fiske's "textual productivity" and digital fandom: Web 2.0 democratization versus fan distinction?', *Journal of Audience and Reception Studies*, 10(1): 130–153.

Hobbs, J. and Robbins, D. (1991). 'The boy done good: football violence, changes and continuities', *Sociological Review*, 39(3): 551–579.

Hobsbawm, E. (1983). 'Introduction: inventing traditions', in: E. Hobsbawm and T. Ranger (eds), *The Invention of Tradition*, pp. 1–14. Cambridge: Cambridge University Press.

Hobsbawm, E. (1990). *Nations and Nationalism since 1980: Programme, Myth, Reality*. Cambridge: Cambridge University Press.

Hochschild, A.R. ([1983] 2003). *The Managed Heart: Commercialization of Human Feeling*. Berkeley: University of California Press.

Hochstetler, A.; Copes, H. and Forsyth, C.J. (2013). 'The fight: symbolic expression and validation of masculinity in working class tavern culture', *American Journal of Criminal Justice*, 39(3): 493–510.

Hodges, A. (2014). 'The hooligan as "internal" other? Football fans, ultras culture and nesting intra-orientalisms', *International Review for the Sociology of Sport*, published online 24 March, https://doi.org/10.1177/1012690214526401.

Hodges, A. (2018). *Fan Activism, Protest and Politics: Ultras in Post-Socialist Croatia*. Abingdon: Routledge.

Hodges, A. and Brentin, D. (2018). 'Fan protest and activism: football from below in South-eastern Europe', *Soccer and Society*, 19(3): 329–336.

Hodges, A. and Stubbs, P. (2016). 'The paradoxes of politicisation: fan initiatives in Zagreb, Croatia', in: A. Schwell, N. Szogs, M.Z. Kowalska and M. Buchowski (eds), *New Ethnographies of Football in Europe: People, Passions, Politics*, pp. 55–74. Basingstoke: Palgrave Macmillan.

Hogan, B. (2010). 'The presentation of self in the age of social media: distinguishing performances and exhibitions online', *Bulletin of Science, Technology and Society*, 30(6): 377–386.

Hognestad, H. (1997). 'The Jambo experience: an anthropological study of Hearts fans', in: G. Armstrong and R. Giulianotti (eds), *Entering the Field: New Perspectives on World Football*, pp. 193–210. Oxford: Berg.

Hognestad, H. (2003). 'Long-distance football support and liminal identities among Norwegian fans', in: N. Dyck and E. Archetti (eds), *Sport, Dance and Embodied Identities*, pp. 97–114. Oxford: Berg.

Holiga, A. (2014). 'Croatia fans' act of terrorism was a planned cry for attention', *Guardian*, 17 November. Available online at: www.theguardian.com/football/blog/2014/nov/17/croatia-fans-terrorism-italy-planned-cry-attention [Accessed 1 February 2019].

Hollanda, B.B. de and Teixeira, R. (2017). 'Brazil's organized football supporter clubs and the construction of their public arenas through FTORJ and

ANATORG', in: C. Brandt, F. Hertel and S. Huddleston (eds), *Football Fans, Rivalry and Cooperation*, pp. 76–91. London: Routledge.

Holt, R. (1989). *Sport and the British: A Modern History*. Oxford: Oxford University Press.

Honigstein, R. (2012). 'Black cloud over Köln as the shambolic club goes down in smoke', *Guardian*, 7 May. Available online at: www.theguardian.com/football/blog/2012/may/07/koln-raphael-honigstein [Accessed 28 February 2019].

Hourcade, N. (2002). 'L'engagement politique des supporters "ultras" français. Retour sur des idées reçues', *Politix*, 13(50): 107–125.

Hourcade, N. (2008). 'Supporters extremes, violences et expressions politiques en France', in: T. Busset, C. Jaccoud, J.-P. Dubey and D. Malatesta (eds), *Le football à l'épreuve de la violence et de l'extrémisme*, pp. 87–106. Lausanne: Antipodes.

H-Side (n.d.). 'About us', Skonto FC Fan Club website. Available online at: www.h-side.lv/info.php?id=mums (in Latvian) [Accessed 4 May 2019].

Ibraheem, D.A. (2015). 'Ultras Ahlawy and the spectacle: subjects, resistance and organised football fandom in Egypt', unpublished PhD thesis. Cairo: American University in Cairo.

Immordino-Yang, M.H. and Damasio, A. (2007). 'We feel, therefore we learn: the relevance of affective and social neuroscience to education', *Mind, Brain, and Education*, 1(1): 3–10.

Jackson, S.A. and Csikszentmihalyi, M. (1999). *Flow in Sports: The Keys to Optimal Experiences and Performances*. Champaign, IL: Human Kinetics.

James, C.L.R. (1963). *Beyond a Boundary*. London: Hutchinson.

Jary, D., Horne, J. and Bucke, T. (1991). 'Football "fanzines" and football culture: a case of successful "cultural contestation"', *Sociological Review*, 39(3): 581–597.

Jasper, J.M. (1997). *The Art of Moral Protest*. Chicago: University of Chicago Press.

Jasper, J.M. (1998). 'The emotions of protest: affective and reactive emotions in and around social movements', *Sociological Forum*, 13(3): 397–424.

Jenkins, H. (1992). *Textual Poachers: Television Fans and Participation Culture*. New York and London: Routledge.

Jenkins, H. (2008). *Convergence Culture*. New York: New York University Press.

Joern, L. (2006). *Homo Fanaticus: Passionerede fodboldsupportere* [Homo Fanaticus: Impassioned Football Supporters]. Slagelse: Bavnebanke.

Johnston, L. (2000). 'Riot by appointment: an examination of the nature and structure of seven hard-core football hooligan groups', in: D. Canter and L. Alison (eds), *The Social Psychology of Crime: Groups, Teams and Networks*, pp. 153–188. Aldershot: Ashgate.

Jones, K.W. (2008). 'Female fandom: identity, sexism, and men's professional football in England', *Sociology of Sport*, 25(4): 516–37.

Jones, T. (2016). 'Inside Italy's ultras: the dangerous fans who control the game', *Guardian*, 1 December. Available online at: www.theguardian.com/world/2016/dec/01/nside-talys-ultras-the-dangerous-fans-who-control-the-game [Accessed 28 February 2010].

Kassimeris, C. (2011). 'Fascism, separatism and the ultràs: discrimination in Italian football', *Soccer and Society*, 12(5): 677–688.

Kassimeris, C. and Xinari, C. (2018). 'Searching for identity through football: the Nicosia derby', *Soccer and Society*, 19(5–6): 730–744.

Katz, J. (1988). *Seductions of Crime: Moral and Sensual Attractions in Doing Evil*. New York: Basic Books.

Katz, J. (1999). *How Emotions Work*. Chicago: University of Chicago Press.

Kawohl, J. (2016). 'Profisport 4.0 – Wohin rollt die Fußballbundesliga?', discussion paper. Berlin: University of Applied Sciences.

Kemper, T. (1978). *A Social Interactional Theory of Emotions*. New York: Wiley.

Kemper, T., ed. (1990). *Research Agendas in the Sociology of Emotions*. New York: State University of New York Press.

Kennedy, D. (2013). 'A contextual analysis of Europe's ultra football supporters movement', *Soccer and Society*, 14(2): 132–153.

Kennedy, H. (2006). 'Beyond anonymity, or future directions for Internet identity research', *New Media and Society*, 8(6): 859–876.

Kimmel, M. (2003). 'Masculinity as homophobia', in: A. Ferber and M. Kimmel (eds), *Privilege: A Reader*, pp. 58–70. Boulder: Westview.

King, A. (1997a). 'The postmodernity of football hooliganism', *British Journal of Sociology*, 48(4): 576–593.

King, A. (1997b). 'The lads: masculinity and the new consumption of football', *Sociology*, 31(2): 329–346.

King, A. (1998). *The End of the Terraces*. Leicester: Leicester University Press.

King, A. (2000). 'Football fandom and post-national identity in the New Europe', *British Journal of Sociology*, 51(3): 419–442.

King, A. (2001). Violent pasts: collective memory and football hooliganism', *Sociological Review*, 49(4): 569–585.

King A. (2003). *The European Ritual: Football in the New Europe*. Aldershot: Ashgate.

King, A. and Rond, M. de (2011). 'Boat race: rhythm and the possibility of collective performance', *British Journal of Sociology*, 62(4): 565–585.

King, C. (2004). *Offside Racism: Playing the White Man*. Oxford: Berg.

Klugman, M. (2008). 'Loves, suffering and identification: the passions of Australian football league fans', *International Journal of the History of Sport*, 26(1): 321–344.

Klugman, M. (2009). *Passion Play: Love Hope and Heartbreak at the Footy*. Melbourne: Hunter.

Kossakowski, R. (2013). 'Proud to be Tukker. A football club and the building of local identity: the case of FC Twente Enschede', *Sociological Review*, 62(3): 107–127.

Kossakowski, R. (2017a). 'From the bottom to the Premiership: the significance of the supporters' movement in the governance of football clubs in Poland', in: B. García and J. Zheng (eds), *Football and Supporter Activism in Europe: Whose Game Is It?*, pp. 233–255. Basingstoke: Palgrave.

Kossakowski, R. (2017b). 'Where are the hooligans? Dimensions of football fandom in Poland', *International Review for the Sociology of Sport*, 52(6): 692–711.

Kossakowski, R. (2017c). From communist fan clubs to professional hooligans: a history of Polish fandom as a social process', *Sociology of Sport*, 34(3): 281–292.

Kossakowski, R. (2017d). *Od chuliganów do aktywistów. Polscy kibice i zmiana społeczna* [From hooligans to activists. Polish football fans and social change]. Kraków: Universitas.

Kossakowski, R., Antonowicz, D. and Jakubowska, H. (forthcoming). 'The reproduction of hegemonic masculinity in football fandom. An analysis of the performance of Polish ultras', in: R. Magrath, J. Cleland and E. Anderson (eds), *The Palgrave Handbook of Masculinity and Sport*, pp. 517–536. London: Palgrave Macmillan.

Kossakowski, R. and Besta, T. (2018). 'Football, conservative values, and a feeling of oneness with the group: a study of Polish football fandom', *East European Politics and Societies and Cultures*, 32(4): 866–891.

Kossakowski, R. and Bieszke, L. (2017). 'The pacts, the death of the Pope and boycotts: the modes of cooperation in Polish football', in C. Brandt, F. Hertel and S. Huddleston (eds), *Football Fans, Rivalry and Cooperation*, pp. 17–32. London: Routledge.

Kossakowski R., Szlendak T. and Antonowicz, D. (2018). 'Polish ultras in the post-socialist transformation', *Sport in Society*, 21(6): 854–869.

Kreisky, E. and Spitaler, G. (2006). *Arena der Männlichkeit. Über das Verhältnis von Fußball und Geschlecht* [Arena of Masculinity. On the Relation Between Football and Gender]. Frankfurt: Campus.

Krugliak, M. and Krugliak, O. (2017). 'The unlikely alliance of Ukrainian football ultras', in: C. Brandt, F. Hertel and S. Huddleston (eds), *Football Fans, Rivalry and Cooperation*, pp. 170–184. London: Routledge.

Kušnierová, D. (2014). 'Ultras in Trnava: history, activities and ideology', *Ethnologia Actualis*, 14(2): 59–96.

Kytö, M. (2011). '"We are the rebellious voice of the terraces, we are Çarşı": constructing a football supporter group through sound', *Soccer and Society*, 12(1): 77–93.

Lande, B. (2007). 'Breathing like a soldier: culture incarnate', *Sociological Review*, 55(1_supp): 95–108.

Lazarus, R. (1994). *Passion and Reason: Making Sense of Our Emotions*. New York: Oxford University Press.

Leary, M.R. and Kowalski, M. (1990). 'Impression management: a literature review and two-component model', *Psychological Bulletin*, 107(10): 34–47.

Le Bon, G. (1896). *The Crowd: A Study of the Popular Mind*. New York: Macmillan.

Ledoux, J. (1999). *The Emotional Brain: The Mysterious Underpinnings of Emotional Life*. London: Phoenix.

Lemmings, D. and Brooks, A. (2014). *Emotions and Social Change: Historical and Sociological Perspectives*. New York: Routledge.

Lengua, G. (2018). 'Roma, scritte contro Pallotta, gli ultras: "Siamo stanchi". Stasera curva in silenzio 10 minuti', *Il Messaggero*, 16 December. Available online at: www.ilmessaggero.it/sport/calcio/striscioni_pallotta_comunicato_ultras-4176517.html [Accessed 21 December 2018].

Lestrelin, L., Basson J.-C. and Helleu, B. (2013). 'Sur la route du stade: mobilisations des supporters de football', *Sociologie*, 3(4): 291–315.

Lestrelin, L., Sallé, L. and Basson, J.-C. (2006). 'The trajectories leading to supporting at a distance: the Olympique de Marseille case study', *European Journal for Sport and Society*, 3(2): 125–141.

Lindgren, S. (2017). *Digital Media and Society*. London: SAGE.

Lipman-Blumen, J. (1976). 'Toward a homosocial theory of sex roles: an explanation of the sex segregation of social institutions', *Signs*, 1(3): 15–31.

Llopis-Goig, R. (2007). 'Female football supporters' communities in Spain: a focus on women's peñas', in: G. Baldwin, K. Moore and J. Magee (eds), *Women, Football and Europe*, pp. 173–189. Oxford: Meyer & Meyer Sport.

Llopis-Goig, R. (2015). *Spanish Football and Social Change*. Basingstoke: Palgrave Macmillan.

Lomas, T. (2018). 'The flavours of love: a cross-cultural lexical analysis', *Journal for the Theory of Social Behaviour*, published online 3 January, https://doi.org/10.1111/jtsb.12158.

Lutz, C. (1986). 'Emotion, thought, and estrangement: emotion as a cultural category', *Cultural Anthropology*, 10(2): 244–263.

Lutz, C. (1988). *Unnatural Emotions: Everyday Sentiments on a Micronesian Atoll and Their Challenge to Western Theory*. Chicago: Chicago University Press.

Lutz, C. and White, G.M. (1986). 'The anthropology of emotions', *Annual Review of Anthropology*, 15: 405–436.

MacIntyre, A. (1985). *After Virtue: A Study in Moral Philosophy*. London: Gerald Duckworth and Co.

Maffesoli, M. (1996). *The Time of the Tribes*. London: SAGE.

Magazine, R. (2007). *Golden and Blue like My Heart: Masculinity, Youth and Power among Soccer Fans in Mexico City*. Tucson: University of Arizona Press.

Magazine, R. and González, S.F. (2017). 'The criminalization of Mexican football fans and the emergence of the "Movement of United Mexican Supporters"', in: C. Brandt, F. Hertel and S. Huddleston (eds), *Football Fans, Rivalry and Cooperation*, pp. 92–107. London: Routledge.

Magrath, R. (2017). '"To try and gain an advantage for my team": homophobic and homosexually themed chanting among English football fans', *Sociology*, published online 10 May, https://doi.org/10.1177/0038038517702600.

Maguire, J. (1999). *Global Sport: Identities, Societies, Civilizations*. Cambridge, MA: Polity.

Maltby, M. (2019). 'Bayern Munich charged over "F*** VAR" banner displayed during Liverpool defeat', *Daily Mirror*, 16 March. Available online at: www.mirror.co.uk/sport/football/news/bayern-munich-charged-over-f-14143970 [Accessed 10 May 2019].

Mann, L. (1989). 'Sports crowds and the collective behavior perspective', in J.H. Goldstein (ed.), *Sports, Games, and Play*, 2nd edn, pp. 299–331. Hillsdale: Erlbaum.

Marchi, V. (2005). *Il Derby del Bambino Morto: Violenza e Ordine Pubblico nel Calcio*. Rome: Deriveapprodi.

Marschik, M. (2003). *Frauenfußball und Maskulinität* [Women's Football and Masculinity]. Münster: LIT.

Marsh, P., Rosser, E. and Harré, R. (1978). *The Rules of Disorder*. London: Routledge & Kegan Paul.

Marshall, E. (2013). 'The ultimate price: 14 year-old fan killed by Corinthians supporters' firework', *Daily Mirror*, 23 February. Available online at: www.mirror.co.uk/sport/football/news/kevin-beltran-espada-14-year-old-1726963 [Accessed 4 March 2018].

Martin, S. (2004). *Football and Fascism: The National Game Under Mussolini*. Oxford: Berg.

Marwick, A.E. and Boyd, D. (2010). 'I tweet honestly, I tweet passionately: Twitter users, context collapse, and the imagined audience', *New Media and Society*, 13(1): 114–133.

Marx, K. (1970). *The German Ideology*. London: Lawrence and Wishart.

Mason, T. (1980). *Association Football and English Society 1863–1915*. Brighton: Harvester Press.

Mason, T. (1988). *Sport in Britain*. London: Faber and Faber.

Massumi, B. (2002). *Parable of the Virtual: Movement, Affect, Sensation*. Durham, NC: Duke University Press.

Mathers A (2014). 'Book review: Manuel Castells, *Networks of Outrage and Hope: Social Movements in the Internet Age*', *Sociology*, 48(5): 1063–1064.

Mauro, M. (2016). *The Balotelli Generation: Issues of Inclusion and Belonging in Italian Football and Society*. New York: Peter Lang.

Mauss, M. (1967). *The Gift: Forms and Functions of Exchange in Archaic Societies*. New York: Norton.

McGaugh, J.L. (2006). *Emotion and Memory*. New York: Columbia University Press.

McGinniss, J. (1969). *The Selling of the President 1968*. New York: Trident Press.

McLuhan, M. (1964). *Understanding Media: The Extensions of Man*. New York: McGraw-Hill.

McManus, J. (2014). 'Been there, done that, bought the T-shirt: Beşiktaş fans and the commodification of football in Turkey', *International Journal of Middle East Studies*, 45(1): 3–24.

Mead, G.H. (1934). *Mind, Self and Society*. Chicago: University of Chicago Press.

Melucci, A. (1996). *Challenging Codes: Collective Action in the Information Age*. Cambridge: Cambridge University Press.

Melucci, A. and Mier, P. (1989). *Nomads of the Present: Social Movements and Individual Needs in Contemporary Society*. Philadelphia: Temple University Press.

Menary, S. (2007). *Outcasts! The Lands that FIFA Forgot*. Studley: Know the Score Books.

Menezes, J. de (2018). 'Lazio "ultras" tell women to stay away from their "sacred space" inside Stadio Olimpico stadium', *Independent*, 20 August. Available online at: www.independent.co.uk/sport/football/european/lazio-fans-ultras-women-stay-away-sacred-space-stadium-stadio-olimpico-flyers-a8499496.html [Accessed 1 March 2019].

Meng, M.D., Stavros, C. and Westberg, K. (2015). 'Engaging fans through social media: implications for team identification', *Sport, Business and Management*, 5(3): 199–217.

Merkel, U. (2007). 'Milestones in the development of football fandom in Germany: global impacts on local contests', in: S. Brown (ed.), *Football Fans Around the World: From Supporters to Fanatics*, pp. 59–77. Abingdon: Routledge.

Merkel, U. (2012). 'Football fans and clubs in Germany: conflicts, crises and compromises', *Soccer and Society*, 13(3): 359–376.

Merleau-Ponty, M. (1971). *Sense and Non-Sense*. Evanston: Northwestern University Press.

Messner, M.A. (1988). 'Sports and male domination: the female athlete as contested ideological terrain', *Sociology of Sport*, 5(3): 197–211.

Messner, M.A. (1992). *Power at Play: Sports and the Problem of Masculinity*. Boston: Beacon Press.

Messner, M.A. (1997). *Politics of Masculinities*. Thousand Oaks: SAGE.

Meštrović, S. (1997). *Postemotional society*. London: SAGE.

Meuser, M. (2008). 'It is a man's world', in: G. Klein and M. Meuser (eds), *Ernste Spiele: Zur politischen Soziologie des Fußballs* [Serious Games: On the Political Sociology of Football], pp. 123–135. Bielefeld: Transcript.

Mewett, P. and Toffoletti, K. (2011). 'Finding footy: female fan socialisation', *Sport in Society*, 14(5): 670–684.

Mezahi, M. (2019). 'In Algeria's Bordj Bou Arreridj, political art takes centre stage', Al Jazeera News, 28 April. Available online at: www.aljazeera.com/news/2019/04/algeria-bordj-bou-arreridj-political-art-takes-centre-stage-190428055122476.html [Accessed 9 May 2019].

Mignon, P. (2002). 'Another side to French exceptionalism: football without hooligans?', in: E. Dunning, P. Murphy, I. Waddington and A.E. Astrinakis (eds), *Fighting Fans: Football Hooliganism as a World Phenomenon*, pp. 62–74. Dublin: University College Press.

Milekic, S. (2018). 'Croatian football federation fined for swastika on the pitch', *Balkan Insight*, 8 March. Available online at: www.balkaninsight. com/en/article/croatian-football-federation-sanctioned-for-swastika-incident -03–08–2018 [Accessed 4 March 2019].

Miller, T. (2008). '"Step away from the croissant": Media Studies 3.0', in: D. Hesmondhalgh and J. Toynbee (eds), *The Media and Social Theory*, pp. 213–230. London: Routledge.

Mills, R. (2009). '"It all ended in an unsporting way": Serbian football and the disintegration of Yugoslavia, 1989–2006', *International Journal of the History of Sport*, 26(9): 1187–1217.

Mills, R. (2013). 'Fighters, footballers and nation builders: wartime football in the Serb-held territories of the former Yugoslavia, 1991–1996', *Sport in Society*, 16(8): 945–972.

Millward, P. (2008). 'The rebirth of the football fanzine – using e-zines as data source', *Journal of Sport and Social Issues*, 32: 299–310.

Millward, P. (2009). 'Rivalries and racisms: "closed" and "open" Islamophobic dispositions amongst football supporters', *Sociological Research Online*, 13(6): 1–17.

Millward, P. (2011). *The Global Football League*. London: Palgrave.

Millward, P. (2012). 'Reclaiming the Kop? Analysing Liverpool supporters' 21st century mobilisations', *Sociology*, 46(4): 633–648.

Millward, P. and Poulton, G. (2014). 'Football fandom, mobilization and Herbert Blumer: a social movement analysis of F.C. United of Manchester', *Sociology of Sport*, 31(1): 1–22.

Mintert, S.M. (2015). 'Football, feminisation, fans – explorative studies in a European context', PhD thesis. Copenhagen: Copenhagen University Press.

Mintert, S.M. and Pfister, G. (2014). 'The Female Vikings, a women's fan group in Denmark: formation and development in the context of football and fan histories', *International Journal of the History of Sport*, 31(13): 1639–1655.

Mintert, S.M. and Pfister, G. (2015). 'The FREE project and the feminization of football: the role of women in the European fan community', *Soccer and Society*, 16(2–3): 405–421.

Moreira, V., Zucal, J.G. and Hijós, N. (2017). 'Rivalry, passion and coop-eration between Argentinean club supporters', in: C. Brandt, F. Hertel and S. Huddleston (eds), *Football Fans, Rivalry and Cooperation*, pp. 62–75. London: Routledge.

Müller, F., Zoonen, L. van and Roode, L. de (2007). 'Accidental racists: experi-ences and contradictions of racism in local Amsterdam soccer fan culture', *Soccer and Society*, 8(2–3): 335–350.

Muro, G. (2015). '"We don't sing the manager's name lightly… Alan Pardew has already earned his chant" – Crystal Palace's Holmesdale Fanatics', *Evening Standard*, 9 January. Available online at: www.standard.co.uk/sport/football/ we-don-t-sing-the-manager-s-name-lightly-alan-pardew-has-already-earned-his-chant-crystal-palaces-9967795.html [Accessed 5 March 2019].

Murphy, P., Dunning, E. and Williams, J. (1988). 'Soccer crowd disorder and the press: processes of amplification and de-amplification in historical per-spective', *Theory, Culture and Society*, 5: 645–693.

Murphy, P., Williams, J. and Dunning, E. (1990). *Football on Trial: Spectator Violence and Development in the Football World*. London: Routledge.

Nash, R. (2000). 'Contestation in modern English football spectatorship: the independent supporters association movement', *International Review for the Sociology of Sport*, 35(4): 465–486.

Newman, L. (2014). 'A world of ultras: Panathinaikos', *These Football Times*, 22 November. Available online at: https://thesefootballtimes.co/2014/11/22/a-world-of-ultras-panathinaikos/ [Accessed 21 February 2019].

Newson, M. (2017). 'Football, fan violence, and identity fusion', *International Review for the Sociology of Sport*, published online 18 September, https://doi.org/10.1177/1012690217731293.

Ngai, S. (2007). *Ugly Feelings*. Cambridge, MA: Harvard University Press.

Nielsen, C.A. (2010). 'The goalposts of transition: football as a metaphor for Serbia's long journey to the rule of law', *Nationalities Papers*, 38(1): 87–103.

Nielsen, C.A. (2013). 'Stronger than the State? Football hooliganism, political extremism and the gay pride parades in Serbia', *Sport in Society*, 16(8): 1038–1053.

Nowell-Smith, G. (1979). 'Television – football – the world', *Screen*, 19: 45–59.

Nuhrat, Y. (2013). 'Playing by the book(s): the unwritten rules of football in Turkey', *FairPlay, Revista de Filosofía, Ética y Derecho del Deporte*, 1(1): 89–112.

Nuhrat, Y. (2018a). 'Contesting love through commodification: soccer fans, affect, and social class in Turkey', *American Ethnologist*, 45(3): 392–404.

Nuhrat, Y. (2018b). 'Ultras in Turkey: othering, agency, and culture as a politi-cal domain', *Sport in Society*, 21(6): 870–82.

Numerato, D. (2015). 'Who says "No to Modern Football"? Italian supporters, reflexivity, and neo-liberalism', *Journal of Sport and Social Issues*, 39(2): 120–138.

Numerato, D. (2018). *Football Fans, Activism and Social Change*. London: Routledge.

Oltermann, P. (2017). 'Borussia Dortmund's "Yellow Wall" stands tall in face of attack on team', *Guardian*, 12 April. Available online at: www.theguardian.com/football/2017/apr/12/borussia-dortmunds-yellow-wall-stands-tall-in-fa ce-of-attack-on-team [Accessed 28 February 2019].

Ortner, S. (2006). *Anthropology and Social Theory*. Durham, NC: Duke University Press.

Panskepp, J. (1998). *Affective Neuroscience: The Foundations of Animal and Human Emotion*. New York: Oxford University Press.

Papacharissi, Z. (2002). 'The presentation of self in virtual life: characteristics of personal home pages', *Journalism and Mass Communication Quarterly*, 79(3): 643–660.

Pearson, G. (2012). *An Ethnography of English Football Fans: Cans, Cops and Carnivals*. Manchester: Manchester University Press.

Pennant, C. (2003). *Congratulations You Have Just Met the ICF*. London: Blake Publishing.

Perasović, B. and Mustapić, M. (2018). 'Carnival fans, hooligans and "Against Modern Football" movement: life within the ultras subculture in the Croatian context', *Sport in Society*, 21(6): 960–976.

Perryman, M., ed. (2002). *Hooligan Wars, Causes and Effects of Football Violence*. London: Mainstream.

Pfister, G., Lenneis, V. and Mintert, S.M. (2013). 'Female fans of men's football – a case study in Denmark', *Soccer and Society*, 14(6): 850–871.

Pfister, G., Mintert, S.M. and Lenneis, V. (2018). '"One is not born, but rather becomes a fan": the socialization of female football fans – a case study in Denmark', in: G. Pfister and S. Pope (eds), *Female Football Players and Fans, Football Research in an Enlarged Europe*, pp. 211–240. London: Palgrave.

Pilz, G.A. and Wölki-Schumacher, F. (2010). *Overview of the Ultra Culture Phenomenon in the Council of Europe Member States in 2009*. Hannover: Leibniz University.

Pisker, L. (2018). 'Ultra-nationalism tarnishes Croatian football success', *NewsMavens*, 19 July. Available online at: https://newsmavens.com/news/smoke-signals/1745/ultra-nationalism-tarnishes-croatian-football-success [Accessed 15 April 2019].

Podaliri, C. and Balestri, C. (1998). 'The ultras, racism and football culture in Italy', in: A. Brown (ed.), *Fanatics! Power, Identity, and Fandom in Football*, pp. 88–100. London: Routledge.

Pope, S. (2012). '"The love of my life": the meaning and importance of sport for female fans', *Journal of Sport and Social Issues*, 37(2): 176–195.

Pope, S. (2017). *The Feminisation of Sports Fandom: A Sociological Study*. London: Routledge.

Portelli, A. (1993). 'The rich and poor in the culture of football', in: S. Redhead (ed.), *The Passion and the Fashion*, pp. 77–87. Aldershot: Avebury.

Portes, A. (1998). 'Social capital: its origins and applications in modern sociology', *Annual Review of Sociology*, 24: 1–24.

Poulton, E. (2005). 'English media representation of football-related disorder: "brutal, short-hand and simplifying"?', *Sport in Society*, 8(1): 27–47.

Poulton, E, (2006). '"Lights, camera, aggro!": readings of "celluloid hooliganism"', *Sport in Society*, 9(3): 403–426.

Poulton, E. (2007). 'Fantasy football hooliganism', *Popular Media, Culture and Society*, 29(1): 151–164.

Poulton, E. (2008). '"I predict a riot": forecasts, facts and fiction in "football hooligan" documentaries', *Sport in Society*, 11(2/3): 330–348.

Poulton, E. (2012a). '"Not another football hooligan story"? Learning from narratives of "true crime" and desistance', *Internet Journal of Criminology*. Available online at: https://docs.wixstatic.com/ugd/b93dd4_2cb08a4b24874dd68dc1e999ee1e9147.pdf [Accessed 5 August 2019].

Poulton, E. (2012b). '"If you had balls, you'd be one of us!" Doing gendered research: methodological reflections on being a female academic researcher in the hyper-masculine subculture of "football hooliganism"', *Sociological Research Online*, 17(4): 1–13.

Poulton, E. (2013). 'Culture of production behind the (re)production of football hooligan culture', *Continuum*, 28(4): 770–784.

Probyn, E. (2005). *Blush: Faces of Shame*. Minneapolis: University of Minnesota Press.

Putnam, R. (2000). *Bowling Alone: The Collapse and Revival of American Community*. New York: Simon and Schuster.

Putnam, R., Leonardi, R. and Nanetti, R. (1993). *Making Democracy Work*. Princeton: Princeton University Press.

Raab, A. (2012). 'Soccer in the Middle East: an introduction', *Soccer and Society*, 13(5–6): 619–638.

Ranc, D. (2009). 'Local politics, identity and football in Paris', *Modern and Contemporary France*, 17(1): 51–65.

Rappaport, R.A. (1999). *Ritual and Religion in the Making of Humanity*. Cambridge: Cambridge University Press.

Ratna, A. (2011). '"Who wants to make aloo gobi when you can bend it like Beckham": British Asian females and their racialised experiences of gender and identity in women's football', *Soccer and Society*, 12(3): 382–401.

Ratna, A. (2014). '"Who are ya?" The national identities and belongings of British Asian football fans', *Patterns of Prejudice*, 48(3): 286–308.

Ratna, A. and Samaya, F.S., eds (2018). *Sport, Race and Gender: The Politics of Ethnic 'Other' Girls and Women*. Abingdon: Routledge.

Reddy, W.M. (2001). *The Navigation of Feeling: A Framework for the History of Emotion*. Cambridge: Cambridge University Press.

Redhead, S. (1993). *The Passion and the Fashion: Football Fandom in New Europe*. Aldershot: Avebury.

Redhead, S. (1997). *Post-Fandom and the Millennial Blues: The Transformation of Soccer Culture*. London: Routledge.

Redhead, S. (2007a). 'This sporting life: the realism of *The Football Factory*', *Soccer and Society*, 8(1): 90–108.

Redhead, S. (2007b). 'Those absent from the stadium are always right: accelerated culture, sport media and theory at the speed of light', *Journal of Sport and Social Issues*, 31(3): 226–241.

Redhead, S. (2007c). 'Emotional hooligan: post-subcultural research and the histories of Britain's football gangs', *Entertainment and Sports Law Journal*, 5(2): 5.

Riesman, D. (1961). *The Lonely Crowd: A Study of the Changing American Character*. New Haven: Yale University Press.

Robson, G. (2000). *No One Likes Us, We Don't Care: The Myth and Reality of Millwall Fandom*. Oxford: Berg.

Roversi, A. (1991). 'Football violence in Italy', *International Review for the Sociology of Sport*, 26(4): 311–331.

Roversi, A. and Balestri, C. (2000). 'Italian ultras today: change or decline?', *European Journal on Criminal Policy and Research*, 8(2): 183–199.

Ruddock, A. (2005). 'Let's kick racism out of football – and the lefties too!', *Journal of Sport and Social Issues*, 29(4): 369–385.

Russell, D. (1997). *Football and the English: A Social History of Association Football in England, 1863–1995*. Preston: Carnegie.

Rydgren, J. (2007). 'The power of the past: a contribution to a cognitive sociology of ethnic conflict', *Sociological Theory*, 25(3): 225–244.

Sandoval, M. and Fuchs, C. (2010). 'Towards a critical theory of alternative media', *Telematics and Infomatics*, 27(2): 141–150.

Sandvoss, C. (2003). *A Game of Two Halves: Football, Television, Globalisation*. London: Routledge.

Sandvoss, C. (2004). 'Technological evolution or revolution? Sport online live Internet commentary as postmodern cultural form', *Convergence*, 10(3): 39–54.

Schechner, R. (2003). *Performance Theory*. New York and London: Routledge.

Scheff, T.J. (1992). *Catharsis in Healing, Ritual, and Drama*. Berkeley: University of California Press.

Schietti, J. (2017). 'Egypt's football ultras fight on in battle over stadiums', *Al Araby*, 25 October. Available online at: www.alaraby.co.uk/english/indepth/2017/10/25/egypts-football-fans-persist-with-their-battle-over-stadiums [Accessed 4 March 2018].

Schmitz, J. (1997). 'Structural relations, electronic media and social change: the public electronic network and the homeless', in: S.G. Jones (ed.), *Virtual Culture: Identity and Communication in Cyberspace*, pp. 80–101. London: SAGE.

Scott, J.W. (1986). 'Gender: a useful category of historical analysis', *American Historical Review*, 91(5): 1053–1075.

Selmer, N. (2004). *Watching the Boys Play: Frauen als Fußballfans*. Kassel: Argon

Sennett, R. (1976). *The Fall of Public Man*. Cambridge: Cambridge University Press.

Sennett, R. (2012). *Together: The Rituals, Pleasures and Politics of Cooperation*. London: Allen Lane.

Servon, L. (2008). *Bridging the Digital Divide: Technology, Community, and Public Policy*. Oxford: Blackwell.

Shilling, C. (1991). *The Body and Social Theory*. London: SAGE.

Shilling, C. (2002). 'The two traditions in the sociology of emotions', *Sociological Review*, 50(2): 10–32.

Simmel, G. (1950). *The Sociology of George Simmel*. London: Free Press of Glencoe.

Sinclair, R.C., Hoffman, C., Mark, M.M., Martin, L.L. and Pickering, T.L. (1994). 'Construct accessibility and the misattribution of arousal', *Psychological Science*, 5(1): 15–19.

Sindbæk, T. (2013). '"A Croatian champion with a Croatian name": national identity and uses of history in Croatian football culture – the case of Dinamo Zagreb', *Sport in Society*, 16(8): 1009–1024.

Smith, A.D. (1986). *The Ethnic Origins of Nations.* Oxford, Blackwell.

Smith, B. and Lord, J. (2017). 'Personal ethics of today's sport fans: connecting cultural values, ethical ideologies, and ethical intentions', in C.L. Campbell (ed.), *The Customer is NOT Always Right? Marketing Orientations in a Dynamic Business World. Proceedings of the 2011 Biennial World Marketing Congress.* New York: Springer.

Solomon, R.C. (1993). *The Passions: Emotions and the Meanings of Life.* Cambridge: Hackett.

Spaaij, R. (2006). *Understanding Football Hooliganism: A Comparison of Six Western European Football Clubs.* Amsterdam: Amsterdam University Press.

Spaaij, R. (2008). 'Men like us, boys like them: violence, masculinity, and collective identity in football hooliganism', *Journal of Sport and Social Issues*, 32(4): 369–392.

Spaaij, R. and Anderson, A. (2010). 'Soccer fan violence: a holistic approach. A reply to Braun and Vliegenthart', *International Sociology*, 25(4): 561–579.

Spaaij, R. and Viñas, C. (2005). 'Passion, politics and violence: a sociohistorical analysis of Spanish ultras', *Soccer and Society*, 6(1): 79–96.

Spaaij, R. and Viñas, C. (2013). 'Political ideology and activism in football fan culture in Spain: a view from the far left', *Soccer and Society*, 14(2): 183–200.

Stearns, P.N. and Stearns, C.Z. (1985). 'Emotionology: clarifying the history of emotions and emotional standards', *American Historical Review*, 90(4): 813–836.

Stearns, P.N. and Stearns, C.Z. (1986). *Anger: The Struggle for Emotional Control in America's History.* Chicago: Chicago University Press.

Stefanini, M. (2009). *Ultras: Identità, Politica e Violenza nel Tifo Sportivo da Pompei a Raciti a Sandri.* Milan: Boroli.

Stone, C. (2007). 'The role of football in everyday life', *Soccer and Society*, 8(2/3): 169–184.

Stone, C. (2013). *Football – A Shared Sense of Belonging.* Sheffield: FURD.

Stott, C., Hutchinson, P. and Drury, J. (2001). '"Hooligans" abroad? Intergroup dynamics, social identity and participation in collective "disorder" at the 1998 World Cup Finals', *British Journal of Social Psychology*, 40: 359–384.

Stott, C. and Pearson, G. (2007). *Football 'Hooliganism': Policing and the War on the 'English Disease'.* London: Pennant Books.

Stott, C. and Reicher, S. (1998). 'How conflict escalates: the inter-group dynamics of collective football crowd "violence"', *Sociology*, 32(2): 353–377.

Sugden, J.P. and Tomlinson, A. (1998). *Fifa and the Contest for World Football: Who Rules the People's Game?* Cambridge: Polity.

Sugden, J. and Tomlinson, A. (1999). *Great Balls of Fire: How Big Money Is Hijacking World Football.* Edinburgh: Mainstream Publishing.

Sülzle, A. (2005). 'Fußball als schutzraum für männlichkeiten? Ethnographische anmerkungen zum spielraum für geschlechter im stadion' [Football as refuge for masculinities? Ethnographic comments on space for gender in the stadium], in: A. Hagel, N. Selmer and A. Sülzle (eds), *Gender Kicks: Texte zu Fußball und Geschlecht*, pp. 37–53. Frankfurt: Koordinationsstelle Fanprojekte.

Sülzle, A. (2007). 'Titten unterwegs. Weibliche fankulturen im männerfußball' [Female fan cultures in men's football], *Bulletin Texte des ZtG*, 33: 54–64.

Sülzle, A. (2011). *Fußball, Frauen, Männlichkeiten: Eine ethnographische Studie im Fanblock* [Football, Women, Masculinities: An Ethnographic Study in the Fan Stands]. Frankfurt: Campus.

Tanaka, T. (2004). 'The positioning and practices of the "feminised fan" in Japanese soccer culture through the experience of the World Cup Korea/Japan 2002', *Inter-Asia Cultural Studies*, 5(1): 52–62.

Tarrow, S. (1995). 'Europeanisation of conflict: reflections from a social movement perspective', *West European Politics*, 18(2): 223–251.

Tarrow, S. (1998). *Power in Movement: Social Movements and Contentious Politics*. Cambridge: Polity.

Taylor, I. (1971a). 'Soccer consciousness and soccer hooliganism', in: S. Cohen (ed.), *Images of Deviance*, pp. 134–164. Harmondsworth: Penguin.

Taylor, I. (1971b). 'Football mad: a speculative sociology of soccer hooliganism', in: E. Dunning (ed.), *The Sociology of Sport: A Selection of Readings*, pp. 352–377. London: Frank Cass.

Taylor, R. (1992). *Football and Its Fans: Supporters and Their Relationship with the Game 1885–1985*. Leicester: Leicester University Press.

Taylor, Rt. Hon. Lord Justice (1990). 'The Hillsborough Stadium Disaster', final report. London: HMSO.

Taylor, V. (1989). 'Social movement continuity: the women's movement in abeyance', *American Sociological Review*, 54(5): 761–775.

TenHouten, W.D. (2007). *A General Theory of Emotions and Social Life*. London and New York: Routledge.

Testa, A. (2009). 'The ultras: an emerging social movement?', *Review of European Studies*, 1(2): 54–63.

Testa, A. (2013). 'Normalization of the exception: issues and controversies of the Italian counter-hooliganism legislation', *Sport in Society*, 16(2): 151–166.

Testa, A. and Armstrong, G. (2010). *Football, Fascism and Fandom: The Ultras of Italian Football*. London: A & C Black.

Tharoor, I. (2014). 'How Israeli soccer hooligans fanned flames of hate', *Washington Post*, 10 July. Available online at: www.washingtonpost.com/news/worldviews/wp/2014/07/10/how-israeli-soccer-hooligans-fanned-flames-of-hate/?noredirect=on&utm_term=.1c7f217d5bee [Accessed 21 March 2019].

Thomas, P. (2010). 'Marching altogether? Football fans taking a stand against racism', in: J. Long and K. Spracklen (eds), *Sport and Challenges to Racism*, pp. 185–198. Basingstoke: Palgrave Macmillan.

Tilly, C. (2004). *Social Movements, 1769–2004*. London: Paradigm.

Tocqueville, A. de (1969). *Democracy in America*. Garden City: Doubleday.

To My Kibice! (2015). 'Wisła Kraków–Lech Poznań', *To My Kibice!*, 1: 7.

To My Kibice Plus (2013). '1.FC Magdeburg', *To My Kibice Plus*, 3(41): 38–41.

Tonkin, E. (1995). *Narrating Our Pasts: The Social Construction of Oral History*. Cambridge: Cambridge University Press.

Tönnies, F. (2001). *Gemeinschaft und Gesellschaft*. Cambridge: Cambridge University Press.

Topal, F. (2010). 'Ultra Kültürü ve Türkiye' [Ultra culture and Turkey], *Birgün*, 19 August. Available online at: www.birgun.net/haber-detay/ultra-kulturu-ve-turkiye-10142.html [Accessed 21 September 2018].

Totten, M. (2014). 'Sport activism and political praxis within the FC Sankt Pauli fan subculture', *Soccer and Society*, 16(4): 453–468.

Touraine, A. (1981). *The Voice and the Eye*. Cambridge: Cambridge University Press.

Touraine, A. (1983). *Solidarity: Poland 1980–81*. Cambridge: Cambridge University Press.

Trail, G., Fink, J. and Anderson, D. (2003). 'Sport spectator consumption behaviour', *Sport Marketing Quarterly*, 12(1): 8–17.

Tsoukala, A. (2009). *Football Hooliganism in Europe: Security and Civil Liberties in the Balance*. Basingstoke: Palgrave Macmillan.

Turkle, S. (1995). *Life on the Screen: Identity in the Age of the Internet*. New York: Simon and Schuster.

Turner, J.H. (2000). *On the Origins of Human Emotions: A Sociological Inquiry in to the Evolution of Human Affect*. Stanford: Stanford University Press.

Turner, V. (1974). 'Liminal to liminoid, in play, flow, and ritual: an essay in comparative symbology', *Rice Institute Pamphlet – Rice University Studies*, 60(3): 53–92.

Turner, V. ([1969] 1997). *The Ritual Process: Structure and Anti-Structure*. Chicago: Aldine Transaction.

Ultras Leverkusen (n.d.). 'Ultra in Lev'. Available online at: http://ultras-lev erkusen.de/ultra-in-lev/ (in German) [Accessed 25 February 2019].

Ultras-Tifo (2015). 'Czech club fined for anti-Islam banners', *Ultras-Tifo*, 14 August. Available online at: www.ultras-tifo.net/news/3696-czech-clubs-fined-for-anti-islam-banners.html [Accessed 28 February 2019].

Van der Kolk, B. (2014). *The Body Keeps the Score: Brain, Mind, and Body in the Healing of Trauma*. New York: Penguin Books

Van Dijk, J. (2005). *The Deepening Divide*. London: SAGE.

Van Hiel, A., Hautman, L., Cornelis, I. and Clerq, B. de (2007). 'Football hooliganism: comparing self-awareness and social identity theory explanations', *Community and Applied Psychology*, 17(3): 169–186.

Varela, S. (2014). '"Drunk and proud", from the streets to the stands: America Football Club fans, aguante and alcohol consumption in Mexican football fandom', *International Review for the Sociology of Sport*, 49(3–4): 435–450.

Viersa (2010). 'Ultras Sur Real Madrid – Atlético de Madrid 2008/2009 tifo' [video], YouTube, uploaded 22 April. Available online at: www.youtube. com/watch?v=przGLXabsUQ [Accessed 4 March 2019].

Vimieiro, A.C. (2015). 'Football supporter cultures in modern-day Brazil: hypercommodification, networked collectivisms and digital productivity', unpublished PhD thesis. Brisbane: Queensland University of Technology.

Vukušić, D. and Miošić, L. (2018). 'Reinventing and reclaiming football through radical fan practices? NK Zagreb 041 and Futsal Dinamo', *Soccer and Society*, 19:3: 440–452.

Wachs, F.L. (2003). '"I was there…": gendered limitations, expectations, and strategic assumptions in the world of co-ed softball', in: A. Bolin and J. Granskog (eds), *Athletic Intruders: Ethnographic Research on Women, Culture, and Exercise*, pp. 177–200. Albany: State University of New York Press.

Wacquant, L. (2004). *Body and Soul: Notebooks of an Apprentice Boxer*. Oxford: Oxford University Press.

Wanmonster (2011). 'ELEPHANT ARMY ULTRAS. Ultras PAHANG. Jatuh dan bangun bersama PAHANG. Tak akan undur!' [blog], 7 April. Available online at: http://kucingkenagigit.blogspot.com/2011/04/elephant-army-ultr as-ultras-pasukan.html [Accessed 5 March 2019].

Wann, D.L., Melnick, M.J., Russell, G.W. and Pease, D.G. (2001). *Sport Fans: The Psychology and Social Impact of Spectators*. London: Routledge.

Weber, M. (1978). *Economy and Society: An Outline of Interpretive Sociology*. Berkeley: University of California Press.

Wetherell, M. (2012). *Affect and Emotions: A New Social Science Understanding*. London: SAGE.

Williams, J. (2007). *Beautiful Game: International Perspectives on Women's Football*. London: Berg.

Williams, J., Dunning, E. and Murphy, P. (1989). *Hooligans Abroad: The Control of English Fans in Continental Europe*. London: Routledge.

Wilman, M. (2014). 'Malmö FF får nya böter för Juventusmatchen', *Sydsvenskan*, 15 December. Available online at: www.sydsvenskan.se/2014-12-15/malmo-ff-far-nya-boter-for-juventusmatchen [Accessed 4 March 2019].

Wilson, B. (2007). 'New media, social movements, and global sport studies: a revolutionary moment and the sociology of sport', *Sociology of Sport*, 24(2): 457–477.

Winands, M., Grau, A. and Zick, A. (2017). 'Sources of identity and community among highly identified football fans in Germany: an empirical categorisation of differentiation processes', *Soccer and Society*, 20(2): 216–231.

Zaimakis, Y. (2018). 'Football fan culture and politics in modern Greece: the process of fandom radicalization during the austerity era', *Soccer and Society*, 19(2): 252–270.

Zalgiris (n.d.). 'Pietų IV', Zalgiris Vilnius website. Available online at: www. fkzalgiris.lt/ (in Lithuanian) [Accessed 2 May 2019].

Zanker, P. (1990). *The Power of Images in the Age of Augustus*. Ann Arbor: University of Michigan Press.

Zerubavel, E. (1996). 'Social memories: steps to a sociology of the past', *Qualitative Sociology*, 19(3): 283–299.

Ziesche, D. (2018). '"The East" strikes back: Ultras Dynamo, hyper-stylization, and regimes of truth', *Sport in Society*, 21(6): 883–901.

Index

EU authorised representative for GPSR:
Easy Access System Europe, Mustamäe tee 50,
10621 Tallinn, Estonia
gpsr.requests@easproject.com

www.ingramcontent.com/pod-product-compliance
Lightning Source LLC
Jackson TN
JSHW060035280625
86840JS00004B/29